Smi[t]
Maritime Museums
of North America

now available in 3 parts

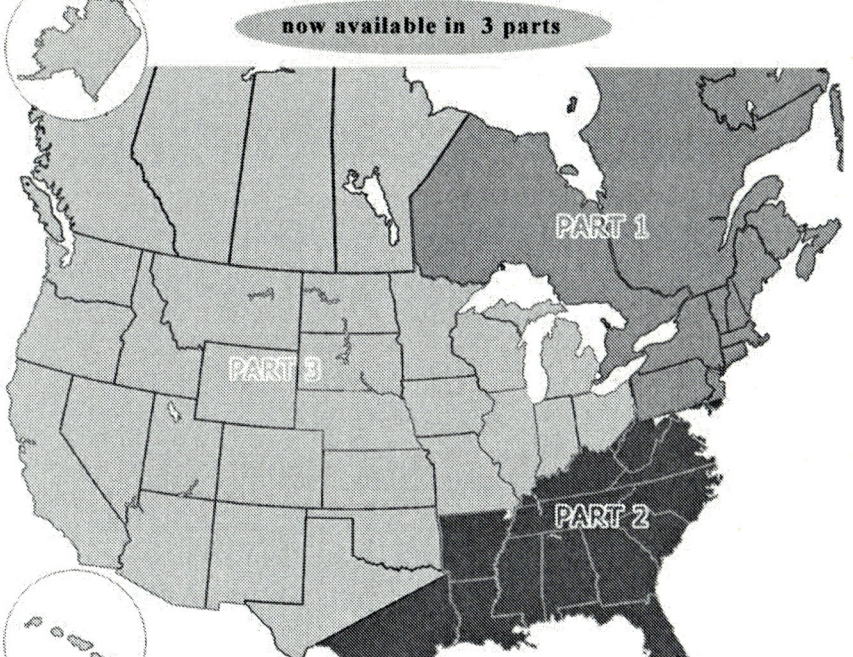

PART 1	CANADIAN MARITIME PROVINCES / NEW ENGLAND / MID-ATLANTIC (with 276 museum entries)
PART 2	SOUTHERN GULF COAST (with 142 museum entries)
PART 3	MID-WEST / CANADA / WEST COAST (with 211 museum entries)

Graphics by *pixel* SHOWCASE

SMITH'S GUIDE TO MARITIME MUSEUMS OF NORTH AMERICA

Part 1
Canadian Maritime Provinces
New England/Mid-Atlantic

Maritime and Selected Lighthouse,
Canal, and Canal Lock Museums

By

Robert H. Smith

© 2002 by Robert H. Smith. All rights reserved.

No part of this book may be reproduced, restored in a retrieval system, or transmitted by means, electronic, mechanical, photocopying, recording, or otherwise, without written consent from the author.

ISBN: 0-7596-9043-X (ebook)
ISBN: 0-7596-9044-8 (Paperback)

This book is printed on acid free paper.

Cover: The 1857 Marshall Point Lighthouse at Post Clyde, Maine, is a brick/granite lighthouse originally equipped with a 5th order Fresnel lens. On shore is the bell tower built in 1898 containing a 1,000 pound bronze bell. Replaced by a fog horn in 1969, the bell is on display in the keeper's house. (Photo by Rick Totton)

1stBooks - rev. 9/18/02

Dedication

To my wife Helen,
whose help and assistance
made it possible
to complete this work.

The Rideau Canal, built by Lt. Col. John By between 1826 and 1832, begins with a flight of eight locks from the Ottawa River in Ontario, Canada. The Commissariat building alongside the canal is now the Bytown Historical Museum   (Photo R. H. Smith)

A sparkling Venice Water Taxi berthed next to only one of four Lyman Cruisers ever built by the famous Lyman Boatworks of Sandusky, Ohio, are preserved at the Antique Boat Museum in Clayton, New York. (Photo R. H. Smith)

CONTENTS

AUTHOR'S PREFACE xi
MARITIME MUSEUM WEBSITE INFORMATION xiii
LIST OF MUSEUMS BY REGION xv
LIST OF ILLUSTRATIONS xxvii
GUIDE TO MARITIME MUSEUMS 1
CANADA 1
MAINE 51
NEW HAMPSHIRE 71
VERMONT 74
MASSACHUSETTS 76
RHODE ISLAND 117
CONNECTICUT 131
NEW YORK 139
NEW JERSEY 182
PENNSYLVANIA 196
DELAWARE 203
CANAL PARKS 210
ALPHABETICAL LIST OF MUSEUMS 211
SUBJECT INDEX CONTENTS 219
ABOUT THE AUTHOR 239

AUTHOR'S PREFACE

"Which is the best maritime museum?" This is the most common question I receive. And my answer is always: "Each maritime museum is important and each has its own story — its own reason for having been founded. Yes, some are large museums with vast collections of artifacts, vessels, and wonderful archives. Others are smaller with equally important artifacts, collections, libraries, and paintings too.

Every museum was established because of an important maritime historical fact or facts. The interested and dedicated people who expended enormous amounts of energy, time, and funding to create each museum, did so to make it possible for succeeding generations to more fully understand and appreciate our maritime historical past. And why "our museum" is important to preserve that history for now and the future.

One of the important attributes of collecting and archiving our maritime history is the increasing interest in genealogy. Where did our ancestors come from, why did they come, and how did they get here? Most, of course came by boat or ship, and almost all experienced great hardship. We ask: What kind of ships? How big or how small? What were the people and the mariners like?

As we and our children search for answers to help understand about how our ancestors arrived on the North American continent, our maritime museums stand ready to aid them, to help understand and appreciate the past.

We can be grateful for the dedication of everyone who has helped preserve our maritime history. Every time you visit a museum please express your thanks to those who greet you — they will appreciate it more than you might realize.

It is with great pleasure that I present this these three editions of maritime, lighthouse, canal, and canal lock museums in North America for your reading, museum visitation, and research.

Robert H. Smith
2002

NOTE

MARITIME MUSEUM WEBSITE INFORMATION

A large number of the entries in *Smith's Maritime Museums of North America* have their own websites and these have been included in:

ROBERT H. SMITH'S MASTER INDEX
TO
WORLD WIDE MARITIME AND RELATED MUSEUM WEBSITES

Those interested in maritime history and heritage have found Smith's master index to over 700 world-wide websites to be invaluable.

The website can be found using the following address on the Internet:
http://www.maritimemuseums.net

LIST OF MUSEUMS BY REGION

Part 1 of 3
CANADIAN MARITIME PROVINCES/NEW ENGLAND/ MID-ATLANTIC

Part 1
Canadian Maritime Provinces
New England/Mid-Atlantic
CANADA
New Brunswick
Newfoundland
Nova Scotia
Ontario
Québec
Prince Edward Island
USA
Maine
New Hampshire
Vermont
Massachusetts
Rhode Island
Connecticut
New York
New Jersey
Pennsylvania
Delaware
British
PART 2
SOUTHERN/GULF
Maryland
Virginia
Washington, D.C.
West Virginia
North Carolina
South Carolina
Kentucky
Tennessee
Arkansas
Georgia
Florida

Alabama
Mississippi
Louisiana
Texas
Part 3
Mid-West/Canada/
West Coast
CANADA
Alberta
Manitoba
USA
Michigan
Ohio
Indiana
Wisconsin
Illinois
Minnesota
Iowa
Missouri
North Dakota
South Dakota
Nebraska
Oklahoma
WEST COAST
CANADA
Columbia
Yukon Territory
COAST USA
Alaska
Washington
Oregon
California
Hawaii

Part 1
CANADIAN MARITIME PROVINCES
THROUGH MID-ATLANTIC

CANADIAN AND MARITIME PROVINCES

NEW BRUNSWICK
Grand Manan	Grand Manan Museum and Walter B. McLaughlin Marine Gallery	2
Hopewell Cape	Albert County Museum	1
Saint John	New Brunswick Museum	3
Shippagan	Aquarium and Marine Centre	1

NEWFOUNDLAND
Musgrave Harbour	Fishermen's Museum	3
St. John'	Newfoundland Museum	4

NOVA SCOTIA
Annapolis Royal/ Clark's Harbour	O'Dell House Museum	14
Barrington	Seal Island Light Museum	16
Bridgewater	HMCS *Fraser* (DDE)	11
Centerville	Archelaus Smith Museum	5
Halifax	HMCS *Sackville* (K-181)	11
	Maritime Command Museum	12
	Maritime Museum of the Atlantic	12
Hantsport	Churchill House and Marine Memorial Room Museam	7
LaHave Island	LaHave Island Marine Museum	10
Liverpool	Queens County Museum	15
Louisbourg	Atlantic Statiquarium Marine Museum	6
Lunenburg	Fisheries Museum of the Atlantic	9
Mahone Bay	Settler's Museum	17
Maitland	Lawrence House	10
Parrsboro	Ottawa House By-the-Sea	14
Port Greville	Age of Sail Heritage Center	5
St. Peters	St. Peters Canal	16
Shag Harbour	"Chapel Hill" Museum	7
Shelburne	The Dory Shop	8
Yarmouth	Yarmouth County Museum	19

ONTARIO

Chaffeys Lock	The Lockmaster's House Museum	28
Collingwood	Collingwood Museum	22
Elgin	Jones Falls Defensible Lockmaster's House	27
Hamilton	*Hamilton-Scourge* Project	26
Kingston	Marine Museum of the Great Lakes at Kingston	29
Mallorytown	St. Lawrence Islands National Park/ Brown's Bay Wreck	40
Manitowaning	Assiginack Historical Museum and SS *Norisle* Heritage Park	20
Mattawa	Voyageur Heritage Centre Samuel de Champlain Provincial Park	43
Merrickville	Merrickville Blockhouse Museum	30
Midland	Huronia Museum	26
Milford	Mariners' Park Museum	29
Mooretown	Moore Museum	31
Ottawa	Bytown Historical Museum	21
Owen Sound	Owen Sound Marine-Rail Heritage Museum	34
Penetanguishene	Discovery Harbour	23
Peterborough	The Canadian Canoe Museum	21
	Peterborough Centennial Museum and Archives	36
	Peterborough Hydraulic Lift Lock and Visitor Center	37
Port Carling	Muskoka Lakes Museum	32
Port Colborne	Port Colborne Historical and Marine Museum	38
Port Dover	Port Dover Harbour Museum	38
Prescott	The Forwarders' Museum	24
St. Catharines	St. Catharines Museum	39
Sault Ste. Marie	Museum Ship *Norgoma*	32
	St. Mary's River Marine Center	41
Smiths Falls	Rideau Canal Museum	39
Thunder Bay	Old Fort William	33
Tobermory	Fathom Five National Marine Park	24
Toronto	HMCS *Haida* Naval Museum	25
	The Pier: Toronto's Waterfront Museum	42
	Toronto Port Authority	43
Wasaga Beach	Nancy Island Historic Site	33
Welland	Welland Historical Museum	44

QUÉBEC

Coteau-du-Lac	Coteau-du-Lac National Historic Site	47
L'islet-sur-Mer	Bernier Maritime Museum (Musée Maritime Bernier)	44

Montréal	David M. Stewart Museum	46
Pointe-au-Père	Pointe-au-Père Sea Museum	48
Québec	Cartier-Brébeuf National Historical Park (Parc Historique National Cartier-Brébeuf)	45
	Grosse Ile and the Memorial National Historic Site	47
	Port of Québec in the Nineteenth Century National Historic Site (Lieu Historique National le Port de Québec au XIXe Siècle)	49

PRINCE EDWARD ISLAND

Port Hill	Green Park Shipbuilding Museum	50
Souris	Basin Head Fisheries Museum	49

USA

MAINE

Bar Harbor	Islesford Historical Museum	58
Bath	Maine Maritime Museum	61
Boothbay	Grand Banks Schooner Museum	56
Boothbay Harbor	Boothbay Region Historical Society	51
Brunswick	The Peary-MacMillan Arctic Museum	65
Cape Elizabeth	Portland Head Light	67
Eastport	Border Historical Society	53
	Quoddy Maritime Museum	68
Friendship	Friendship Museum	56
Greenville	Moosehead Marine Museum	62
Islesboro	Sailor's Memorial Museum and Lighthouse	68
Kennebunk	Brick Store Museum	54
Kennebunkport	Kennebunkport Maritime Museum	59
Kittery	Kittery Historical and Naval Museum	60
Lubec	The Old Sardine Village Museum	63
Machiasport	Gates House	56
Newfield	Willowbrook at Newfield	71
Northeast Harbor	The Great Harbor Maritime Museum	57
Pemaquid Point	Fishermen's Museum and Pemaquid Point Lighthouse	55
Port Clyde	Marshall Point Lighthouse Museum	61
Portland	Osher Map Library	64
Rockland	Shore Village Museum	70
Searsport	Penobscot Marine Museum	65
South Berwick	Counting House-Old Berwick Historical Society	54

South Portland	Portland Harbor Museum	66
Yarmouth	Museum of Yarmouth History	63
York	John Hancock Warehouse and Wharf/	58
	Old York Historical Society	58

NEW HAMPSHIRE

Portsmouth	John Paul Jones House	71
	Port of Portsmouth Maritime Museum	72
	Portsmouth Athenaeum	73
	Strawbery Banke Museum	73
Wolfeboro Falls	New Hampshire Antique & Classic Boat Museum	72

VERMONT

Basin Harbor	Lake Champlain Maritime Museum	74
Shelburne	Shelburne Museum, Inc.	75

MASSACHUSSETTS

Amesbury	Lowell's Boat Shop	92
Beverly	Beverly Historical Society and Museum	77
Boston	Boston Marine Society	78
	Boston Tea Party Ship and Museum	78
	Charlestown Navy Yard	81
	Museum of Science	97
	The Old State House - The Bostonian Society	102
	USS *Constitution*	112
	USS *Constitution* Museum	113
Buzzard's Bay	Capt. Charles H. Hurley Library	80
Cambridge	Hart Nautical Collections	87
Cohasset	Cohasset Maritime Museum	81
Eastham	Salt Pond Visitor Center	108
Edgarton	Martha's Vineyard Historical Society and Museum	95
Essex	Essex Shipbuilding Museum	84
Fall River	Battleship Cove	76
	Marine Museum at Fall River	93
	The PT Boat Museum and Library	103
Falmouth	Falmouth Historical Society Museums	86
Gloucester	Gloucester *Adventure (schooner)*	86
	Cape Ann Historical Museum	79
Hull	Hull Lifesaving Museum	90
Lowell	Middlesex Canal Museum	97
Marblehead	Marblehead Historical Society	92
	1768 Jeremiah Lee Mansion	111

Marion	*Mary Celeste* Museum	96
Medford	Medford Historical Society Museum	96
Milton	Captain Robert Bennet Forbes House	80
Nantucket	Egan Institute of Maritime Studies	83
	Nantucket Life-Saving Museum	98
	Whaling Museum	115
New Bedford	Lightship *New Bedford*	91
	New Bedford Free Public Library	99
	New Bedford Whaling Museum	99
	SS *Nobska* (Coastal Steamer)	107
	Schooner *Ernestina* Commission	109
Newburyport	Custom House Maritime Museum of Newburyport	82
North Truro	Truro Historical Society Museum	111
Osterville, Cape Cod	Osterville Historical Society	102
Plymouth	Pilgrim Hall Museum	104
	Plimoth Plantation	106
Provincetown	Expedition *Whydah (Pirate Ship)*	85
Quincy	United States Naval Shipbuilding Museum	114
Rockport	Sandy Bay Historical Society and Museums	109
Salem	Peabody Essex Museum	103
	Salem Maritime National Historic Site	108
	New England Pirate Museum	100
Scituate	The Maritime & Irish Mossing Museum	94
	Scituate Lighthouse	110
Wellflelet	Historical Society Museum	88
	Old Harbor Life-Saving Station	101
Woods Hole	Woods Hole Historical Collection	116
Yarmouth Port	Historical Society of Old Yarmouth	90

RHODE ISLAND

Block Island	Block Island Southeast Light & Museum	119
Bristol	Herreshoff Marine Museum/Hall of Fame	120
East Greenwich	Varnum Memorial Armory	130
Jamestown	Beavertail Lighthouse & Museum	118
	The Jamestown Museum	121
Kingston	University of Rhode Island, Special Collections	130
Newport	The International Yacht Restoration School	120
	Museum of Newport History	122
	Museum of Yachting	123
	Naval War College Museum	124
	Rose Island Lighthouse & Museum	128

Providence	Singlehanded Sailors Hall of Fame 129
	Alfred S. Brownell Collection of Atlantic Coast Fishing Craft Models 117
	Providence (Replica Sloop) 126
	The Rhode Island Historical Society Library 127
Woonsocket	Chafee Blackstone National Corridor 119

CONNECTICUT
Bridgeport	HMS *Rose* (Replica Ship) 132
	The *Glacier* Society Museum 132
Deep River	Stone House 137
Essex	The Connecticut River Museum 131
Groton	*Nautilus* and Submarine Force Museum 135
Middletown	Submarine Library Museum 138
Mystic	Mystic Seaport Museum 134
New London	Custom House Museum 131
	U.S. Coast Guard Museum 138
Norwalk	The Maritime Aquarium 133
Plainville	Plainville Historic Center 137
Stonington	The Old Lighthouse Museum 136

NEW YORK
Albany	*Half Moon* Visitor Center/ New Netherland Museum 158
	New York State Canal System 168
	USS *Slater* Museum (Destroyer Escort) 180
Bellport	Barn Museum 142
Blue Mountain Lake	Adirondack Museum 139
Bronx	Maritime Industry Museum/Fort Schuyler 163
Brooklyn	Waterfront Museum and Showboat Barge 181
Buffalo	Buffalo and Erie County Naval and Military Park 142
	Lower Lakes Marine Historical Society 162
Camillus	Sims' Store Museum 175
Canastota	Canastota Canal Town Museum 143
Captree	Fire Island Lighthouse Preservation Society 155
Centerport	Vanderbilt Mansion, Marine Museum 180
Chittenango	Chittenango Landing Canal Boat Museum 146
City Island	City Island Nautical Museum 146
Clayton	Antique Boat Museum 141
Cold Spring Harbor	Whaling Museum 148

xxii

Location	Site	Page
Crown Point	Crown Point State Historic Site	148
Cuddebackville	Neversink Valley Area Museum/ D and H Canal Park	165
Dunkirk	Dunkirk Historical Lighthouse and Veteran's Park	151
East Hampton	East Hampton Town Marine Museum	153
Greenport	East End Seaport Maritime Museum	152
Fort Hunter	Fort Hunter - Schoharie State Historic Site	156
High Falls	Delaware and Hudson Canal Museum	150
Hyde Park	Franklin D. Roosevelt Library/Museum	156
Kings Point	American Merchant Marine Museum U.S. Merchant Marine Academy	140
Kingston	Hudson River Maritime Museum	158
Lockport	Lockport Canal Museum	160
Massena	Dwight D. Eisenhower Lock	152
Mayville	Chautauqua Lake Historic Vessels Co.	144
Montauk	Montauk Point Lighthouse Museum	164
New York City	*Intrepid* Sea-Air-Space Museum	159
	Museum of the City of New York	164
	The New-York Historical Society	166
	Ocean Liner Museum	170
	South Street Seaport Museum	177
Northport	Northport Historical Museum	170
Oswego	H. Lee White Marine Museum	157
	Oswego Maritime Foundation	171
Plattsburg	Clinton County Historical Museum	147
Port Jefferson	Mather House Museum	163
Poughkeepsie	Hudson River Sloop *Clearwater, Inc.*	159
Riverhead	Suffolk Historical Museum	179
Rome	Erie Canal Village	154
Sackets Harbor	Sackets Harbor Battlefield State Historic Site	172
Sag Harbor	Sag Harbor Whaling Museum	173
Saugerties	Saugerties Lighthouse Museum	174
Sodus Point	Sodus Bay Lighthouse Museum	176
Southampton	Southampton Historical Museum	178
Southold	Nautical Museum at Horton Point Lighthouse	165
Staten Island	The Noble Collection	169
Syracuse	Canal Society of New York State	143
	Erie Canal Museum	154
Waterford	Tugboat *Urger*	179
West Sayville	Long Island Maritime Museum	161
Whitehall	Skenesborough Museum	175

NEW JERSEY

Atlantic City	Absecon Lighthouse	182
	Historic Gardner's Basin	188
Barnegat Light	Barnegat Lighthouse	184
Camden	Battleship *New Jersey*	185
Cape May	Cape May County Historical and Genealogical Society Museum in the John Holmes House	186
Edgewater	*Binghampton* (Ferry)	185
Greenwich	John Dubois Maritime Museum	189
Hackensack	New Jersey Naval Museum/ Submarine USS *Ling*	192
Highlands	Fort Hancock Museum	187
	Twin Lights State Historic Site	195
Keyport	Steamboat Dock Museum	194
Linwood	Linwood Maritime Museum	190
Morristown	Canal Society of New Jersey Museum at Waterloo Village	186
North Wildwood	Hereford Inlet Lighthouse	188
Ocean City	Ocean City Historical Museum	193
Paterson	Paterson Museum	193
Somers Point	Atlantic County Historical Society Museum	182
Toms River	Toms River Seaport Society	195
Tuckerton	Barnegat Bay Decoy and Baymen's Museum	183

PENNSYLVANIA

Easton	National Canal Museum/Hugh Moore Park	200
Erie	Erie Maritime Museum (Homeport U.S. Brig *Niagara*)	198
	Watson Curtze Mansion and Planetarium	203
Greenville	The Canal Museum	197
New Hope	New Hope Canal Boat Company	201
Philadelphia	American Philosophical Society Library	196
	Cigna Museum and Art Collection	197
	Independence Seaport Museum	199
	Philadelphia Ship Preservation Guild	201
Pittsburgh	USS *Requin* (SS-481) (Submarine)	202
Wyomissing	C. Howard Hiester Canal Center	196

DELAWARE

Bethany Beach	Indian River Life-Saving Station	206
Fenwick Island	DiscoverSea Shipwreck Museum	205
Georgetown	Treasures of the Sea Exhibit	208

Lewes	Cannon Ball Marine Museum	203
Port Penn	Port Penn Interpretive Center	207
Wilmington	*Kalmar Nyckel* Shipyard & Museum	206

LIST OF ILLUSTRATIONS
(For Part 1)

Bytown Historical Museum, Ottawa, Canada vi
Classic Venice Taxi, Antique Boat Museum, NY vii
Boston's Tea Party Ship *Beaver II* xxix
USS *Cassin Young* (DD) Charlestown Navy Yard, Boston xxx
Sodus Point Lighthouse, Upstate New York xxxi
The Falls on the St. Lawrence near Quebec 18
The first lock canal on the St. Lawrence River - Quebec 19
Basin Head Fisheries Museum on Prince Edward Island, Canada 35
Nancy Island Lighthouse, Ontario, Canada 36
St. Lawrence Bateau (boat) model – Forwarders' Museum 52
Maine Marine Museum, Bath, ME 53
Lighthouse Fresnel – Lens Collection, Shore Village Museum 69
Colcester Reef Lighthouse – Shelburne Museum 70
Top: Lowell's Boat Shop Museum at Amesbury, MA 89
Bottom: Lobster Boat Model – Penobscot Maritime Museum 89
Mayflower at Plimoth, Plymouth, MA 105
Expedition *Whydah* Pirate Ship Museum, Provincetown, MA 106
Naval War College Museum, Newport, RI 125
Seaman Church Institute and Whale Museum, Newport, RI 126
Top: Old Lighthouse, Stonington, CT 145
Bottom: Ship Models at Buffalo/Erie County Naval Museum 145
Top: Erie Canal Locks 1, 2, and 3 at Hudson River – Cohoes, NY 167
Bottom: Suffolk Marine Museum, Long Island, NY 167
Francis Life Car Exhibit – Independence Seaport Museum 190
Barnegat at Lighthouse, Long Beach, NJ 191
Admiral Dewey's *Olympia* at Penn's Landing, Philadelphia 192

Swede Longboat at the *Kalmar Nyckel* Shipyard, Wilmington 204
Boston Light, Boston Harbor 205
Dory boat building at Lowells BoatShop (1793), Amesbury, MA 209

The Tea Party Ship *Beaver II* (replica) and her crew recreates dumping of dutied tea chests (340, each weighing 400 pounds), into the Harbor at Boston on the night of December 16, 1773. A visit to this museum you can "Take-a-Stand" by voicing your opinion in the Protest Room. (Photo: R. H. Smith)

The USS *Cassin Young* (DD), built in 1943 in San Pedro, California for the US Navy saw action in the Pacific. Preserved afloat at the old Charlestown Navy Yard in Boston Harbor where her owner, the National Park Service, presents her to visitors where she is berthed near "Old Ironsides." (Photo R. H. Smith)

Because Sodus Bay was considered an ideal harbor from the time of the first settlers in the late 1700s, in 1824 Congress appropriated $4,500 to construct a lighthouse tower and keeper's residence at Sodus Bay. Farm products and other commodities were exported by commercial captains transporting cargoes aboard schooners and steamers to ports on Lake Ontario. (Photo Bob Glasheen)

GUIDE TO MARITIME MUSEUMS

NEW BRUNSWICK - CANADA

HOPEWELL CAPE, NEW BRUNSWICK - CANADA

Albert County Museum
Albert County Historical Society
12 Hopewell Cross Road
Hopewell Cape, New Brunswick E4H 3G9 Canada
(506) 734-2003 E-mail: albertcountymueum@nb.aibn.com
Location: Hopewell Cape is on Rte. 114 (the Tidal Trail), midway between Moncton and Fundy National Park. The Museum is in an old jail house on west bank of Petitcodiac River.
Highlights: Local historical items, ship models,
Website: www.albertcountymuseum.ca
General Information: Albert County Museum, founded in 1957, is a "Museum in a gaol" (former County Jail built in 1845). In addition to the "dungeon," mineral samples and early furnishings, the Museum contains maritime exhibits.

Many wooden sailing ships were built in Albert County. Among them was Rear-admiral Peary's *Roosevelt*, the ship that carried him on his successful and historic voyage in 1909 to discover the North Pole. Also available for visitors is a report on the Gaius Turner shipyard along with a complete listing of the ships built in Albert County. Models and photographs of wooden ships and the plans and tools used in building the ships are on display here.

Admission: Entry fee. Open June 15-mid-September, Monday-Sunday, 9:30 A.M.-5:30 P.M., **(See also:** The Peary-MacMillan Arctic Museum in Maine.)

SHIPPAGAN, NEW BRUNSWICK - CANADA

Aquarium and Marine Centre
(Centre Marin de Shippagan)
100 Aquarium Street
Shippagan, New Brunswick E8S 1H9 Canada
(506) 336-3013 Fax: (506) 336-3057 E-mail: aquarium@gnb.ca
Location: Reached by traveling north on provincial Highway 11 and Local Highway 345, the aquarium is located near the northeast end of New Brunswick, the Arcadian peninsula, overlooking the Bay of Chaleur.
Highlights: Life of the fisherman and a new aquarium, the "touch-tank," where you can touch the aquatic life, harbor seals, gift shop, 1904 lighthouse, seafood specialty restaurant, marina, **Website:** www.gnb.ca/aquarium

Robert H. Smith

General Information: Shippagan (the Micmac Indian word for "Passage of Ducks") Aquarium and Marine Centre is a fascinating complex that explores the underwater life and world of fishing in the Gulf of St. Lawrence, which is home to many fish species. From the powerful wolf fish with its threatening jaw to the graceful lumpfish, you will meet typical local fish in more than thirty tanks. Over 800 slides and a twenty-minute commentary reveal the stormy history of fishing in the Gulf, the waters of which have been the object of many revelries and much greed from the twelfth century to modern time.

A life-size fishing boat wheelhouse equipped with electronic instruments (some of them operating while visitors watch) makes one realize the importance of electronics for today's commercial fisherman. Gear, photographs, and diagrams complete the exhibition on fishing and its techniques.

Activities: Audiovisual presentation of fishing industry of the Gulf of Saint Lawrence, interpretation on fisheries and biology of sealife. The seals are fed everyday at 11 A.M. and 4 P.M.

Admission: Entry fee. Open daily, 10 A.M. to 6 P.M. May-September.

GRAND MANAN, NEW BRUNSWICK - CANADA

Grand Manan Museum
1141 Route 776
Grand Manan New Brunswick
E5G 4E9 Canada
(506) 662-3524 Fax: (506) 662-3009

Location: I-95 to Bangor, Maine, exiting on to SR-9. Follow SR-9 ninety-five miles into Calais, Maine, where you exit onto Rte. 1, Canada. After approximately twenty-three miles, turn on to Rte. 785 toward Blacks Harbour. The Museum is located in Grand Harbour, Grand Manan Island, roughly nineteen miles off the coast of Maine in the Bay of Fundy, a thirty-mile (one and one-half-hour) ferry boat ride south from Blacks Harbour.

Highlights: Maritime history, Grand Manan Archives, over 300 taxidermy birds collected on the Island, sales desk,

General Information: Founded in 1967, the Grand Manan Museum exhibits a collection of local history and geology; the "Moses" collection of birds of Grand Manan Island; and a marine gallery that investigates the history of local fishing. In addition, navigation, shipbuilding techniques, commerce, and shipwrecks are depicted through the use of marine charts, paintings, photographs, and artifacts. The lens and mechanism of the old Gannet Rock Lighthouse are also on display.

The Museum houses the Grand Manan Archives and the sales desk has several original island publications.

Activities: Summer nature school; during July and August slide shows/talks twice weekly.

Admission: Entry fee. Open Monday-Saturday, 10 A.M..-4:30 P.M., Sunday, 1 P.M.-5 P.M., June 15-end of September. Open year round by appointment. Call for information.

New Brunswick Museum
277 Douglas Avenue
Saint John, New Brunswick E2K 1E5 Canada
(506) 643-2300 Fax: (506) 643-2360 E-mail: nbmuseum@nb.aibn.com
Location: The Museum is situated on Douglas Avenue just five minutes west of downtown Saint John in historic Market Square. Coming from the south on Rte. 1, take the Catherwood exit to Raynes Avenue, then turn north onto Douglas. If you're coming from the north, exit at Mills Street, then turn west onto Douglas.
Highlights: New Brunswick history, New Brunswick Paleontology, New Brunswick animals/whales, ship models and portraits, scrimshaw, gift shop,
Website: www.gnb.ca/culture
General Information: The New Brunswick Museum, founded in 1842, provides an exciting look at the history of New Brunswick, focusing on industries, geology, marine live and decorative art. The family Discovery Gallery provides a hands-on interactive "Port Live" exhibit. The Museum and Parks Canada will open "Wind, wood, and Sail: Shipbuilding in the 19th Century," a new marine history exhibition.

Fully accessible, the Museum is connected by a pedway system to hotels, restaurants, and attractions.

Activities: The Library and Archives are located at 277 Douglas Avenue, five minutes from uptown Saint John, on St. Patrick's Street. Group tours and rates are available — required time is 2 to 3 hours. Shorter tours are available.

Admission: Entry fee. Open Monday-Wednesday and Friday, May 15-October 31, 9 A.M.-5 P.M.; Thursday, 9 A.M.-9 P.M.; Saturday-Sunday, 12 Noon-5 P.M. November 1-May 14, open Tuesday, Wednesday, and Friday, 9 A.M.-5 P.M.; Thursday, 9 A.M.-9 P.M., Saturday-Sunday, 12 Noon-5 P.M. Closed Mondays.

NEWFOUNDLAND - CANADA

MUSGRAVE HARBOUR, NEWFOUNDLAND-CANADA

Fishermen's Museum
4 Marine Drive
Musgrave Harbour, Newfoundland A0G 3J0 Canada
(709) 655-2119

Robert H. Smith

Location: Ferry to Port Aux Basques from North Sydney, Cape Breton Island. Take Rte. 1 north by northeast approximately 300 miles to the intersection of Rte. 330. Bear north about thirty-six miles on Rte. 330 into Musgrave Harbour on the road to the shore.

Highlights: Artifacts reflecting life of fishermen in area, ship models, books, newspapers,

General Information: The Fishermen's Museum is housed in a building built in 1910, designed by Sir William Coaker, founder of the Fishermen's Protective Union. Collections include: items pertaining to fisheries; ship models, such as miniature fishing boats; engines; photographs; and logbooks from the lighthouse (1902) that contain accounts of local shipwrecks. See also displays of a sleigh hearse that carried the body of Dr. Frederick Banting, co-discoverer of insulin, after a 1941 plane crash near Musgrave Harbour tragically claimed his life, 40-foot by 8-foot outside mural depicting the past and present fishing industry.

Activities: Conducted tours.

Admission: Entry fee. Open daily 10 A.M.-7 P.M., June-September.

ST. JOHN'S, NEWFOUNDLAND - CANADA

Newfoundland Museum
285 Duckworth Street
P.O. Box 8700
St. John's, Newfoundland A1B 4J6 Canada
(709) 729-2329 Fax: (709) 729-2179 E-mail: kwalsh@mail.gov.nf.ca

Location: Follow Rte. 2 to Gower Street and turn off at Duckworth Street to the Museum's downtown location.

Highlights: Natural history, archaeology, **Website:** www.nfmuseum.com

General Information: The Newfoundland Museum, founded in 1887, explores the diverse flora and fauna of the land and sea. These include objects related to underwater archaeology, navigation, cartography, sea disasters and the development of the fishing industry, and maritime trade where the visitor can learn about the European migratory fishermen who first frequented our shores 500 years ago, and about those who decided to stay, establishing fishing communities that survive to this day. The collection is highlighted by a Mariner's astrolabe dated 1628.

Activities: Education and public programs

Admission: Entry fee. Open mid-September-mid-June, Tuesday-Friday, 9 A.M.-4:45 P.M., Saturday, 9:30 A.M.-4:45 P.M., Sunday, 12:00 P.M.-4:45 P.M., closed Mondays and Saturday, holidays. Mid-June-Mid-September, Open daily, 9 A.M.-4:45 P.M.. Closed statutory holidays, year-round.

NOVA SCOTIA - CANADA

PORT GREVILLE, NOVA SCOTIA-CANADA

Age of Sail Heritage Center
P.O. Box 14
Port Greville, Nova Scotia BOM 1T0
(902) 348-2030
Location: The Centre is on Route 209, approximately 15 km west of Parrsboro.
Highlights: Lumbering and shipbuilding, Gift Shop
   General Information: Operated by the Greville Bay Shipbuilding Society the Age of Sail Heritage Centre, overlooking the tidal Greville River, pays tribute to the heritage of the communities along the Minas Channel from the Bay of Fundy to Cobequid Bay and ultimately Truro, Nova Scotia. History of lumbering and shipbuilding are brought to life through pictures, videos, story telling, artifacts, and hands-on exhibits along with activities for children.
   Activities: To further your enjoyment, visit our Blacksmith Shop and Tearoom Gift Shop.
   Admission: Entry fee. Open June through Labor Day, 10 A.M. - 6 P.M., six days a week - closed Mondays. Open weekends in May, September, and October.

CENTREVILLE, NOVA SCOTIA - CANADA

Archelaus Smith Museum
Archelaus Smith Historical Society
Clark's Harbour, Nova Scotia B0W 1P0 Canada
(902) 745-2411 or 3361 or 3227
Location: Cape Sable Island is about 155 miles southwest of Halifax. The Museum is located in Centreville, roughly three miles south of the junction of Rtes. 3 and 330 across the Cape Sable Island Causeway.
Highlights: Boat building, fishing industry,
Website: www.bmhs.ednet.ns.ca/tourism/smith.htm
   General Information: The Archelaus Smith Museum, founded in 1970, exhibits artifacts pertaining to the marine involvement of the community such as the fishing industry and boat building. Other displays include artifacts from the shipwrecks and works by local artists that illustrate the history of Cape Sable Island and genealogical information.
   Activities: Research projects
   Admission: No entry fee. Open daily, 9:30 A.M.-5:30 P.M., June 15-late September.

Robert H. Smith

LOUISBOURG, NOVA SCOTIA - CANADA

Atlantic Statiquarium Marine Museum
1328 Main Street
P. O. Box 316
Louisbourg, Nova Scotia B0A 1M0 Canada
(902) 733-2220/2721
Location: Once on Cape Breton Island (northeastern Nova Scotia), take either Rte. 105 or Rte. 4 to Sydney, then travel south on Rte. 22 to Louisbourg. The Museum is on the ground floor of a building (c. 1895) on Main Street.
Highlights: Early local fishery artifacts, shipwreck artifacts, ship models

General Information: The ocean embraces a rich world which, for the most part, remains hidden from our eyes by the restless surface of its water. It's a world full of secrets into which the Atlantic Statiquarium Marine Museum will give you a glimpse.

In this unique Museum, founded in 1977, you will be pleasantly introduced to many creatures and objects from the local marine environment. See the recovered sunken treasure of the *Le Chameau*, wrecked in 1725, and other historic shipwrecks of particular interest to divers and history buffs.

See also the exhibits featuring ship models, marine artifacts, and many items used by local fishermen until just a few years ago. Visitors can observe sea-creatures and their behaviour from close-up at the saltwater aquarium. Their fossilized ancestors on display give evidence of life in the seas during times that predate even dinosaurs.

Activities: Reproductions in pewter.
Admission: Entry fee. Open daily, 10 A.M.-7 P.M., June and September; 10 A.M.-9 P.M., July-August.

HANTSPORT, NOVA SCOTIA - CANADA

Churchill House and Marine Memorial Room Museum
P.O. Box 101
Hantsport, Nova Scotia B0P 1P0 Canada
(902) 684-3461
Location: Churchill House is located in Hantsport, forty-two miles north by northwest from Halifax (just beyond Windsor) on Rte. 101.
Highlights: Churchill House and Museum, ship models
  General Information: The Churchill House and Marine Room Museum, founded in 1967, is housed in the home (c. 1860) of Ezra Churchill, a Nova Scotia shipbuilder. The Marine Memorial Room, overlooking the Avon River, takes the visitor back to early shipbuilding days when many a fine vessel was launched to sail the seven seas. At one time, Hantsport was rated fifth in the world as a builder of fine ships, a total of 120 having been built there.
  Exhibits include shipbuilding tools, nautical instruments, old logs, ship models, and pictures.
  Admission: No entry fee, but donations accepted. Open daily, 10 A.M.-noon and 1 P.M.-5 P.M., July 2 - September 1.

SHAG HARBOUR, NOVA SCOTIA - CANADA

"Chapel Hill" Museum
Shag Harbour, Shelburne County
Shag Harbour, Nova Scotia B0W 3B0 Canada
(902) 723-2377 or 723-2830
Location: East from Yarmouth 62 klms on Rte. 103, then south six klms to Shag Harbour. The Museum is on Rte. 3, a main road.
Highlights: Lobster fishing history
  General Information: In 1971 the doors of the United Baptist Church closed. In this edifice more than a century of joys and sorrows of the people were shared. In 1979, After the church had been closed for 8 years, the Chapel Hill Historical Society saved the building and with the aid of donations and Government grants, the building was restored into a local history museum.
  The Museum maintains a collection of local documents, papers, farming and fishing implements; a collection of various types of magazines and scrapbooks for reference materials, a fisherman's loft featuring lobster fishing equipment, and trawling equipment. And a unique collection is displayed of deformed lobster claws, most resulting from injuries occurring in fights with other lobsters.
  Admission: No entry fee. Donations accepted. Open daily 10 A.M.-5 P.M., June 12-September 15.

Robert H. Smith

SHELBURNE, NOVA SCOTIA - CANADA

The Dory Shop
Dock Street
P. O. Box 39
Shelburne, Nova Scotia B0T 1W0 Canada
(902) 875-3219 Fax: (902) 875-4141
Location: Shelburne lies approximately 175 klms (109 miles) southwest of Halifax on Rte. 103. The shop is in the waterfront historic district on one-way (east) Dock Street.
Highlights: History of dory building
　　General Information: The Dory Shop, also known as the John Williams Dory Shop, was originally established in 1880 as part of the dory-building industry which, at one time, included at least seven shops along the Shelburne waterfront building thousands of dories — some shipped all over the world.

　　In 1877 Isaac Coffin Crowell designed, patented, and built what was to become the famous Shelburne dory based on a design brought here originally by Portuguese fishermen. Known for its exceptional strength, it was the dory preferred by Gloucester and other fishermen. John Williams served his apprenticeship under the guidance of Isaac Crowell.

　　When the John Williams Dory Shop was in operation, both the first and third floors were devoted to the storage of lumber, while the dories were built on the second floor. A visitor to the Dory Shop would have seen a number of dories in various stages of completion — an early version of the assembly line. The Dory Shop operated from 1880 to 1970, employed between 5 and 7 men building about 350 of these small work boats each year for both Canadian and American fishing schooners. The Dory Shop was affected by the decline in dory production and ceased operations in 1971. It was reopened in 1983 as a branch of the Nova Scotia Museum and is now operated for the Museum by the Shelburne Historical Society.

　　Activities: Demonstration of dory building.
　　Admission: Entry fee, but donations accepted. Open daily, June 1-September 30, 9:30 A.M.-5:30 P.M.

Smith's Guide to Maritime Museums of North America
LUNENBURG, NOVA SCOTIA - CANADA

Fisheries Museum of the Atlantic
68 Bluenose Drive
P. O. Box 1363
Lunenburg, Nova Scotia B0J 2C0 Canada
(902) 634-4794 Fax: (902) 634-8990 E-mail: fma@gov.ns.ca
Location: The town of Lunenburg lies approximately sixty-five miles southwest of Halifax on Rte. 103. The Museum is at 68 Bluenose Drive on the historic Lunenburg waterfront.
Highlights: The *Theresa E. Conner*, last of Lunenburg salt bank schooners, *The Cape Sable* (steel-hulled side trawler/dragger), aquarium, Dory Shop, Hall of Inshore Fisheries, Schooner *Bluenose* exhibit and memorabilia, theatre of archival films and videos, research library (1000 volumes), photographic archives (10,000 images), *Dorymates* (bi-annual newsletter), gift shop, restaurant and deli

General Information: The Fisheries Museum of the Atlantic, founded in 1967, originally began aboard the *Theresa E. Conner*, built in 1938, the last of the salt-banking schooners to operate out of Lunenburg. Also at the Museum's docks is *The Cape Sable*, built in 1962, one of the fresh fish draggers of the Lunenburg fishing fleet. The whole community of Lunenburg continues to thrive on the fishing industry.

A visitor to this Museum will find staff ready to answer any and all questions on all aspects of the fishing industry. And they conduct, all day long, a wide variety of talks on, for instance, lobsters, the cod fishery, trawl-line dories, dory building and launching, and much more.

The five buildings, which were originally part of W. C. Smith and Company's fish operations, houses exhibits dealing with the Atlantic Canadian fishing industry, including inshore fishing vessels and an aquarium of fish representative of the types important to the industry; Documentation Centre and research library; photographic archives; education centre; and a Parks Canada exhibit dealing with the Grand Banks fisheries during the Age of Sail. A theatre, gift shop, and restaurant are also on the grounds.

Activities: Films dealing with the fisheries; demonstrations of small boat construction; dory construction; dory rowing; fish filleting; net mending and knot tying; bait bag making; lobster trap making; rope and wire splicing; "hands on" participation in many activities; quilting; rug hooking; various school programmes.

Admission: Entry fee. Open daily, 9:30 A.M.-5:30 P.M., June 1-October 15; off season by appointment.

Robert H. Smith

LAHAVE ISLAND, NOVA SCOTIA - CANADA

LaHave Island Marine Museum
100 Bell Island Road
P.O. Box 69
La Have, Nova Scotia B0R 1C0 Canada
(902) 688-2973 or (902) 688-3192 (Fax too) E-mail: limms@auracom.com
Location: Travel seventy-two miles southwest of Halifax on Rte. 103. At exit 15 and at the junction of Rte. 331 on the lighthouse route, turn east toward
 Petite Rivière and Rissers Beach Provincial Park to Crescent Beach - the road to the LaHave Islands.
Highlights: Maritime history
 General Information: The LaHave Island Marine Museum, founded in 1972, is housed in what was previously a church and now houses a collection of marine artifacts.
 Admission: No entry fee, but donations accepted. Open mid-June-August 31, 10 A.M.-5:30 P.M., Sunday-Friday; Saturdays, 9 A.M. - 4 P.M. September and may upon request (902) 688-3192

MAITLAND, NOVA SCOTIA - CANADA

Lawrence House
Mail: Nova Scotia Museum Maitland, Nova Scotia 1747 Summer Street
(902) 261-2628 Halifax, Nova Scotia B3H 3A6 Canada
Location: From Truro travel south/southwest on Rte. 102 to the junction with Rte. 236. Head toward South Maitland, then north two miles into Maitland.
Highlights: Shipbuilding history
 General Information: The Lawrence House, established as a museum in 1967, is located in the home of William D. Lawrence, designer and builder of the largest three-masted ship in Canada. Furnishings and memorabilia in the house relate to the Lawrence family and ship building in the Cobequid Bay area. The house is both a national and provincial historic site.
 Typical of the grand homes of shipbuilders, shipowners, and captains, the Lawrence House was built about 1870, when Maitland and other towns in Nova Scotia were prosperous shipbuilding communities. In the early 1870s a number of vessels over 1,000 tons were being built; but Lawrence wanted to design an even larger one. In the fall of 1872, the keel was laid for a great ship the *William D. Lawrence*, and with the assistance of his brother Lockhart as master builder, his son John as foreman, and a workforce of 75 men, Lawrence began to make his dream a reality. On October 27, 1874, over 4,000 people flocked to Maitland to witness the launching of the 2,459-ton ship.
 Activities: Tours

Admission: No entry fee, but donations accepted. Open Monday-Saturday, 9:30 A.M.-5:30 P.M., Sunday, 1 P.M.-5:30 P.M., May 15-October 31.

BRIDGEWATER, NOVA SCOTIA - CANADA

HMCS *Fraser* (DDE-233, later DDH-233)
Box 233, Unit 17
450 LaHave Street
Bridgewater, NS B4V 3T2
(902) 543-1169 Fax: (902) 624-1537 E-mail: saguenay@fox.nstn.ca
Location: The Fraser is located at Bridgewater some 10 miles upriver from the Atlantic Ocean and 18 miles west of Lunenburg.
Highlights: The HMCS *Fraser*,
Website: www.maritime.org/hnsa-fraser.htm
Website: www.geocities.com/CapeCanaveral/9411/fraser/
General Information: The HMCS *Fraser* is the last surviving ship of the St. Laurent-class destroyer escorts. When first operational, they were known as the "Cadillacs" of the NATO fleet. Their unusual underwater surface and rounded hulls allowed them to actively hunt submarines at speeds of up to 18 knots, in any weather or sea condition. *Fraser* was towed to her new home of Bridgewater on December 18, 1997 where she is the cornerstone of a marina and coastal cruise liner port on the Bridgewater waterfront.
Admission: Contact Museum for information.

HALIFAX, NOVA SCOTIA - CANADA

HMCS *Sackville* (K-181)
The Canadian Naval Memorial Trust
P.O. Box 99000 Station Forces
Halifax, NS B3K 5X5 Canada
(902) 429-2132 (June to September), (902) 429-0550 x2837 (October to May)
Fax: (902) 427-1346 E-mail: co@hmcssackville-cnmt.ns.ca
Location: The ship is located in downtown Halifax, behind the Maritime Museum of the Atlantic
Highlights: HMCS *Sackville*, *Action Stations* Newsletter,
Website: www.hmcssackville-cnmt.ns.ca/
General Information: The HMCS *Sackville* (K-181) is the last remaining corvette of the 236 that were laid down in Canada and Britain during WW II. Her operational career was spent escorting convoys between St. John's, Newfoundland, and Londonderry, Northern Ireland. After the war, the *Sackville* was laid up in reserve. But in 1952, the ship was reactivated and spent the next 30 years engaged in oceanographic, hydrographic, and fisheries research. Retired

Robert H. Smith

from the Royal Canadian Navy in 1982, *Sackville* was transferred to the Canadian Naval Corvette Trust and restored to her 1944 appearance. And on May 4, 1985, *Sackville* was formally dedicated as the Canadian Naval Memorial.

Admission: Entry fee. Open: Monday to Saturday, 10 A.M.- 5:30 P.M. and 12:00 Noon - 5:30 P.M. on Sundays.

HALIFAX, NOVA SCOTIA - CANADA

Maritime Command Museum
Canadian Forces Base Halifax
Halifax, Nova Scotia B3K 2X0 Canada
(902) 427-8250 E-mail: nstn1674@fox.nstn.ca
Location: The Museum occupies Admiralty House, which lies between North, Gottingen, Russell, and Barrington Streets, five blocks north of Citadel Hill in Halifax.
Highlights: History of the Royal Canadian Navy, library
General Information: Founded in 1974, the Maritime Command Museum is located in Admiralty House, which was built between 1814 and 1818. This Georgian-style house first served as the official residence of the Commander in Chief of the British North American Station. Over the years it has been used as a summer residence, a hospital, and a wardroom.

The main objective of the Maritime Command Museum is to collect, preserve, and display the artifacts and history of the Canadian Maritime Military Forces in war and peace. Exhibits focus mainly on the history and development of the Canadian Navy since its inception in 1910 through to current operations as well as the Royal Navy's presence and influence on Halifax since 1759.

The Museum also maintains a library and archives relevant to naval history and the Dockyard since 1759. In addition, the Museum houses a permanent collection displaying the history of the Royal Canadian Navy, which was founded on May 4, 1910.

Activities: Guided tours
Admission: No entry fee. Open year round Monday-Friday, 10:00 A.M.- 4 P.M.; July-August, Sunday, 1 P.M. to 5 P.M.

HALIFAX, NOVA SCOTIA - CANADA

Maritime Museum of the Atlantic
1675 Lower Water Street
Halifax, Nova Scotia B3J 1S3 Canada
(902) 424-7490 Fax: (902) 424-0612 E-mail: lunnge@gov.ns.ca
Location: The Museum is on the waterfront on Lower Water Street in Halifax, Nova Scotia.

Highlights: The CSS *Acadia* (retired Canadian hydrographic survey vessel built in 1913), William Robertson & Son Ship Chandlery, "Age of Steam," "Navy and " Days of Sail" galleries, ship models, small craft collection, library (4,000 titles and 20,000 photographs), HMCS *Sackville*, a Flower Class Corvette from WW II and Canada's naval memorial-owned and operated by the Canadian Naval Memorial Trust — is berthed at an adjacent wharf June to September. **Website:** http://maritime.museum.gov.ns.ca

General Information: Maritime Museum of the Atlantic, founded in 1948, exhibits nautical history through a wide range of marine artifacts, from ship's hardware (as exhibited in the turn-of-the-20th century ship chandlery) to over seventy-five small craft and an 846-ton steamship, CSS *Acadia*, Canada's first purpose-built hydrographic survey vessel.

The Museum also has over 350 ship models, a large collection of navigational instruments, and shipwright's tools. Its research library contains over 4,000 titles, 20,000 photographs, and a small collection of vessel plans.

The exhibit *"Titanic* and Halifax" contains a collection of wooden pieces retrieved from the water in the aftermath of the ship's sinking in 1912 as well as some other items taken from bodies of passengers that were brought to Halifax.

The latter items were carefully catalogued to assist people in their search for family members that met their fate in this tragic disaster. 150 of those who died in this tragedy are buried in Halifax cemeteries.

Other exhibits include "Halifax Wrecked" comprised of displays recounting the devastating explosion that occurred in Halifax Harbour in 1917. The collision of two ships one carrying explosives destined for Europe during WW I killed 2,000, injured 10,000, and destroyed homes that housed 20,000 people; it leveled the densely populated north end of the city. And a new permanent exhibit, "Shipwreck Treasures of Nova Scotia" is scheduled to open in June, 2001.

The Museum is the marine history branch of the Nova Scotia Museum and, together with the Fisheries Museum of the Atlantic in Lunenburg, collects, preserves, and interprets the material culture of the marine history of the Atlantic Provinces.

Activities: Regular interpretive programs and tours May 1 - October 31, school programs, workshops, events, special spring oceanography program, and research associates.

Admission: Admission charged year round, lower off-season rates Nov. through April. Open daily May 1 through Oct. 31, Mon.- Sat. 9:30 A.M.- 5:30 P.M. (8 P.M. Tuesdays), Sun. 1 P.M.- 5:30 P.M.; Open Tues. - Sun. Nov. 1 - April 30, Tues.- Sat. 9:30 A.M. - 5 P.M. (8 P.M. Tuesdays), Sun. 1 P.M.-5 P.M. CSS *Acadia*: open May - Oct. (not Tuesday evenings).

Robert H. Smith

ANNAPOLIS ROYAL, NOVA SCOTIA - CANADA

O'Dell House Museum
136 St. George Street
Annapolis Royal, Nova Scotia B0S 1A0 Canada
(902) 532-7754 Fax: (902) 532-0700 E-mail: kirbywr@gov.ns.ca
Location: From the ferry landing at Digby, Annapolis Royal is approximately 25 klm northwest on Hwy 1.
Highlights: Local maritime history
    General Information: The O'Dell House Museum is located at the head of the old ferry slip and faced the is housed in the building that once faced the wharves and shipyards on which Annapolis Royal thrived. Two rooms of the display — ship's models, paintings, tools, etc. — highlight the local shipbuilding and mercantile history of the town. As well, the Museum's archival/genealogical resource centre features photo and family histories which related to this topic.
    Admission: Entry fee. Open year-round; hours vary.

PARRSBORO, NOVA SCOTIA - CANADA

Ottawa House By-the-Sea
Shore Historic Society
Partridge Island
Parrsboro, Nova Scotia, B0M 1S0 Canada
(902) 254-3266
Location: From Moncton, New Brunswick, take Rte. 2 east/southwest through Sackville into Amherst. Parrsboro lies about 61 klms south of Amherst on Rte. 2. In town, follow Main Street to Partridge Island Road.
Highlights: Shipbuilding history,
Website: www.town.parrsboro.ns.ca/history.oh.htm
    General Information: Ottawa House By-the-Sea, founded in 1979 as a museum, is the sole remnant of the original Partridge Island settlement. Once an inn, the house was built more than 200 years ago by James Ratchford, a prominent trader in the early history of Parrsboro.
    Ottawa House is devoted to the shipbuilding and maritime heritage of the area. Exhibits include a collection of shipbuilding tools, photographs of many of the important vessels launched from local yards, and artifacts from the days of sail. Rooms on the second floor reflect the home's appearance during Sir Charles Tupper's residency.
    Activities: Museum tours
    Admission: Entry fee. Open daily, 10 A.M.-6 P.M., mid-June-mid-September.

Smith's Guide to Maritime Museums of North America
LIVERPOOL, NOVA SCOTIA - CANADA

Queens County Museum
109 Main Street
P. O. Box 1078
Liverpool, Nova Scotia B0T 1K0 Canada
(902) 354-4058 Fax: (902) 354-2050 E-mail: rafusela@gov.ns.ca
Location: Situated in the southwest tip of Nova Scotia, Liverpool is approximately eighty-five miles west of Halifax on Rte. 103. The Museum is one block south of the town's center intersection on Main Street.
Highlights: Shipbuilding history, privateer history,
Website: www.geocities.com/Paris/2669/

    General Information: Built in 1980, Queens County Museum is adjacent to the 200-year-old Simon Perkin House and is designed to resemble the original buildings surrounding it.

    The Museum provides a cultural history intrinsically linked to the forests where its importance in the eighteenth and nineteenth centuries in Queens County has been well recorded. Simon Perkin's painstaking account of the cultural and economic events of the day is a landmark Colonial document unique in North America and on permanent display.

    The Main Gallery exhibit introduces Queens County with displays of its natural setting of land, rivers, and ocean. The exhibit demonstrates historically how mankind and nature have combined to yield the lifestyle of today's residents. And an important part of the collections is the cultural heritage of the Micmac or Eastern Woodland Indians. The contribution these "first peoples" have made to the cultural mosaic and survival of this country are preserved in a variety of Micmac artifacts and stone drawings on exhibit.

    Adjacent to the Queens County Museum is the over-200-year-old Simon Perkin's house where he lived, worked, and chronicled the events of his community including his small-share participation in privateer enterprises.

    The Museum's collections of artifacts and records also pertains to the history of residents and industries in the county since 1760; the development of local fishing, lumbering, and shipbuilding; and the period of the privateers. History buffs and genealogy enthusiasts will find the Museum a worthwhile place to visit. And the Queens County Historical Society maintains extensive archives in The Thomas Raddall Research Centre, interestingly designed for the family historian.

    Admission: No entry fee, but donations accepted. Open June 1-October 15 daily, 9:30 A.M.-5:30 P.M., Sundays, 1 P.M.-5:30 P.M. October 15-May 31, open Monday-Saturday, 9 A.M.-5 P.M., closed Sunday.

Robert H. Smith

ST. PETERS, NOVA SCOTIA - CANADA

St. Peters Canal
P.O. Box 8
St. Peters, Nova Scotia B0E 3B0 Canada
(902) 535-2118
Location: St. Peters is 33 klms east of Port Hawkesbury on Rte. 4. *Highlights:* Working canal,
General Information: St. Peters Canal is 800-meters (2600-feet)-long and links the Atlantic Ocean with Bras d'Or Lake — it is unique. Work started on the canal in 1854 and was completed in 1869. The canal also boasts the only functioning lock system in Nova Scotia. View interpretive exhibits, enjoy a picnic lunch, or experience the canal by pleasure craft. The canal was declared a Canadian National Historic Site.

BARRINGTON, NOVA SCOTIA - CANADA

Seal Island Light Museum
Barrington, Nova Scotia B0W 1E0
(902) 637-2185 E-mail: maxwelbm@gov.ns.ca
Location: Barrington is 45 klms southeast of Shelburne. The lighthouse is located across the road from the Tourist Information Centre in Barrington.
Highlights: Fresnel lenses, local history artifacts,
Website: www.bmhs.ednet.ns.ca/cshs/sil.htm
General Information: The Seal Island Light Museum is a 35-foot replica of the 67-foot lighthouse on Seal Island. The island is located approximately 20 miles southeast of Cape Sable Island at the elbow of the Fundy inlet where tides rank the highest in the world. When the light on Seal Island was first lit in 1831, it was just a vat of seal oil on a metal base. The seal oil was lit and used as a beacon. In 1892, the seal oil was replaced with a 5-wick-kerosene light, and in 1902, to a kerosene vapor light.

The 2nd-order Fresnel light was fixed for 76 years, but in 1907, a revolving mechanism, counter clockwise, was installed, giving three flashes and one blank, with flashes occurring every 10 seconds. Finally, in 1959, the lighthouse became electrically operated with the use of a generator electric light was installed, all in the original Fresnel lens.

In May 1979 the automated light took over for the old light and the lightkeeper. Earlier, in 1977, citizens of southwest Nova Scotia learned about the replacement of the Seal Island Light and petitioned to the Minister of Transport. It resulted in the Cape Sable Historical Society raising the necessary funds to construct the replica lighthouse. The complicated operating mechanism and the lantern were dismantled and transported by helicopter to Cape Sable Island where they were turned over to municipal authorities and subsequently to the Society.

The Light Museum was opened in 1985, providing an historical background to this important light. Along with other important artifacts is a 4th-order Fresnel lens from Bon Portage Island and other items relating to local shipping.

Admission: Entry fee. Open June to September, Monday-Saturday from 9:30 A.M.-5:30 P.M. On Sunday, from 1 P.M. to 5:30 P.M.

MAHONE BAY, NOVA SCOTIA - CANADA

Settler's Museum
578 Main Street
P. O. Box 583 Mahone Bay
Mahone Bay, Nova Scotia B0J 2E0 Canada
(902) 624-6263 (Phone/Fax) E-mail: mbsm@ns.sympatico.ca
Location: Mahone Bay lies approximately forty-four miles southwest of Halifax via Rte. 103.
Highlights: Ship models, China collection,
Website: www3.ns.sympatico.ca/mbsm
General Information: The Settler's Museum, founded in 1978, contains a collection of early shipbuilding tools and ship models from local shipyards and houses the Inglis-Quinlan china collection. Also displayed are materials used by first settlers of the district: clothing, kitchen equipment, furniture, pictures, quilts, and dishes.

Activities: Meetings, activity days; lectures

Admission: No entry fee, but donations accepted. Open June-Labour Day, Tuesday-Saturday 10 A.M.-5 P.M., Sunday, 1 P.M.-5 P.M. Closed Mondays.

Robert H. Smith

In the early 1800s, these low but turbulent rapids, at Coteau-du-lac, blocked the ascent of people and supplies to the West and the Great Lakes where the Delisle and St. Lawrence Rivers meet. (Photo R. H. Smith)

The first lock canal in North America was built at the point of Coteau-du-Lac in 1780, by-passing the low rapids in the St. Lawrence. Unique boats and figures, outlined in steel, positioned in and around this canal, give the visitor a real sense of perspective of its original use. (Photo R. H. Smith)

YARMOUTH, NOVA SCOTIA - CANADA

Yarmouth County Museum
22 Collins Street
Yarmouth, Nova Scotia B5A 3C8 Canada
(902) 742-5539 Fax: (902) 749-1120 E-mail: ycn0056@ycn.library.ns.ca
Location: Located on the southwestern tip of Nova Scotia, Yarmouth is approximately 192 miles southwest of Halifax on Rte. 103. Ferries leave from Portland and Bar Harbor, Maine. The Museum is located at 22 Collins street near downtown Yarmouth.
Highlights: Ship portrait collection, library/archives, bookshop,
Website: ycn.library.ns.ca/museum/yarcomus.htm
  General Information: The Yarmouth County Museum contains in its exhibits and records a picture of the continuity of life in one of Canada's oldest seaport communities. Yarmouth was founded in 1761 by settlers from New England. Shipping and allied trades made the town prosperous in the nineteenth century, and in the 1870's was one of Canada's leading seaports, per capita of population, in number and tonnage of sailing ships.

Robert H. Smith

The Museum 's collection of ship paintings — the third largest in Canada — and models, the period rooms, costumes, and pioneer artifacts, all tell their own story for visitors. The Museum also boasts a fine research library and archive with ship logs and other important ship information.

Awards include: 1982 Award of Merit, American Association for State and Local History and 1989 Canadian Parks Service Heritage Award.

Activities: Historical Society meeting held monthly. The Museum operates two other important sites: Next door is the Pelton-Fuller House (Fuller Brush) open to visitors year round. And in the downtown area, the Killam Brother's, Canada's oldest shipping office open during the summer.

Admission: Entry fee. Open Monday-Saturday, 9 A.M.-5 P.M., Sunday, 2 P.M.-5 P.M. Winter hours, Tuesday-Saturday, 2 P.M.-5 P.M.

ONTARIO - CANADA

MANITOWANING, ONTARIO - CANADA

Assiginack Historical Museum and
SS *Norisle* Heritage Park
SS *Norisle* (Great Lakes ship))
c/o Municipal Clerk, Box 147
Manitowaning, Ontario P0P 1N0 Canada
(705) 859-3196 or 859-3977 Fax: 705-859-2416

Location: Manitowaning is on the eastern side of Manitoulin Island in northern Lake Huron, about 140 miles east of Mackinaw City, Michigan. Approachable from the north via Canadian Rte. 69 to Little Current. Follow island Rte. 6 south twenty miles to Manitowaning.

Highlights: The SS *Norisle* (Great Lakes Steamship)

General Information: The Assiginack Historical Museum, founded in 1955, is housed in what was once a jail, built in 1878, and contains general displays of marine historical interest.

Located on the same grounds are a pioneer blacksmith's shop, barn, home, and school. Manitowaning Roller Mills, built 1885 as a gristmill, exhibits an agricultural display. The SS *Norisle* tour gives a full view of the workings of a large Great Lakes ship.

Activities: Tours during July and August, small-craft docking available adjacent to Heritage Park and full small-craft services, shopping, and restaurants nearby.

Admission: Entry fee. Open daily, 10 A.M.-5 P.M., June, July, and August; August and September.

Smith's Guide to Maritime Museums of North America

OTTAWA, ONTARIO - CANADA

Bytown Museum
P.O. Box 523, Station B.
Ottawa, Ontario K1P 5P6 Canada
(613) 234-4570 Fax: (613) 234-4846 E-mail: bytownmuseum@ncf.ca
Location: The Museum is in the Commissariat Stores Building which stands beside the Ottawa Locks, the northern eight-lock entrance to the Rideau Canal from the Ottawa River. Take the steps down from Wellington Street in the glen between Parliament Hill and the Château Laurier Hotel alongside the Rideau Canal.
Highlights: Rideau Canal history, archives, library,
  General Information: Lt. Col. John By of the British Army's Royal Engineers was the founder of Bytown, which was to become Ottawa and developed between 1826 and 1832 around the major works at the Ottawa River Terminus of the Rideau Canal. The Bytown Museum's major permanent exhibit depicts John By's personal and military life and information on the construction of the Rideau Canal. Other exhibits include a lumberman's shanty, pioneer kitchen, Victorian parlour, and toy store.
  The Rideau Canal, conceived in the wake of the War of 1812 to be a wartime supply route to Kingston and the Great Lakes, is a chain of beautiful lakes and canal cuts. Winding its way through varying landscapes, the Rideau Canal stretches a distance of 202 kms (124 miles) from Kingston, at the head of Lake Ontario, to Ottawa, Canada's capital city.
  Visitors will view personal and household possessions from the earliest days of settlement in the Ottawa area. The Canadian Parks Service presents a self-guided exhibit called "The Builders of the Rideau Canal" on the ground floor of the Commissariat building.
Admission: Entry fee. Open April 1-mid-May, Monday-Friday, 10 A.M.-4 P.M., closed on Tuesday; mid-May-mid-October, Monday-Saturday, 10 A.M.-4 P.M., Sunday, 12 P.M.- 4 P.M., closed on Tuesday; mid-October-end of November, Monday-Friday, 10 A.M.-2 P.M., closed on Tuesday; end of November 29-April 1, by reservation only.

PETERBOROUGH, ONTARIO - CANADA

The Canadian Canoe Museum
910 Monaghan Road
Peterborough, Ontario K9J 5K4 Canada
(705) 748-9153 1-866-34-CANOE Fax: (705) 748-0616
Location: Peterborough is sixty-two miles northeast of Toronto, a 90-minute drive.

Robert H. Smith

Highlights: Kanawa International (canoe) Collection, Gift Shop,
Website: www.canoemuseum.net/

General Information: The Canadian Canoe Museum is where you will discover the enduring significance of the canoe to the people of Canada in North America's only canoe museum. With more than 600 canoes and kayaks and 1,000 related artifacts, the Museum's collection is the largest of its kind.

Experience a dramatic waterfall upon entering, hear creation stories inside a traditional Mi'Kmaq wigwam, or try your hand building a birch bark canoe in the new Preserving Skills Gallery. Feel what it was like living as a voyageur during the Fur Trade era, plan a prospecting expedition from the Klondike gold rush days, and enjoy the cottage lifestyles of the early 19th century. The canoe is the ultimate link to Canada's rich cultural heritage, connecting the people, the past, and the unique Canadian landscape.

Admission: Entry fee. Memberships available. Open year-round: Summer hours, May-October, 10 A.M.-4 P.M. 7-days a week; Winter hours, November-April, Monday-Friday, 10 A.M.-4 P.M. Saturday/Sunday, 1 P.M.-4 P.M.

COLLINGWOOD, ONTARIO - CANADA

Collingwood Museum
P. O. Box 556
45 St. Paul Street
Collingwood, Ontario L9Y 4B2 Canada
(705) 445-4811 Fax: (705) 445-9004 E-mail: cm-chin@georgian.net
Location: At the juncture of Federal Highways 401 and 400 on the top end of Toronto, proceed north on Highway 400 to the City of Barrie (about 60 miles) to Provincial Highway 27. Follow Highway 27 northwest about 8 miles to Highway 26. Proceed west on Highway 26 into Collingwood (about 35 miles). The Town of Collingwood, population 12,500, is located on the shores of
Georgian Bay. The Museum is located in Memorial Park at Highway 26 and St. Paul Street, two blocks east of the community is downtown.

Highlights: Nineteenth-century ship models, videos, temporary exhibits, research, special events, archive, Museum store

General Information: The Collingwood Museum, founded in 1904 as the Huron Institute, is housed in a reproduction 1873 railway station, known as "The Station." Exhibits are devoted to the community and area history, the town is extensive boat and shipbuilding heritage, and the Petun Indians, who lived in the area from approximately 1600 to 1650s. Numerous 19th century ship models, archives, research opportunities and Museum store are part of the operation.

The Museum maintains an archive of extensive marine publications, particularly in relation to Collingwood. Appointments to access the archives is required.

Activities: Films, group tours (by appointment only). The Museum's special events throughout the year include traditional Christmas celebrations.

Admission: Entrance fee. Open May 24th weekend to Canadian Thanksgiving, Monday to Saturday 9 am to 5 P.M, Sunday noon to 5 P.M. Canadian Thanksgiving to May 24th weekend, open Monday, Tuesday, Friday 9 am to 5 P.M., Saturday 10 A.M. to 5 P.M., and Sunday noon to 5 P.M.

PENETANGUISHENE,* ONTARIO - CANADA

Discovery Harbour
Discovery Harbour
93 Jury Drive
Penetanguishene, Ontario, L9M 1G1 Canada
Tel: (705) 549-8064 Fax: (705) 549-4858
E-mail: hhp@DiscoveryHarbour.on.ca
* pn: Pen-et-ANG-wish-een. An Abenaki Indian word meaning "Place of the rolling white sands."

Location: Coming from Toronto, follow Hwy. 400 North 90 miles to Hwy. 93. Take Hwy. 93 north directly to Penetanguishene (Hwy 93 turns into Penetanguishene's main street). Take the main street to the bottom of the hill towards the water, turn right and follow the Blue Ship logos to Discovery Harbour. The museum is on an old British naval base.

Highlights: The historic ships: *Bee* (schooner), *Perseverance* (bateau), and *Tecumseh*, Mr. Chiles' Chandlery Store, Captain Roberts' Table restaurant, *The Ship's Bell* (quarterly newsletter),

Website: www.discoveryharbour.on.ca/english/

General Information: Discovery Harbour — A Centre for Marine Heritage — was founded in 1971 and located on the shores of beautiful Penetanguishene Bay. Come board authentic ships and chat with friendly guides and period-costumed staff. The site maintains a collection of 15 reconstructed and restored buildings, historic naval and military properties, original officer's quarters, a period and reproduction collection, maps and manuscripts, and replicas of the historic ships *Bee*, *Tecumseh*, and *Perseverance* built in 1802 at Point aux Pins, was burned in 1814 at Sault Ste. Marie by U.S. forces during the War of 1812..

Activities: Guided tours, historical demonstrations and dramas, education programmes, ship displays, "midday Sailaway" and "Sailor's Sunset" afternoon and evening sailing programmes, and horse-drawn wagon rides.

Admission: Entry fee. Open Monday-Friday, 9 A.M.-5 P.M., Victoria Day to

Robert H. Smith

TOBERMORY, ONTARIO - CANADA

Fathom Five National Marine Park
P.O. Box 189
Tobermory, Ontario N0H 2R0 Canada
(519) 596-2503 Fax: (519) 596-2552 E-mail: bruce_fathomfive@pch.gc.ca
Location: Fathom Five Park is located in the Bruce Peninsula National Park at the northern end of Rte. 6 about 300 kms northwest of Toronto on Georgian Bay.
Highlights: Shipwreck sites,
Website: arkscanada.pch.gc.ca/parks/ontario/fathomfive/fathom_five_e.htm
   General Information: Built in 1852, the schooner *John Walters* is a true old timer. This 108-foot wooden schooner met its fate off Russell Island circa 1883.
   The remains of this vessel lie in shallow water (maximum 15 feet), making it a site suitable for both novice divers and snorkelers.
   Fathom Park protects the historical shipwrecks, aquatic ecosystem, and island archipelago at the mouth of Georgian Bay. Nearby is Flowerpot Island with hiking trails and picnicking and six tent sites available.
   Wreck sites include the schooner *China* wrecked in 1883, the schooner *John Walters* wrecked in 1883, the steamer *W. L. Wetmore* sunk in 1901, the schooner/barge *James C. King* sunk in 1901, the steamer *Newaygo* wrecked in 1903, the schooner *Philo Schoville* wrecked in 1889, the schooner *Charles P. Minch* driven onto the rocks in 1898, and the barque *Arabia* that foundered in 1884. There are 12 other wreck sites to dive. Divers must check in at the Diver Registrations Centre open 7-days-a-week from June to Labour Day Reduced hours at other times of year. There is a hyperbaric chamber at the local medical clinic.

PRESCOTT, ONTARIO - CANADA

The Forwarders' Museum
Water and Centre Streets
P.O. Box 2179
Prescott, Ontario K0E 1T0 Canada
(613) 925-5788
Location: Prescott is eighty miles northeast from Kingston east toward Montreal on the St. Lawrence River. The Museum is on the waterfront in Prescott in Forwarders' Building.
Highlights: History of freight forwarders along the St. Lawrence River
   General Information: The Forwarders' Museum, opened in 1978, was established to preserve the history of the freight forwarders who moved all the goods from the "civilized" world to the settlers on the frontier via boat. Goods

and travelers were put ashore on the docks at Prescott, where the forwarders' building, now the museum, stands. Goods needing protection were stored in the lower level of the building, and offices occupied the upper floor.

The operators of the several forwarding companies were the entrepreneurs of their day and contracted to send the travelers and their goods to their destinations at Brockville, Kingston, York (Toronto), and other ports on the lakes. Huge rafts of squared timbers (some rescued from the lake bottom to be shown at the Museum) came down river (St. Lawrence), tied up a Prescott to "tighten their chains" before venturing through the rapids. Other larger vessels that could not navigate the lower St. Lawrence rapids off-loaded their cargo at Prescott to be reloaded on shallow-draft vessels for the continued transport to the Atlantic Ocean. The restored building maintains a variety of exhibits reflecting the forwarders' work and lifestyle. The Museum will bring history to life before your eyes.

Admission: Entry fee, but donations accepted. Open Sunday-Friday 11 A.M.-5 P.M., Saturdays 10 A.M.-6 P.M.

TORONTO, ONTARIO - CANADA

HMCS *Haida* Naval Museum
Ontario Place Corporation
955 Lakeshore Boulevard West
Toronto, Ontario M6K 3B9 Canada
(416) 314-9755 Fax: (416) 314-9878 E-mail: hnmchin@planteer.com
Location: Permanently berthed at Ontario Place on Lake Shore Boulevard West. From Niagara Falls, Canada Rte. QEW west forty miles to Rte. 403. Then north QEW 55 klms to Ontario Place in Toronto.
Highlights: World War II cutter (restored), *Friends of HMCS Haida* (newsletter), library and archival collection, noon-day gun fires a "salute" to mark 12 noon, gift shop, **Website:** www3.sympatico.ca/hrc/haida/home.htm
General Information: HMCS *Haida* served in World War II and the Korean War. The Museum, founded in 1965, exhibits a collection housed in a Royal Canadian Navy Destroyer and serves as a Naval Memorial and Maritime Museum. The Museum also maintains a library and archival collection with access by appointment only.
Activities: Self-conducted tours with guides stationed at points throughout the ship to answer questions. Special tours for school groups by appointment.
Admission: Entry fee. Open mid May-Labour Day: daily, 10:30 A.M.-7 P.M.

Robert H. Smith

HAMILTON, ONTARIO - CANADA

Hamilton-Scourge **Project**
City Hall
71 Main Street W.
Hamilton, Ontario L8N 3T4 Canada
(905) 526-3967 E-mail: ikerrwil@city.hamilton.on.ca
Location: Hamilton is about forty-six miles west of Niagara Falls on Lake Ontario's waterfront.
Highlights: The *Hamilton* and *Scourge* (1812 schooners resting at the bottom of Lake Ontario), gift shop,
Website: www.hamilton-scourge.city.hamilton.on.ca/
   General Information: The *Hamilton-Scourge* Project, founded in 1980, relates to two armed merchant schooners from the War of 1812 that capsized on Lake Ontario in a squall on August 8, 1813. In 1973, the vessels were discovered intact and perfectly preserved in 300 feet of water, six miles off Port Dalhousie, Ontario.
   Title to the vessels was transferred in 1980 to the City of Hamilton from the U.S. Navy through the U.S. Congress and the Royal Ontario Museum. Work continues to determine the best method to preserve and present these vessels for the long term. Three levels of Canadian Government — municipal, provincial, and federal — are participating in this project.
   Hamilton-Scourge Society is open to membership by the general public, sells related posters, books, "National Geographic" (March 1983) limited edition prints. (Scholars welcome to study at the Project Offices, Monday-Friday, 9 A.M.-5 P.M.)
   Activities: Research on the two schooners; speakers bureau; exhibition programme; interpretation centre open July-August, Wednesday-Sunday, 12 noon-5 P.M.
   Admission: No entry fee. Visitor's Centre open Wednesday-Sunday, noon-5 P.M., July and August.

MIDLAND, ONTARIO - CANADA

Huronia Museum and Huron Indian Village
Little Lake Park
549 Little Lake Park Road
P.O. Box 638
Midland, Ontario L4R 4P4 Canada
(705) 526-2844 Fax: (705) 527-6622 E-mail: hmchin@bconnex.net
1-800-263-7745 - Midland-Penetang Tourism Consortium

Location: The Museum and Village are located in the Town of Midland's Little Lake Park, just off King Street.

Highlights: History of sixty-seven ship wrecks, photograph collection (15,000), library, archival collections on Georgian Bay shipping/fishing, **Website:** www.georgianbaytourism.on.ca/members/huroniamuseum.htm

General Information: The maritime focus of Huronia Museum is on the history of transportation on Georgian Bay as part of the Great Lakes system. It contains artifacts and objects relating to the shipwrecks of the southeastern part of Georgian Bay. In addition an extensive photographic collection relating to Great Lakes marine history is partially displayed.

The Museum is in the Huron Village and Museum complex in Little Lake Park. There is a rich heritage in this part of Ontario, much of it based in the history of marine activities and sailing vessels. The project will culminate in the Georgian Bay Marine Museum and Heritage Harbour.

Admission: Entry fee. Open: January through March, Monday-Saturday, 9 A.M.-5 P.M., closed Sundays; April through June, Monday-Sunday, 9 A.M.-5 P.M.; July/August, Monday-Sunday, 9 A.M.-6 P.M.; September through December, Monday-Sunday, 9 A.M.-5 P.M.

ELGIN, ONTARIO - CANADA

Jones Falls Defensible Lockmaster's House and Blacksmith Shop
Southern Area Interpretation Office
Parks Canada, Rideau Canal
Box 10
Elgin, Ontario K0G 1E0 Canada
(613) 359-5377 Fax: (613) 359-6042

Location: The lockmaster's house is about 2 1/2-miles west from Highway #15 and adjacent to the Rideau Canal and in the Southern Sector/Rideau Canal National Historic Site of Canada.

Highlights: Rideau Canal lockmaster's house

General Information: The lockmaster's house, opened in 1980, is the restored defensible lockmaster's house (Sweeny House) and an operational blacksmith shop (1840s), both furnished with original reproduction artifacts. The gift shop is located in the blacksmith shop.

Admission: No entry fee. Open from the long holiday weekend in May to Thanksgiving weekend (Canadian).

Robert H. Smith

CHAFFEY'S LOCK, ONTARIO - CANADA

The Lockmaster's House Museum
Director: Preston Scott, Seasonal Curator
P.O. Box 50
Chaffeys Lock, Ontario K0G 1C0 Canada
(613) 359-5022
Location: The Museum is located on the Rideau Canal at Chaffey's Lock. From Canada Rte. 401 at the end of U.S. I-81, turn west to Exit 645. Turn north on Rte. 32, 18 kms where Rte. 32 becomes Rte. 15. Continue 18 kms to Rte. 9, near Elgin, turning west for 9 kms (6 miles) to Chaffey's Lock and hamlet.
Highlights: Chaffey's Lock lockstation, swing bridge over lock, gift shop, publications, **Website:** www.rideau-info.com/lockhouse/welcome.html

General Information: The Museum is on the site of a defensible lockmaster's house built in 1844 to defend the canal against US-based raiders, and is now restored to the 1894 period, when the building was modernized by the federal government. The hamlet of Chaffey's Lock is one of the most charming along the beautiful Rideau Canal transiting from Kingston at Lake Ontario to

Ottawa, the capitol of Canada. If you arrive by boat, you will be locked through by locktenders turning cranks to raise or lower the water in the locks and turning other cranks to open the lock gates, all by hand as was done in 1832. Arrival at Chaffeys Lock by boat or auto will enthrall you.

From the swing bridge, one can easily visualize the history of this quiet Lockstation. For over a century steamers passed through the lock gates towing barges loaded with cordwood, cheese, minerals, and grain. The 1872 stone gristmill was the commercial hub of the surrounding countryside. All summer long, farmers lined up in wagons, patiently waiting for their wheat and corn to be ground. At the Lockmaster's House Museum canal life in years gone by is interpreted through exhibits illustrating the daily work of the men and women who settled the shores of the Rideau Lakes and nearby Crosby Township and the Rideau Lakes region, with a special emphasis on the turn of the century (1890-1910). Yearly changing exhibits; audiovisual presentation; and Samuel Chaffey (1793-1827) brochures along with a fine video entitled "The Golden Times" are available.

Admission: No entry fee. Donations appreciated. Open last weekend in June to Labour Day.

KINGSTON, ONTARIO - CANADA

Marine Museum of the Great Lakes at Kingston
55 Ontario Street
Kingston, Ontario K7L 2Y2 Canada
(613) 542-2261 Fax: (613) 542-0043 E-mail: mmuseum@library.queensu.ca
Location: Take I-81 north from Watertown, New York, thirty miles into Canada. At the junction of Rte. 401, bear west eight miles to Kingston on northeast shore of Lake Ontario. The Museum is near the Thousand Islands tourist area five blocks west of Kingston City Hall.
Highlights: Exhibits in historic shipyard structures, museum ship *Alexander Henry*, bed and breakfast, publications, archives and library with over 10,000 titles, gift shop, **Website:** www.marmus.ca
General Information: The Marine Museum of the Great Lakes at Kingston, founded in 1976, maintains exhibits that trace the development of shipping on the Great Lakes — our freshwater seas. Main exhibits on shipbuilding (begun in 1790) are displayed in four buildings along the east side of an 1891 drydock. A stone building, once a powerhouse, has its original machinery still in place that used to operate the heavy drydock gate and the pumps for emptying it.

Artifacts collected by divers and the shipping industry of the Great Lakes are exhibited along with the 3,000-ton, 210-foot icebreaker *Alexander Henry*, acquired in 1985, which operates as a Bed and Breakfast from mid-May to Labour Day. Almost all items in the Museum are related to ships and shipbuilding. Special exhibitions are changed regularly.

An important marine library and archival collection includes over 40,000 builders' drawings of Great Lakes ships as well as nineteenth- and twentieth-century shipping and shipbuilding records.
Activities: Annual lectures.
Admission: Entry fee. Memberships are available. Open January-March, Monday-Friday, 10 A.M.-4 P.M., April-December, open daily 10 A.M.-5 P.M.; Library and archives: open all year by appointment. Bed and breakfast operated mid-May-Labour Day.

MILFORD, ONTARIO - CANADA

Mariners' Park Museum
c/o Mrs. B. Van Dusen
Mariners' Park Marine Society
R.R. 2
Milford, Ontario K0K 2P0 Canada
(613) 476-8392

Robert H. Smith

Location: South Bay is approximately 100 miles east of Toronto near Belleville. Take Rte. 49 south from Rte. 401 ten miles to Rte. 17. Follow it ten miles farther to Milford, turning onto Rte. 9 for one mile to South Bay on Lake Ontario.

Highlights: Artifacts from the *Protostatis, Sheboygan,* and *Acadian* (lake freighters — some of the many local shipwrecks off Prince Edward Island), False Duck Island lighthouse (1828)

General Information: The Mariners' Park Museum, founded in 1966, encompasses several buildings, including one of the oldest lighthouses in Ontario. Displays include fishermen's nets, ships' logs, a map pinpointing the locations of wrecks offshore, and hundreds of other artifacts that depict the area's seafaring history — all that remains of a past era that came abruptly to a close about the beginning of World War II. Nearby is the False Duck Island Lighthouse, where a Fresnel lens of French manufacture is located; its light extinguished for the last time November 3, 1965. The sixty-two-foot-high lighthouse and lantern are memorials to the County's sailors.

The Museum also exhibits a lifeboat from the Greek freighter *Protostatis,* an anchor from the *Sheboygan,* and a wheelhouse form the *Acadian*

Activities: Tours by appointments, Mariners' outdoor church service held annually on the second Sunday in August

Admission: Entry fee. Memberships available. Open weekends, 9 A.M.-5 P.M., Victoria Day-Canada Day (July 1); 9 A.M.-5 P.M. daily Canada Day to Labour Day; weekends from Labour Day to Thanksgiving (Canadian).

MERRICKVILLE, ONTARIO - CANADA

Merrickville Blockhouse Museum
c/o Secretary, Merrickville and District Historical Society
P.O. Box 294
Merrickville, Ontario K0G 1N0 Canada
(no phone listed)

Location: The Merrickville Blockhouse is located on the Rideau Canal in the center of Merrickville at the corner of St. Lawrence and Main Streets.

Highlights: Blockhouse, Rideau Canal, and locks

General Information: The Merrickville Blockhouse Museum, built in 1832 by Lt. Colonel By as a defence for the Rideau Canal, is now a Museum opened in 1980. The largest blockhouse of four built along the canal was constructed to protect the lock station from attack and to provide storage for arms and ammunition. It also served as a barracks for 50 men.

The blockhouse sits beside the Rideau Canal, which was built by the British as an alternate route from the St. Lawrence River. The Americans were a constant concern due to the unsettled boundary between Canada and the U.S. in the Oregon Territory out west. Lt. Col. John By was assigned the task of building the canal, which he did between 1826 and 1832. The canal covers some 202 kms (124 miles) from Ottawa on the Ottawa River to Kingston, Ontario, on the St. Lawrence River.

The military necessity long over, the canal is now one of the favorite inland waterways taking the boater through a series of beautiful lakes and some 49 locks alongside charming villages and lockstations where most of the lock gates are still hand operated.

Today, the Museum is home to many interesting artifacts from the early settlement days of Merrickville and surrounding areas. Later, John Johnston became the locktender, and, while living here, he detested the cold held in by the thick-walled blockhouse. It now houses the Museum and features both military and folk collections gathered from the area.

Admission: Entry fee. Open May-September, Tuesday-Sunday, 10 A.M.- 6 P.M.

MOORETOWN, ONTARIO - CANADA

Moore Museum
94 Moore Line
Mooretown, Ontario N0N 1M0 Canada
(519) 867-2020 Fax: (519) 867-5509 E-mail: 1mason@twp.moore.on.ca
Location: Mooretown is twenty-five minutes south of Sarnia, Ontario. The Museum is located three miles west of Hwy. 40 on Moore Line or two blocks east of the St. Clair Parkway (County Road 33) on Moore Line in Mooretown.
Highlights: Local maritime history
General Information: Moore Museum is a local history museum with nine exhibit buildings, including a one-room schoolhouse, log cabin, Victorian cottage, and a historic church, railroad station, and blacksmith shop located close to the St. Clair River.

Marine history is part of the Museum's collections and include The Marine Room with highlights of the exploration of the St. Clair River which led to the settlement of Moore Township by Europeans. Early settlers often crossed the river to the United States by boat or ferry in the summer and by foot, horse, or sleigh across the ice in the winter.

Exhibited are such marine artifacts as ship's compasses, sextants, and life rings. Also included are a few ship models, a fine diorama of the wreck of the *Edmund Fitzgerald*, the ore freighter that presently lies on the bottom of Lake Superior since November 1975, and the early shipping history of Father Hennepin's *Griffon*.

The wooden 1890 Corunna rear-range light is also on display on the Museum grounds.

Robert H. Smith

Admission: Entry fee. Open Wednesday-Sunday, 11 A.M.-5 P.M., March-June; daily, 11 A.M.-5 P.M., July-August; Monday-Friday, 9 A.M.-4 P.M. September 1-December 15.

SAULT STE. MARIE, ONTARIO - CANADA

Museum Ship *Norgoma*
Station Mall P. O. 23099
Sault Ste. Marie, Ontario P6A 6W6 Canada
(705) 256-SHIP (7447)
Location: Sault Ste. Marie lies on the Canadian-Michigan border where Lakes Huron and Superior meet. The twin cities are about 175 miles west of Sudbury on Canadian Rte. 17. The Museum ship is at the Roberta Bondar Park Marina in Sault Ste. Marie, Ontario.
Highlights: The *Norgoma* (Great Lakes cruise ship), Gift Shop
Website: www.geocities.com/TheTropics/5508/
General Information: The Museum Ship *Norgoma*, founded in 1976, exhibits the motorship *Norgoma*, 188-ft diesel-powered passenger vessel (built in 1950), featuring historical artifacts on the main deck.

The *Norgoma*, presently under volunteer restoration, was the last overnight cruise ship built on the Great Lakes. She ran from Owen Sound to Sault Ste. Marie between 1950 and 1963, after which she served as an auto ferry to Manitoulin Island until 1974.

Activities: Entire ship open for touring.
Admission: Entrance fee. Open daily, May-June 10 A.M.-6 P.M.; July-August, daily, 10 A.M.-8 P.M.; daily, September-October 10 A.M.- 6 P.M.,.

PORT CARLING, ONTARIO - CANADA

Muskoka Lakes Museum
100 Joseph Street
P.O. Box 432
Port Carling, Ontario P0B 1J0 Canada
(705) 765-5367 Fax: (705) 765-6271 E-mail: musklake@muskoka.com
Location: Port Carling is approximately 140 miles north of Toronto. Take te. 400 north eighty-five miles to Victoria Harbour, then Rte. 69 north twenty- five miles to Foots Bay, then east nine miles to Port Carling. The Museum is located in Island Park adjacent to the locks.
Highlights: Canal locks, boat collection, boatbuilding history, gift shop
Website: www.muskoka.com/tourism/mlm/ **AND**
www.wenonah.ca/pages/home.html

General Information: Museum Port Carling where Muskoka Lakes is the home of the Ditchburn launches, runabouts, and the Disappearing Propeller (DISPROS) Boat Co. The Museum maintains a collection of artifacts used by early settlers in the Muskoka area from 1865. Also displayed are artifacts relating to the wooden launches built in Muskoka. The Museum has a room devoted to small boat construction, steamers on the lakes, and is a repository for information on the locks.
Admission: Entry fee. Open daily, 10 A.M.-5 P.M.; Sunday noon-5 P.M., June 1-to Thanksgiving (Canada).

WASAGA BEACH, ONTARIO - CANADA

Nancy Island Historic Site
Wasaga Beach Provincial Park
11-22nd Street, P.O. Box 183
Wasaga Beach, Ontario L0L 2P0 Canada
(705) 429-2728 or 429-2516 Fax: (705) 429-7893
Location: The historic site is located in the Wasaga Beach Provincial Park on the Nottawasaga River and Georgian Bay in the Province of Ontario, Canada.
Highlights: Hull of the *Nancy*, ship models, theatre, museum, lighthouse replica, bateau (flat-bottom freight boat),
Website: www2.georgian.net/~nancyisland/
General Information: Nancy Island Historic Site, founded in 1928, provides a vital moment in history. It is here that the story of the schooner *Nancy* is told.

The *Nancy*, built as a private cargo vessel in 1789 at Detroit which was then British. She was a fur trading vessel but was pressed into service as a British supply ship during the War of 1812. The *Nancy* was burned and sunk by the British to avoid capture in a battle August 14, 1814. Soon after, on September 10th, Admiral Perry defeated the British on Lake Erie. Her hull rested in the river until the charred remains were recovered in 1928. Today, the hull is located inside the museum along with a wide variety of artifacts and ship models.
Admission: Entry fee. Open weekends, 10 A.M.-6 P.M., Victoria Day (near May 24th) through third Friday in June; daily, 10 A.M.-6 P.M., third Friday in June to Labour Day.

THUNDER BAY, ONTARIO - CANADA

Old Fort William
Vickers Heights Post Office
Thunder Bay, Ontario PAT 2Z0 Canada
(807) 577-8461 Fax: (807) 473-2327 E-mail: info@oldfortwilliam.on.ca
Location: The fort is two- and one-half miles south of the junction of Hwys.

Robert H. Smith

11B, 17B, and 61, then two- and one-half miles southwest on Broadway Avenue.
Highlights: Great Lakes history,
Website: www.oldfortwilliam.on.ca/index2.html
   General Information: Thunder Bay was formed with the joining of two cities: Fort William and Port Arthur located on Lake Superior — a major grain-shipping port. Tied closely to the fur trade, Old Fort William, consisting of forty-two carefully constructed historical buildings, was an important inland outpost headquarters of the North West Company, serving from the early nineteenth century. The energy of those early days is recaptured through interpretive guide programs along with guided tours and special events during the winter.
   The Fort includes craft shops that were typical of the early period where today much of the activity and spirit of those early days can be relived. Included is a naval yard, a farm, dairy, Indian encampment, and a site where large cargo birchbark canots (canoes) are built.
   Admission: Seasonal entry fees. Open Mid-May-mid-October, 9 A.M.- 6 P.M., June 17-August 19; Monday-Friday, 10 A.M.- 4 P.M. Please refer to website or e-mail for further information.

OWEN SOUND, ONTARIO - CANADA

Owen Sound Marine-Rail Heritage Museum
1165 First Avenue West
Owen Sound, Ontario N4K 4K8 Canada
(519) 371-3333 Fax: (519) 371-8628
E-mail: marinerail@city.owen-sound.on.ca
Location: Owen Sound is 120 miles northwest from Toronto on Hwy. 10. The museum is one- and one-half blocks north of 10th Street.
Highlights: Boat models, CNR/CPR memorabilia, special exhibits & displays,
Website: www.city.owen-sound.on.ca/marinerail
   General Information: The Marine and Rail Museum explains the role each industry played in shaping the area's economic history. Displays include models of boats, trains, flags, charts, propellers, ship wheels, uniforms, and tools. A library is open to the public.
   Admission: Entry fee. Open Monday-Friday, 9 A.M.- 4 P.M.; Saturday-Sunday, 11 P.M.-3 P.M. (Longer hours June, July, August.)

Smith's Guide to Maritime Museums of North America

Located in a former fishing port, the Basin Head Fisheries Museum on Prince Edward Island, founded in 1973, tells the story of the inshore fishery.
(Photo R. H. Smith)

Robert H. Smith

Near this lighthouse replica on Nancy Island, the hull of the schooner *Nancy* was burned and sunk by the British to avoid capture in a battle August 14, 1814. It now rests here in the museum on Nancy Island. (Photo courtesy Nancy Island Lighthouse)

PETERBOROUGH, ONTARIO - CANADA

Peterborough Centennial Museum and Archives
300 Hunter Street E. Armour Hill
P.O. Box 143
Peterborough, Ontario K9J 6Y5 Canada
(705) 743-5180 Fax: (705) 743-2614

Location: Peterborough is 135 kilometers northeast of Toronto. The lock is accessible either by footpath along the waterway or via Hunter Street East.
Highlights: Hydraulic lift lock, Trent Severn Waterway, archives, Peterborough canoes, **Website:** www.kawartha.net/~jleonard/home.htm

General Information: The Peterborough Centennial Museum is in the region known as the home of the "Canadian" canoe, as it was in this area in the 1850s where this new type of canoe was developed out of the traditional birch bark and dugout canoe technologies. There were a number of local manufacturers from about 1860 up to 1960.

The Museum portrays the settlement and domestic life of Peterborough through various collections and exhibits. The archives contain local records, historical photographs, maps, and waterway charts. The Museum overlooks the Trent Canal lock and has several examples of Peterborough-built canoes in its collection.

Admission: By donation. Open Monday-Friday, 9 A.M.-5 P.M., weekends and holidays, noon-5 P.M. The Archives are open by appointments.

PETERBOROUGH, ONTARIO - CANADA

Peterborough Hydraulic Lift Lock and Visitor Center
Hunter Street E.
Peterborough, Ontario K9J 6Z6 Canada
(705) 750-4950 E-mail: ftsw@ptbo.igs.net
Location: The lock is on the Trent-Severn Waterway in Peterborough.
Highlights: Hydraulic lift lock, Trent-Severn Waterway and archives,
Website: http://collections.ic.gc.ca/waterway/rg_eng_i/ptboll.htm

General Information: The Peterborough Hydraulic Lift Lock was built between 1896 and 1904 on the Trent-Severn Waterway, which meanders 240 miles (386 kms) across Central Ontario, linking the Bay of Quinte (Trenton) with Georgian Bay to the west. The concrete and steel monolith slowly emerged. The purpose was to overcome the considerable rise between Little Lake and the Otonabee River at Nassau Mills, with the Waterway providing a through-route from the Great Lakes to the West.

To visualize a lift lock think of two giant out-door water-filled chambers (like cake pans) 140 feet long and 33 feet wide with a water depth of 8 feet.

When one chamber is at the upper level (65 feet above the lower chamber), the gates are opened, boats float into it. It is a counterbalance to the lower chamber, and they move opposite to each other — full of water and boats — up/down some 65 feet. Once in their proper positions, the end-gates are opened to allow the barges/boats to float out and travel on to their destinations.

Robert H. Smith

This lift lock is the highest in the world of its type. The lock is operated mid-May through October, and a working model of the lock can be seen in the Visitor Centre. Nearby, the Peterborough Centennial Museum and Archives overlook the lift lock. The Trent-Severn Waterway is a historical canal operated and maintained by Parks Canada.
Admission: Entry fee. Open daily, 10 A.M.-5 P.M., May-October.

PORT COLBORNE, ONTARIO - CANADA

Port Colborne Historical and Marine Museum
P. O. Box 572
Port Colborne, Ontario L3K 5X8 Canada
(905) 834-7604
Location: Port Colborne lies 30 miles directly west of Buffalo, New York, on Canadian Rte. 3.
Highlights: Welland Canal, wheelhouse from steam tug *Yvonne Dupré Jr.*, Arabella's Tearoom, lifeboat from SS *Hochelaga*
   General Information: The Port Colborne Historical and Marine Museum, founded in 1974, is housed in a Georgian Revival-style home built in 1869. It exhibits artifacts pertaining to the early history of this area, including the Welland Canal; a heritage village site with an 1818 log school house; blacksmith sho p c. 1880's; 1946 wheelhouse; 1915 tea room; and an 1850's loghouse.
   Canal Days is held on Canada's Civic Holiday Weekend (the first Monday in August) and features marine displays, an outdoor art and craft show, demonstrations, entertainment, and food.
   Activities: Group tours, Canal Days, and a Christmas Festival held the first Sunday in December. Arabella's Pie Social, last Sunday in May.
   Admission: No entry fee for the Museum and village. Various fees for special events. Open daily, noon-5 P.M., May-December.

PORT DOVER, ONTARIO - CANADA

Port Dover Harbour Museum
44 Harbour Street Box 1298
Port Dover, Ontario N0A 1N0 Canada
(519) 583-2660 E-mail: portdover.museum@norfolkcounty.on.ca
Location: Port Dover lies approximately seventy-two miles west of Niagara Falls on Lake Erie. Take Rte. 3 to Jarvis, then Rte. 6, south thirteen miles to Port Dover.
Highlights: Schooner trade history, freshwater commercial fishing history
   General Information: Founded in 1976, at the Port Dover Harbour Museum, you can visit an original Port Dover fisherman's net shanty, peer into the iron

wheelhouse of the lake freighter *William P. Snyder, Jr.,* enjoy exhibits on the legends and lore of Long Point and Lake Erie — shipwrecks, salvage, and rescues; and learn a little more about what makes this area such a special part of Canada's "South Coast."
Admission: No entry fee, but donations accepted. Open: Summer hours; Tuesday-Saturday, 11 A.M.-7 P.M., Sundays, 1 P.M.-6 P.M.; Holiday Mondays, 1 P.M.-6 P.M.

SMITHS FALLS, ONTARIO - CANADA

Rideau Canal Museum
34B Beckwith Street South
Smiths Falls, Ontario, K7A 2A8 Canada
(613) 284-0505, Fax: (613) 284-0505 E-mail: rcmchin@superaje.com
Location: From Ottawa travel southwest on Rte. 7 approximately 30 miles to Rte. 15. Then bear south sixteen miles to Smiths Falls. From Watertown, New York, north on I-87 29 miles to Canadian Route 401. Then east 37 km to Rte. 29; turn north some 32 miles to Smiths Falls. Museum is in heart of the Rideau.
Highlights: The Rideau Canal,
Website: www.rideau-info.com/museum/index.html
General Information: The Rideau Canal Museum, opened in 1991, offers five floors of a unique blend of historic displays, artifacts, and modern technology to interpret one of the first engineering triumphs of Canadian History: the building and development of the Rideau Canal. This recreational waterway, which links Kingston and Ottawa, was built by Lt. Col. John By between 1826 and 1832 as a military alternative route where blockhouses provided protection from a feared American invasion.

Housed in a restored mill, the Museum provides a 20-foot (6m) animated detailed model of the waterway, a Look-Out Tower, a Tunnel of History, user-friendly computer quizzes, information mini-theatre programmes, and a narrated slide presentation. During high season, interpretive walks along the canal provide an interesting view of the old winches and massive gates, which still operate as they did 160 years ago.

Admission: Entry fee. Open daily, mid-May- July, 10 A.M.-5 P.M.; July-August, 10 A.M.-8 P.M.; September-mid-October, 10 A.M.-4:30 P.M.

ST. CATHARINES, ONTARIO - CANADA

St. Catharines Museum
1932 Government Road
St. Catharines, Ontario L2R 7C2
(905) 984-8880 Fax: (905) 984-6910 E-mail: muslk3@niagara.com

Robert H. Smith

Location: Welland Canals Centre at Lock 3 on the Welland Canal. Exit at QEW at Glendale Ave. West and follow the Welland Canals Centre signs for approximately 1 km. (2/3 mile.)
Highlights: History of four-sequential Welland Canals and city that grew up around them, video presentation, Ontario Lacrosse Hall of Fame and Museum, Black History Tour *Follow the North Star*, Lock 3 viewing platform, Tourist Information Centre, Gift Shop, Snack Bar and full service restaurant,
Website: www.lock3.com

General Information: St. Catherines was built around the Canal. At the St. Catherines Museum, one can learn about the history of the four Welland Canals; how they were built and how they operate. William Hamilton Merritt (1793-1862), was the driving force behind the engineering marvel of the Welland Canal. The Canal was built first in 1829, with 39 locks and wooden gates. The second and third canals were opened in 1845 and 1887. In 1932, the forth canal was completed. It has a total of eight locks and is 43 kilometres (27 miles) long. Portions of the old canal can still be seen today in downtown St. Catherines and Port Dalhousie, complete with lock tender shanties.

Activities: *The Welland Canals Past and Present* 12-minute video presentation, play in the "hands-on" Discover Room, tour the *Follow the North Star* exhibit which recounts the history of the Underground Railroad and the rich heritage of Niagara's African Canadians, visit the Library/Archives and extensive photograph collection, lectures, special events, guided tours to all pre-booked groups, educational programming, Discovery Park is being developed to expand the Museum walls out of doors.

Admission: Entry fee. Open daily, 9 A.M.-5 P.M.; Winter weekend hours 11 A.M.-4 P.M.; Extended hours 9 A.M.-8 P.M. from Canada (July 1) to Labour Day. Closed Christmas Day, Boxing Day, and New Years Day.

MALLORYTOWN, ONTARIO - CANADA

St. Lawrence Islands National Park/Brown's Bay Wreck
2 County Road 5
R.R. 3
Mallorytown, Ontario K0E 1R0 Canada
(613) 923-5261 Fax: (613) 923-1021 E-mail: ont_sli@pch.gc.ca
Location: Take I-81 north from Watertown, New York, to Canada and east on 1000 Islands Parkway to Mallorytown Landing and to the St. Lawrence Islands National Park. The Park is a collection of twenty-five islands between the cities of Kingston and Brockville.
Highlights: 1812 gunboat (a flat-bottomed clinker-built, i.e., with overlapping planks/plates like the clapboards on a house),
Website: www.parkscanada.gc.ca/sli

General Information: "When I was a youngster, we used to go skating in Brown's Bay in the winter time, and if the ice was clear of snow and the moon was full, you could see a ship frozen in the ice with its copper fasteners shining like gold," noted a Museum publication. Her ribs black against the green of the River, children used her as a diving platform, duck hunters built blinds on her bow, and fishermen lost many a lure to her oaken sides. The old wreck lay quietly in the silt and sand of Brown's Bay.

In the mid 1960s, national park staff arranged for the hulk to be raised, and, because of certain markings, she was thought to be a gunboat and probably dated around 1817. Gunboats usually mounted two cannons, were powered by sail and oar, carried supplies and escorted troops, scouted the shore, and in time of hostilities, harassed larger vessels. Although hundreds were in service on the Great Lakes, both shores of the Atlantic, the Baltic, and the Mediterranean seas, the gunboats have vanished, except for a few rare hulks such as this one.

The St. Lawrence Islands National Park was founded in 1904. The 54-foot gunboat went on display in 1968 in a special display building and cradle at St. Lawrence Islands National Park headquarters on the beautiful St. Lawrence River.

Activities: Guided tour and exhibit of the gunboat.

Admission: Entry fee. Open daily, June 30-September 3, other times by appointment.

SAULT STE. MARIE, ONTARIO - CANADA

St. Mary's River Marine Center
Museum Ship *Norgoma*
Station Mall, P.O. Box 23099
Sault Ste. Marie, Ontario P6A 6W6 Canada
(705) 245-SHIP (7447) (seasonal)
Location: Sault Ste. Marie lies on the Canadian-Michigan border where Lakes Huron and Superior meet. The twin cities are about 175 miles west of Sudbury, Ontario, on Hwy 17 and at the top of I75 in the U.S. The Museum ship is at the Roberta Bondar Park Marina in Sault Ste. Marie, Ontario.
Highlights: The *Norgoma* (Great Lakes cruise ship),
General Information: The St. Marys River Marine Centre was founded in 1976 and exhibits the motor ship *Norgoma*, a 188-foot diesel-powered passenger vessel (build in 1950), featuring historical artifacts on the main deck. The *Norgoma*, presently under volunteer restoration, was the last overnight cruise ship built on the Great Lakes. She ran from Owen Sound to Sault Ste. Marie between 1950 and 1963, afterwhich she served as an auto ferry to Manitoulin Island until 1974.

Robert H. Smith

The St. Marys River's rapids at Sault St. Marie, were first discovered by Etienne Brule in 1622, and the first permanent mission was founded by Père Marquette in 1669. A canal was built and the area became an important transportation center for Great Lakes traffic. The canal, closed for some time due to deterioration and lack of need because of the larger American "Soo Locks" next to it. Its now rebuilt to handle mostly pleasure craft and the recreational lock opened in 1998.

The Visitor Centre maintains 1,100 engineering drawings and land plans related to development and operation of the canal. Also available for research are eight feet of archival files and documents and a site-specific artifact collection.

Publications: "The Sault Ste. Marie Canal: A Chapter in the History of Great Lakes Transport."

Admission: Entry fee. Open daily 10 A.M.-8 P.M., mid-May to September.

TORONTO, ONTARIO - CANADA

The Pier: Toronto's Waterfront Museum
245 Queens Quay West
Toronto, Ontario M5B 2K9 Canada
(416) 338-7437 Fax: (416) 392-1767 E-mail: thepier@city.toronto.on.ca
Location: The Museum is located in the heart of Tronoto's waterfront.
Highlights: The *Ned Hanlan* (tugboat), boatbuilding library (1200 volumes and periodicals),
Website: http://toronto.com/E/V/TORON/0020/62/14/cs1.html

General Information: The Pier, located right in the heart of Toronto's waterfront, in a restored 1930s shipping warehouse, is an interactive, family-friendly center that explores the history of Toronto Harbour. Friendly staff help visitors learn about the language of steamship whistles, examine beautiful ship models and water craft or try their hand at rowing as they learn about Ned Hanlan,

Toronto's first great international sports hero.

In the Discovery Zone, parents and children play together as they explore the technology and history of the harbour. The working boat shop gives everyone a chance to learn about traditional wooden boatbuilding. Throughout the year The Pier offers special theme exhibits and events as well as group and education programs, including traditional wooden boat building classes. Exhibits include: whistles; animated triple-expansion engine (operating May to October); underwater archaeology display; ship models; historic small craft. The eighty-foot steel steam tug *Ned Hanlan*, built in 1932, is restored and dry docked beside the Museum.

Admission: Entry fee. Open seven days a week from mid-March to October 31. Group tours and education programs can be booked all year round.

TORONTO, ONTARIO - CANADA

Toronto Port Authority Archives
60 Harbour Street
Toronto, Ontario M5J 1B 7 Canada
(416) 863-2008 Fax: Same E-mail: mdale@torontoport.com
Location: The archives are located in Toronto, Ontario.
Highlights: Extensive archives of official documents,
Website: www.torontoport.com/thc/archives.asp

General Information: The Toronto Port Authority Archives maintains a wide variety of information which includes: annual reports, 1853 to the present; minutes of the Board of Commissioners, 1887-1970s; harbour dues, manifest and tonnage registers, 1848-1970s; financial records, 1850-1980s; harbour police logbooks; correspondence, legal documents, photographs, and engineering and architectural drawings concerning waterfront development, the construction and administration of Sunnyside Beach and Amusement Area and the Toronto Island and Malton Airports, the development of the St. Lawrence Seaway, and the activities of North American port and harbour associations.

Publications include: Stinson, Jeffrey, "The Heritage of the Port Industrial District," Toronto: Toronto Harbour Commissioners, 1990.

Admission: No entry fee. Open all year by appointment.

MATTAWA, ONTARIO - CANADA

Voyageur Heritage Centre
Samuel de Champlain Provincial Park
P.O. Box 147
Mattawa, Ontario P0H 1V0 Canada
(705) 744-2276 Fax: (705) 744-0587
Location: The centre is approximately twelve miles west of Mattawa on the Ottawa River.
Highlights: Canoe replica, publications

General Information: The Voyageur Heritage Centre exhibits include: a replica of twelve metre Canot de Maître; furs and trade goods; and description of voyageur history.

Activities: Conducted hikes; canoe hikes, film and slide shows; children's programmes; self-guided hikes; and amphitheater programmes. Self-guided tour description of Voyageur Museum

Admission: Entry fee to park only. Open summer or upon appointment.

Robert H. Smith

WELLAND, ONTARIO - CANADA

Welland Historical Museum
65 Hooker Street
Welland, Ontario L3C 5G9 Canada
(905) 732-2215 E-mail: whmchin@niagara.com
Location: Located in the center of the Niagara Peninsula, the Museum occupies a 1914 school alongside Welland's recreational water-and canal-side park.
Highlights: The Welland Canal, **Website:** www.niagara.com/~whmchin/
General Information: First known as the Seven Mile State, Welland received its first residents in the late 1700s. In 1832, the first Welland Canal was built after an aqueduct was constructed to carry the Welland River over the canal — all of this to bypass Niagara Falls. Soon, the boats being built on the Lakes were too big to fit into the first canal so four other canals were built, each one larger and deeper than the one before. Still, the thirteen 1,000-foot-plus ore ships can't leave the Great Lakes — the newest Welland Canal is too small!

The Welland Historical Museum currently displays Welland and Its Canals, illustrating the effect of the four canals on the city's development; a City Street Gallery filled with urban material from the turn of the century.

Admission: Entry fee. Open Monday-Friday, 10 A.M.-4 P.M., winter; Monday-Saturday, 12 A.M.-4 P.M. summer.

L'ISLET-SUR-MER, QUÉBEC - CANADA

Bernier Maritime Museum
(Musée Maritime Bernier)
55, des Pionniers Est
220 L'Islet-sur-Mer, Québec G0R 2B0 Canada
(418) 247-5001 Fax: (418) 247-5002 E-mail: info@mmq.qc.ca
Location: Approximately sixty miles northeast of Quebec City, L'Islet-sur-Mer lies on south side of St. Lawrence River on Rte. 132.
Highlights: The Ernest Lapointe (icebreaker), Bras d'Or 400 (hydrofoil), Hydro-Québec park, ship models and boatworks, library, gift shop,
General Information: Founded in 1968, the mission of the Musée Maritime du Québec Inc. is to safeguard, study, and promote the maritime heritage of the St. Lawrence River, from it entry point to the Great Lakes to the high seas including the Arctic territories.

Visitors to the Musée du Québec discover not only an exceptional natural site in an enchanting setting on the shores of the St. Lawrence River, but also a cultural site focused on history and the world. The museum offers them a chance to explore our maritime heritage, to the real and contemporary and based on traditions and dreams. On the program: four interactive thematic exhibits, the

Ernest Lapointe icebreaker, the *Bras d'Or 400* hydrofoil, and the Hydro-Québec park and the boatworks, complete with a boat-maker plying his traditional trade in the presence of visitors.

The Museum's collections naturally reflect its dual mandate. The most obvious "artifacts" are its three boats, the sailing ship *J.E. Bernier* II; the icebreaker *Ernest Lapointe*, the pride of the museum's holdings; the Hydrofoil *Bras d'Or 400*, an experimental ship developed for anti-submarine defense. The collections also contain more usual maritime artifacts as navigational instruments and aids, items of rigging and berthing, clothing and accessories, ship's equipment and furnishings, dishes and cutlery, weapons, flags, and scale models. Finally, the museum's holdings also include archival manuscripts, photographs, maps and plans, drawings, and posters.

Activities: Guided tours; animation sessions, documentary films, documentation center, illustration of navigation on the St. Lawrence River and demonstration of ancient maritime techniques.

Admission: Entry fee according to selected activities. Various packages are sold on site. For groups with reservation, the Museum is open at all times. Museum open daily, 10 A.M.-5 P.M., May 20-June 22; open daily, 10 A.M.-5 P.M. June 23-September 3. The rest of the year, 10 A.M.-Noon and 1 P.M.- 4 P.M. Tuesday-Friday. The hydrofoil is open from June 23-September 3. Picnic areas, out-door cafe, and playgrounds are on site.

QUÉBEC, QUÉBEC - CANADA

Cartier-Brébeuf National Historical Park
(Parc Historique National Cartier-Brébeuf)
175, rue de l'Espiany, P.O. Box 2474
Québec, Québec G1K 7R3 Canada
(418) 648-4038

Location: You can reach the park by heading north via Côte d'Abraham and rue Dorchester (follow 175 nord) approximately two miles out from the city center.

Highlights: A 1/20 scale model of a sixteenth-century flagship and a life- sized reproduction of an amerindian loghouse,

Website: www.parcscanada.gc.ca/parks/quebec/brebeuf/en/index.html

General Information: The information center commemorates Jacques Cartier, first European known to have spent a winter in Canada (1535-36), and Jean de Brébeuf, a martyred Jesuit priest. The museum contains documents that illustrate Cartier's second voyage, the mixing of sixteenth-century European and

Robert H. Smith

American Indian cultures, and the initial implantation of the Jesuits in "New France."

Activities: Guided tours of the interpretation centre, hands-on display of navigation instruments, maps and photographs illustrating the site's different historical themes. Special activities from the beginning of July to mid-August.

Admission: Entry fee. Call the museum for information about fees, opening hours, and special activities.

MONTRÉAL, QUÉBEC - CANADA

David M. Stewart Museum
Old Fort - St. Helen's Island
P.O. Box 1200, Station "A"
Montréal, Québec H3C 2Y9 Canada
(514) 861-6701

Location: Via the Jacques Cartier Bridge. By car: take the Jacques Cartier Bridge to the Parc des Iles Exit. This exit is the only one on the bridge and has a very short entry — be prepared. Follow signs for the Fort/Museum's parking. Via Metro: Take Line 4 from Berri-LIQAM Station or Logueuil to Ile Sainte-Hélène Station. A 10-minute walk.

Highlights: Marine Gallery, ship models, book/gift shop through the park gets you there. By bus (in season): Take Bus 169 from Papineau Metro Station to Ile Ste-Hélène stop, then take a brief walk to the Fort.

General Information: Founded in 1955, the David M. Stewart Museum, is housed in an 1822 Arsenal. Among the buildings and exhibits to see are the armory, workshops and cannon store-sheds (even a full-time gun-smith is on site), and ammunition magazines. Other buildings include the powder magazine and barracks.

The fortified arsenal was built by the British to defend the city of Montreal from potential attack by the Americans. The unique artifacts take you back to the life and times of another era, when bold new discoveries were opening vast new frontiers and changing the face of the world. The collections include artifacts, from kitchen utensils to firearms, ancient maps, scientific instruments, and navigational aids and historic documents. During the summer, you'll see the precision drills of two historic regiments who perform 18th-century maneuvers reflecting the daily routine of the troops which were garrisoned in France's New World outposts from 1683 to 1760. And the Olde 78th Fraser Highlanders add another historic dimension to events at the Fort.

Admission: Entry fee. In summer, the Fort/Museum is open from 10 A.M.- 6 P.M. During winter, open until 5 P.M., closed Tuesdays.

Smith's Guide to Maritime Museums of North America

COTEAU-DU-LAC, QUÉBEC - CANADA

Coteau-du-Lac National Historic Site
308A Chemin du Fleuve
Coteau-du-Lac, Québec J0P 1B0 Canada
(450) 763-5631 Fax: (450) 763-1654
Location: Coteau-du-Lac lies along the north side of the St. Lawrence River. From Rte. 40, take Exit 17 south on Rte. 201 past Rte. 20 and 338 to end of road. Turn west 1 klm to site.
Highlights: First lock canal in North America,
Website: www.parcscanada.gc.ca/parks/quebec/coteau/
   General Information: Coteau-du-Lac was a strategic gateway from the days of the nomadic Indian tribes to the 19th century. It is situated on the north side of the St. Lawrence River. In the early 1800s, to avoid the turbulent rapids which blocked the ascent of people and supplies to the West and the Great Lakes, the first lock canal in North America was built at the point of Coteau-du-Lac in 1780, where the Delisle and St. Lawrence Rivers meet. It is remarkable in its short length and simple design.
   British troops passed through on boats and Durham barges. During the armed conflicts of 1776 and 1812, imposing fortifications were built, consisting of a variety of earthworks, defensive buildings, and an octagonal blockhouse.
   Now you can stroll along the short but now-dry canal as far as the fortified bastion to admire the low rapids in the St. Lawrence that the canal by-passed. Unique boats and figures, outlined in steel, positioned in and around this canal, give the visitor a real sense of perspective of its original use.
   Activities: Guided tours and group activities are available daily at the site.
   Admission: Entry fee. Open mid-May to mid-October. Contact for time and fees.

QUÉBEC, QUÉBEC - CANADA

Grosse Ile and the Irish Memorial
National Historic Site
2 rue d'Auteuil
P.O. Box 2474, Postal Terminal
Québec, Québec, G1K 7R3 Canada
(418) 248-8888 1-800-463-6769 E-mail: parcscanada-que@pch.gc.ca
Location: Grosse Ile is in the middle of the St. Lawrence River dominating L'Île-aux-Grues Archipelago. River transportation may be obtained at Berthier sur Mer, Montmagny, Québec City (48 klms).
Highlights: Immigration quarantine station, ice canoe (1920s), Marconi Station (1919), **Website:** www.parkscanada.gc.ca/grosseile

Robert H. Smith

General Information: Situated in the upper St. Lawrence estuary, this island served as a quarantine station from 1832 to 1937 for the port of Quebec, the main gateway to Canada for immigrants until the First World War. In 1847, it was the site of a tragedy when more than 5,000 immigrants, for the most part Irish, fell victims of typhus. Canadian heritage is the focus of this historical site's nineteenth and twentieth century immigration in the development of Canada.

Artifacts reflecting the maritime history of the island include an ice canoe. The canoe dates from the 1954-1955. And a Marconi station dating to 1919 is also on the island. Around 40 historical buildings, some of which are open to the public, are located on the island.

Guided tours are offered and excursions are available, but require reservations.

Admission: The entry fee is included in the transport- carrier's river transport rate. Open early May to October, Wednesday- Sunday. Call for rates and telephone number for carriers.

POINTE-AU-PÈRE, QUÉBEC - CANADA

Pointe-au-Père Sea Museum
1034 du Phare
Pointe-au-Père, Québec G5M 1L8 Canada
(418) 724-6214 Fax: (418) 721-0815 E-mail: museepc@yobetrotter.net
Location: Pointe-au-Père is about five miles east of Rimouski on Rte. 132 (on the south side of the St. Lawrence River, approximately 180 miles northeast of Québec.)
Highlights: The Wreck of the *Empress of Ireland* (Canada's worst maritime tragedy), Pointe-au-Père Aid Center, lighthouse (second highest in Canada),

General Information: Because of its unique location at the frontier between inland waters and the maritime environment, Pointe-au-Père (Father Point) played an important historic role for more than a century. Because of its many navigational aid facilities and a St. Lawrence pilot station, it was well known to navigators by the beginning of the twentieth century. In 1976 the lighthouse and associated buildings were declared a national historic site. Visitors may tour the lighthouse, visit the *Empress of Ireland* Pavilion, the fog horn shed, the first keeper's house, and discover the *Empress of Ireland*, which sank off Rimouski on May 29, 1914, with a loss of 1,012 lives.

Displays include original artifacts, montages, models, dioramas, videos, 3D projection, and photographs depicting the maritime patrimony of the region.

Activities: Illustrations, exhibitions, educational programs, historical research, and historical preservation.

Admission: Entry fee; special fees for groups. Open daily, 9 A.M.-6 P.M., June-October 7 days a week.

QUÉBEC, QUÉBEC - CANADA

Port of Québec in the Nineteenth Century National Historic Site (Lieu Historique National le Port de Québec au XIXe Siècle)
National Historical Site
100 Saint-André Street, P. O. Box 2474
Québec, Québec G1K 7R3 Canada
(418) 648-3300
Location: Overlook the Louise Basin, the centre is located at 100 Saint-André Street in the heart of the Old Port.
Highlights: The history of the Port of Québec in the 19th century
General Information: The Old Port of Québec interpretation Centre has been offering high quality interpretation services since 1984. The hands-on exhibitions relate to the port's principal activities in the nineteenth century: shipbuilding and timber trade. Scale-models, reproductions, soundtracts and mannequins in period costume recreate the hustle and bustle of Québec's harbourfront at the time of tall ship sailing.
Activities: Guided tours of the exhibitions. Guided tour of the port in the 19th century.
Admission: Entry fee. Open May 2nd-September 3rd: everyday, from 10 A.M. - 5 P.M.; September 4th - October 7th: every day from 1 P.M. to 5 P.M.

PRINCE EDWARD ISLAND - CANADA

SOURIS, PRINCE EDWARD ISLAND - CANADA

Basin Head Fisheries Museum
Souris P.O. RR#2
Souris, P.E.I. C0A 2B0 Canada
(902) 357-7233 Fax: (902) 357-7232 (Off season: (902) 368-6600 & Fax: (902) (368-6608) E-mail: basinhead@gov.pe.ca
Location: The Museum is located high on the bluff overlooking (Singing Sand" beach and the Northumberland Strait off Rte. 16, 12-km East of Souris, on Prince Edward Island.
Highlights: View, dioramas, lobster fishery, coastal ecology exhibit, aquariums, and gift shop. **Website:** www.peimuseum.com
General Information: Located in a former fishing port, the Basin Head Fisheries Museum, founded in 1973, tells the story of the inshore fishery through artifacts, dioramas, and photographs that depict the life style of an inshore fisherman through displays of regional small craft and fishing gear. As the lobster industry boomed, canneries sprang up all along the Prince Edward Island coast. In 1903, the Island had 190 canneries. On site are dioramas illustrating

Robert H. Smith

fishing-industry techniques and the variety of boats used and various types of trawl nets, fish sheds, and small-craft.

The large building down by the wharf below the Museum once housed the Smith fish cannery, which put up tins of salt fish and chicken haddy and now houses a coastal ecology exhibit that complements the other exhibits.

Activities: Variety of workshops including art, tole painting, child craft workshops, craft and kite demonstrations, as well Share History Talks. (Call for information.)

Admission: Entry fee. Open daily Spring to Fall, 9 A.M.-5 P.M.; mid-season, 9 A.M.- 6 P.M. Special rates for bus tours.

PORT HILL, PRINCE EDWARD ISLAND - CANADA

Green Park Shipbuilding Museum
Green Park Provincial Park
Port Hill, Tyne Valley RR 1
Prince Edward Island C0B 2C0
Canada
(203) 831-7947 E-mail: lxarsenault@bov.pe.ca

PEI Museum
2 Kent St.
Charlottetown, PEI
Canada C1A 1M6
(203) 892-9127

Location: Take the new Confederation Bridge to Prince Edward Island: toll one way only. Then 8 klms to Rte. 1-A west some 26 klms to Rte. 2. Then west on Rte. 2 a short distance to the intersection to Rte. 12. Turn north on 12 traveling 16 klms into Port Hill and Green Park Provincial Park where the shipyard is located.

Highlights: History of wooden ship building, Annual Blue Berry Social, gift shop

Website:www.peimuseum.com/greenpark.shtml?MUSEUM=greenpark&LANGUAGE=english

General Information: During the nineteenth century, shipbuilding was a major industry on Prince Edward Island. Green Park was the site of an active shipyard. Green Park includes the Green Park Shipbuilding Museum, founded in 1973, tracing the history and craft of shipbuilding in the 1800s in a re-created nineteenth-century wooden shipbuilding yard, and an interpretive centre. The museum includes the restored 1865 Victorian residence of ship owner James Yeo Jr. Exhibits also include carpenter and blacksmith shops, and a partially completed full-size vessel.

Activities: July Blueberry Social, concerts on the Green, and Ghost Story

USA

MAINE

BOOTHBAY HARBOR, MAINE

Boothbay Region Historical Society
72 Oak Street
P.O. Box 272
Boothbay Harbor, ME 04538
(207) 633-3462/0820
Location: At Bath, head east on Rte. 1 ten miles to State Highway 27. Boothbay Harbor is on the peninsula between the Sheepscot and Damariscotta Rivers and shares the peninsula and adjacent islands with a dozen other communities, including Boothbay (settled 1730), of which it was once a part. *Highlights:* Maritime history,
Website: www.mainemuseums.org/htm/museumdetail.php3?orgID=9

General Information: Twenty years before the Pilgrims stepped ashore on Plymouth Rock, English fishermen visited and inhabited numerous spots in the Boothbay Region, including Damariscove Island, Fisherman's Island, and Newagen, the tip of Southport. They caught, salted, and dried codfish to sell to Spain, France, England, and the "wine islands" of Madeira, the Canaries, and the Azores. By 1621 their settlements were so prosperous that when Edward Winslow came east to buy food for the starving Pilgrims, the fishermen at Damariscove supplied him generously and refused payment.

The Boothbay Region Historical Society, housed in a nineteenth-century sea captain's residence of Italianate design with period furnishings, was organized in 1967 for the purpose of bringing together individuals interested in local history and collecting and preserving records and artifacts relating to this region and the people who have lived and worked here.

The Historical Society exhibits documents the artifacts from the Indian days and the periods of active fishing, shipbuilding, and trading, into the present century. Fishing gear, tools, and nautical instruments are displayed, and a guide will be glad to explain their use.

A number of photographs of sailing ships, steamers, and "how it was in the good old days" are mounted and many more are on file. The Society has models of Boothbay vessels built by local artists. The exhibits include implements of the fishing and ship-building industries, plus nineteenth-century household appliances, old photographs, and documents.

Admission: No entry fee. Open all year Saturdays, 10 A.M.-2 P.M.; July-August, Wednesday, Friday, and Saturday, 10 A.M.-4 P.M. Other times by appointment.

Robert H. Smith

The history of the freight forwarders who moved all the goods from the "civilized" world to the settlers on the frontier via boat—the St. Lawrence Bateau. This model is in the Forwarders' Museum, Prescott, Ontario. (Photo R. H. Smith)

This rich seafaring heritage comes to life at the Maine Maritime Museum in Bath, Maine, founded in 1962. On the Museum's grounds is the last shipyard intact in the country where sailing vessels were built. (Photo: Dennis Griggs)

EASTPORT, MAINE

Border Historical Society
P.O. Box 95
Eastport, ME 04631
(207) 853-2328.
Location: Eastport, Maine, is adjacent to Nova Scotia in the southeast corner of the state.
General Information: The Society preserves maritime items of the fishing industry including the boats, the factories, and industry along the U.S. and Canadian shores of Passamaquoddy Bay.
Admission: Open Tuesday-Saturday 1 P.M.-4 P.M., May Day - Labor Day and by appointment.

Robert H. Smith

KENNEBUNK, MAINE

Brick Store Museum
177 Main Street
Kennebunk, ME 04043
(207) 985-4802 E-mail: info@brickstoremuseum.org
Location: Kennebunk lies twenty-five miles south of Portland on Rte. 1, one mile east of I-95. The Museum is located downtown at 117 Main Street.
Highlights: Maritime history, research library, museum gift shop, **Website:** www.brickstoremuseum.org
  General Information: The Brick Store Museum, founded in 1936, is a complex of four restored nineteenth-century buildings, including William Lord's brick store (1825). The Museum contains changing exhibits of fine and decorative arts, historical and maritime collections, and a research library.
  Activities: Architectural walking tours June-October tours every Friday at 2 P.M., 10 June -14 October. Leaving from the Museum, the tours pass by homes in the Kennebunk Historic District (1760-1900).
  Admission: Entry fee. Open Tuesday-Friday 10 A.M.-4:30 P.M. and Saturdays 10 A.M.-4:30 P.M. April 1-December.

SOUTH BERWICK, MAINE

Counting House-Old Berwick Historical Society (c. 1830)
P.O. Box 296
South Berwick, ME 03908
(207) 384-8041 or 207/384-5162 or 207/384-0000
E-mail: rmp@nh.ultranet.com
Location: From Kittery north on Rte. 236 14 miles to South Berwick on corner of Main and Liberty Streets.
Highlights: Gundalow ship models (freight boats), nautical library
  General Information: The Society's 160-year-old restored factory building is situated at the head of navigation on the Salmon Falls River. Shipbuilders tools are exhibited along with ship models, navigational instruments, photos, and other items of a local nature. The Museum displays artifacts from local archaeological "Dig," (1935-1690 Chadbourne Site). Also displayed are gundalow models, photos, and technical drawings on gundalows. The Counting House contains an archive with 3,000 documents and photographs.
  Admission: No entry fee, but donations accepted. Open Saturday-Sunday, 1 P.M.- 4 P.M., July-August-September, also by appointment.

PEMAQUID POINT, MAINE

Fishermen's Museum and Pemaquid Point Lighthouse
Lighthouse Park
Pemaquid Point, ME 04554
(207) 677-2494/2726
Location: Pemaquid Point Lighthouse is located sixty miles northeast of Portland near Boothbay Harbor.
Highlights: Wall-size chart of all coastal lighthouses in Maine, Fresnel lighthouse lens built in France, working half-models of fish boats and a whaler, lobster boat, ship models, **Website:** www.lighthouse.cc/pemaquid/

General Information: The Pemaquid Point Lighthouse was commissioned by John Quincy Adams in 1827. Its 1,000-candlepower beam is visible up to fourteen miles at sea. The town of Bristol owns and maintains the surrounding park and the Fishermen's Museum, now housed in the old lightkeeper's dwelling. The light, though not attended, is a familiar navigational aid to fishermen and all coastal traffic. It is a working light and not open to the public.

Displays at the Fishermen's Museum, opened in 1972, include pictures of lighthouses along the coast of Maine, which are numbered to correspond to a wall-size navigational chart; a bronze buoy bell with iron chain; and a Lyle gun for shooting a lifeline to ships in distress. Also presented are tools used in lobstering and gear for several different methods of harvesting the sea. A lens identical to the one in the tower of the lighthouse is featured.

The Museum exhibits are located in four rooms: the Navigation Room, with navigation displays; the Fish House, with work-benches, tools, and gear used in the lobstering and fishing industries; the Net Room, where several different methods of harvesting fish are displayed, including a small scallop dredge and a sink-gill net used to catch cod and haddock; and the Gallery, where working half-models of fish boats as well as models of a whaler are displayed. A photographic record of the building of a schooner, scrapbooks containing information on fishing, shrimping, and shipwrecks, as well as albums of old postcards, documents, and newspaper articles pertaining to the area, are of special interest.

Admission: No entry fee, but donations accepted. Open Monday-Saturday, 10 A.M.-5 P.M., Sunday, 11 A.M.-5 P.M., Memorial Day-Columbus Day. Other times by appointment.

Robert H. Smith

FRIENDSHIP, MAINE

Friendship Museum
P. O. Box 325
Friendship, ME 04547
(207) 832-4337 E-mail: case@midcoast.com
Location: Friendship is approximately seventy-two miles north of Portland, Maine. Follow Rte. 1 to Waldoboro, and take Rte. 220 south to Friendship.
Highlights: Memorabilia of the town of Friendship
   General Information: Friendship Museum was founded in 1964 and housed in an old brick schoolhouse built in 1850. The Museum contains exhibits on the community and the history of the sailing craft known as the Friendship Sloop.
   Admission: No entry fee, but donations accepted. Open July-Labor Day, Monday-Saturday, 1 P.M.- 4 P.M., Sunday, 2 P.M.-4 P.M.

MACHIASPORT, MAINE

Gates House/Machiasport Historical Society
Route 92
P.O. Box 301
Machiasport, ME 04655
(207) 255-8461
Location: Machiasport lies about ninety-five miles due east of Bangor on Machias Bay. Take Rte. 1 to SR-92. The Society operates the Gates House in town.
Highlights: Ship models, library, genealogy
   General Information: The Gates House, built circa 1800, is a Federal-style house with several rooms furnished in period fashion. The maritime room exhibits include ship models and a maritime library.
   Admission: No entry fee, but donations accepted. Open Tuesday-Saturday, 12:30 P.M.-4:30 P.M., mid-June-mid-September. Closed holidays.

BOOTHBAY, MAINE

Grand Banks Schooner Museum
P. O. Box 123
Boothbay, ME 04537
(207) 633-4727 E-mail: staff@schoonermuseum.org
Location: The Museum is the wooden, auxiliary fishing schooner *Sherman Zwicker*. The schooner is generally docked at the Maine Maritime Museum during the summer at 263 Washington Street, Bath, Maine.
Highlights: The *Sherman Zwicker* (a 142-foot dory schooner),

Website: www.schoonermuseum.org

General Information: Grand Banks Schooner Museum, founded in 1968, preserves and exhibits the schooner *Sherman Zwicker*, a 142-foot dory schooner, as a significant representative of fishing history.

Built in 1942 in Lunenburg, Nova Scotia, this transition vessel, with schooner hull identical to the famous *Bluenose* and a powerful diesel engine, fished for almost twenty years under Capt. Moyle Crouse of Lunenburg. Then Capt. Max Burry from Glovertown, Newfoundland, fished her until 1968, when the schooner was saved from the graveyard, to be restored as a museum.

Completely restored and operational, this historic vessel is accessible both above and below decks to the viewing public. This is the only seaworthy vessel of this type that remains active in waterfront and Tall Ship activities, such as celebrations in Boston and New York City.

The engine room is particularly interesting: much of it is filled with the massive Fairbanks Morse 320-horse-power engine which drives the ship at a cruising speed of 9.5 knots.

Admission: Entry fee. (For further information, see Maine Maritime Museum listing.)

NORTHEAST HARBOR, MAINE

The Great Harbor Maritime Museum
125 Main Street
P.O. Box 145
Northeast Harbor, ME 04662
(207) 276-5262 E-mail: ghmmuse@acadia.net
Location: North East Harbor lies ten miles southwest of Bar Harbor on Mount Desert Island.
Highlights: History of Maine coastal life
General Information: The Great Harbor Collection Museum, founded in 1982, is the result of the hard work and generosity of the local townspeople. Rotating exhibits showing specific aspects of the areas history through photographs, artifacts, and film. Oral histories and children's trips to create art from nature on islands are part of the program.

Special exhibits of maritime interest include models of the steamboats *Rangeley* and *J. T. Morse* as well as "Life at Mt. Desert Rock Lighthouse," a series of glass-plate photographs taken at the Light in 1907.

Activities: Various heritage activities depicting the area's culture
Admission: No entry fee, but memberships available. Open Tuesday-Saturday, seasonal 9 A.M.-5 P.M.

Robert H. Smith

BAR HARBOR, MAINE

Islesford Historical Museum
c/o William Otis Sawtelle Collections and Research Center
Acadia National Park
P.O. Box 177
Bar Harbor, ME 04609
(207) 244-9224 (Summer), 207/288-3338 (year round),
Location: The Islesford Historical Museum is located on Little Cranberry Island within the Town of Cranberry Isles, which is located five miles off the coast of Mount Desert Island. The Museum is accessible by Mailboat or ferry from the village of Northeast Harbor or the Town of Southwest Harbor (both located on Mount Desert Island).
Highlights: Maritime history, island history, Settlement of the Town of Cranberry Isles, Genealogy of the Town of Cranberry Isles,
Website: www.mainemuseums.org/htm/museumdetail.php3?orgID=249
    General Information: The Islesford Historical Museum was founded by Professor William Otis Sawtelle in 1919 in an effort to preserve the maritime and settlement history of the Cranberry Isles. In 1948 the Museum was donated to the National Park Service and became a part of Acadia National Park.

    Exhibits illustrate the maritime history of the region, depict everyday life on an island, and offer a glimpse into the lives of islanders. Rotating exhibits highlight artifacts from the extensive collection.

    The collection contains documents pertaining to the sale of land, town records, ship records, books and ship logbooks, and genealogical records including vital statistics. Additionally, the collection contains furnishings including farming and navigational tools, ship models and name boards, household goods, and children's toys. The collections, not on exhibit, are located at the William Otis Sawtelle Collections and Research Center in Bar Harbor, ME and are accessible (year round) for research by calling or writing to the Museum Curator (207/288-5463) at the above address.

    Admission: No entry fee. Open daily from mid-June to approximately mid-September.

YORK, MAINE

John Hancock Warehouse and Wharf/
Old York Historical Society
P. O. Box 312
York, ME 03909
(207) 363-4974 E-mail: oyhs@oldyork.org

Location: Exit off I-95 onto Rte. 1A in the southeast corner of Maine. The wharf and warehouse are on Lindsay Road and the bank of the York River. *Highlights:* Art Gallery in George Marshall Store,
Website: www.oldyork.org

General Information: John Hancock Warehouse and Wharf were built in the eighteenth century and established as a museum and historical site in 1974. It documents three hundred years of commercial life along the York River. Of the many wharves and warehouses that fronted the river and York Harbor (then Lower Town) in the eighteenth century, the John Hancock Warehouse is the only remaining commercial building from the Colonial period in York.

Guides will lead you through six museum buildings that date from 1740 to 1940 and portray community, commercial, maritime, and family life from those periods. Collections include furnishings and other maritime artifacts from wealthy shipowners and merchants.

Activities: Guided tours, library for research, decorative arts, genealogy, early manuscripts, documents pertaining to York County, and some maritime materials.

Admission: Entry fee. Tickets at Jefferds' Tavern Visitor's Center open Tuesday-Saturday, 10 A.M.-5 P.M., Early June to Columbus Day weekend.

KENNEBUNKPORT, MAINE

Kennebunkport Maritime Museum
Ocean Avenue
P.O. Box 765
Kennebunkport, ME 04046
(207) 967-4195 967-3218

Location: The Museum is located at "The Floats" on the historic Kennebunk River. Follow Rtes. 9 or 35 to Dock Square in Kennebunkport. Turn right onto Ocean Avenue along river and follow approximately one mile to Museum.
Highlights: Navigational instruments, marine paintings, scrimshaw, ship models, museum shop, **Website:** www.ohwy.com/ME/k/kebumamg.htm

General Information: The Museum is located in the fully renovated boathouse of celebrated author, Booth Tarkington. Here you'll find the last remnants of Tarkington's schooner *Regina*, a longtime Kennebunkport landmark, including the ship's wheel, all her bow carvings, her quarterboards, and the ship's name flag.

Displays include: artifacts from throughout New England's seafaring history; eighteenth- and nineteenth-century navigational instruments including quadrants, sextants, chronometers, and spyglasses; a large collection of antique scrimshaw; eighteenth- and nineteenth-century ship models, builders one-half models; and a

Robert H. Smith

collection of marine paintings by Bard, McFarlane, Badger, Jacobsen, Raleigh, and York.
Admission: Entry fee. Open daily, 10 A.M.-4 P.M., May 15-October 15.

KITTERY, MAINE

Kittery Historical and Naval Museum
Rogers Road
P. O. Box 453
Kittery, ME 03904-3080
(207) 439-3080
Location: Just north of Portsmouth, New Hampshire, off I-95 at Exit #2, then Rte 1 North just beyond Kittery Traffic Circle. Kittery is an old sea town where ships were built since earliest days. Even today, the oldest naval shipyard in the country lies in the Piscataqua River, between the New Hampshire shore and Kittery.
Highlights: Artifacts from early seacoast life, genealogy of Kittery families and local culture, 2nd Order Fresnel lens from Boon Island Lighthouse, ship models, video history, gift shop, library
General Information: Kittery Historical and Naval Museum, founded in 1975, has assumed the responsibility of preserving and interpreting the history of the oldest incorporated town in Maine, as well as that of the naval shipyard and related on-shore activities.

Kittery, the "Gateway to Maine," was first settled in 1623. From 1695 to 1749, three English warships were constructed by local craftsmen. In 1776, the first Continental Naval vessel, the *Raleigh*, was launched on the Piscataqua. On June 12, 1800, the Department of the Navy purchased Fernald's Island in Kittery, and established the first government installation of its kind in the U.S.

The Museum exhibits objects and manuscripts related to the history of the town and the Portsmouth Naval Shipyard. At the Museum you will see a thirteen-foot model of the sloop *Ranger*, models of eighteenth-, nineteenth-, and twentieth-century naval vessels, a naval Gatling gun, collections of scrimshaw items, Bellamy carvings and shipwright's paraphernalia. A video presentation outlines Kittery's rich maritime past and highlights many of her early notables. photographs, dioramas, paintings of bygone days, ships plans, and logs. Manuscripts are also available for researchers.
Activities: Special exhibits, lectures, and special events.
Admission: Entry fee: reduced rates for children, seniors, and groups. Open Tuesday-Saturday, 10 A.M.-4 P.M., June-Columbus Day, or by appointment.

BATH, MAINE

Maine Maritime Museum
243 Washington Street
Bath, ME 04530
(207) 443-1316 Fax: (207) 443-1665 E-mail: maritime@bathmaine.com
Location: Follow I-95 to Rte. 1. Head east to Bath (thirty-five miles northeast of Portland near Boothbay) on the west side of the Kennebec River. ***Highlights:*** The *Sherman Zwicker* (Grand Banks Schooner), "Lobstering and the Coast of Maine" exhibit, maritime history exhibit building, small-craft collection, the boat shop (wooden boat building), library (10,000 volumes) on Maine maritime history, **Website:** www.bathmaine.com/

General Information: For centuries mariners have built wooden ships, sailed them to faraway ports, and fished from them on banks and bays for elusive cod and lobster. This rich seafaring heritage comes to life at the Maine Maritime Museum, founded in 1962. The Museum includes a restored ten-acre shipyard with over 1,000 feet of river frontage — it's the last shipyard intact in the country where sailing vessels were built — a boat-building and lobstering exhibit, and a new major exhibit building on Maine's maritime heritage.

Exhibits depict local shipbuilding families and traditions as well as regional history and models; half-models; tools; instruments; trade goods; seamen's possessions; small boats; and dioramas.

Board the Grand Banks schooner *Sherman Zwicker* when she is in port. The shipyard also houses an apprentice shop where traditional boatbuilding skills are taught, exhibits on wood ship construction, and a fine collection of small craft used along the Maine coast and inland waterways.

Activities: Hour-long tours of the Percy & Small Shipyard, where one learns how wooden ships were built, begin April 15. Shipyard demonstrations of blacksmithing, draft horses, ship launchings, treenail making, and signal flags begin June 22. Hour-long river excursions and day-long cruises — seasonal. Two video presentations; training programs in small wooden boat building; group tours by appointment; and an annual symposium on maritime history.

Admission: Entry fee. Open daily, 9:30 A.M.-5 P.M., year-round. Closed Thanksgiving, Christmas, and New Year's Days.

PORT CLYDE, MAINE

Marshall Point Lighthouse Museum
P.O. Box 247
Port Clyde, ME 04855
(207) 372-6450

Robert H. Smith

Location: The Museum is located in Port Clyde. From Rte. 1 in Thomaston take Rte. 131 to Port Clyde, follow the signs to the lighthouse.
Highlights: Lighthouse, gift shop,
Website: www.rickslighthouses.com/marshall_point.htm
General Information: The Marshall Point Lighthouse Museum is in the 1895 keeper's house. It used seven lard-oil lamps with fourteen-inch reflectors. The current tower built in 1858 was equipped with a fifth-order Fresnel lens. A fog bell added in 1898, was replaced by a fog horn in 1969. In 1935 the light was electrified and automated in 1971. The current Keeper's House built in 1895 — deserted in 1980 — was taken over by the local Historical Society and restored.

The Museum was opened on the first floor and now welcomes 10,000 visitors each year. The Museum has exhibits on fishing, lobstering, quarrying, and of course, the lighthouse itself. A set of three-ring scrap books preserve local stories in photos, postcards, newspaper, and magazine articles. They lend a feeling of sharing in family remembrances as they preserve the town's sense of history. As part of the Maine Lights Program the ownership was officially transferred in June 1998. The Museum is an example of successful community involvement and hard work.

Admission: No entry fee. Open June-September, every afternoon 1 P.M. - 5 P.M.; Saturday 10 A.M. - 5 P.M.

GREENVILLE, MAINE

Moosehead Marine Museum
P. O. Box 1151
Greenville, ME 04441
(207) 695-2716 Fax: (207) 695-2367 E-mail: katahdincruise@ctel.net
Location: The Museum is located in the center of Greenville, seventy-five miles northwest of Bangor at the south end of Moosehead Lake.
Highlights: The *Katahdin* (steamboat), The *Katahdin Knots* (newsletter),
Website: www.katahdincruises.com
General Information: The Moosehead Marine Museum, founded in 1976, is a floating museum aboard the Lake Steamer SS *Katahdin*. For many years, before the opening of the road system in the United States, water traffic was the primary mode of transportation around the country, including the area around Moosehead Lake. Steamboats carried livestock, railroad equipment, supplies, and passengers. Steamboat history began there in 1836 with the steamboat *Moosehead*. Many of the boats were built at Greenville and the West Cove shipyard.

Exhibits in the Museum include artifacts and photos concerning the steamboat era on Moosehead Lake, logging, and the Mount Kineo Hotel, considered one of the finest resort properties in the world during its heyday. The

Museum has two rooms of area memorabilia: one room is devoted to the ships of the lake, the other to the great hotel era, the Mount Kineo House in particular.

The SS *Katahdin*, a 1914 lake ferry steamship, used on the last log drive in the Nation, has undergone restoration and is once again carrying passengers on happy voyages on Moosehead Lake.

Activities: Head of Lake Cruises and Mt. Kineo Cruises

Admission: Cruises: Moosehead Lake-Monday-Friday, Daily except Monday & Friday, 12:30 P.M.-4 P.M., Memorial Day - Columbus Day. Other times by appointment rest of year.

YARMOUTH, MAINE

Museum of Yarmouth History
Main Street
P. O. Box 107
Yarmouth, ME 04096
(207) 846-6259
Location: Take exit 16 on I-295 to Rte. 1. Exit onto Rte. 115, the main street in Yarmouth. (Yarmouth is just nine miles north of Portland on Casco Bay.) Merrill Memorial Library houses the Museum.
Highlights: History of Yarmouth and North Yarmouth, book shop
General Information: The Museum of Yarmouth History focuses on the history of both Yarmouth and North Yarmouth, a coastal community settled in 1636. Yarmouth history has always been linked to the sea, especially in the nineteenth century when it was home to many shipyards and sea captains.

Museum exhibits may include photographs, shipbuilding tools, instruments, ship paintings. Research materials include journals, documents.

Admission: Donations welcome. Open Monday-Friday, 1 P.M.-5 P.M., July and August; Tuesday-Friday, 1 P.M.-5 P.M.; Saturday, 10 A.M.-5 P.M., September-June.

LUBEC, MAINE

The Old Sardine Village Museum
Route 189
Lubec, ME 04652
(207) 733-2822
Location: Take I-95 to Bangor, then east on US 1A/1 approximately ninety miles to Whiting, then Rte. 189 eleven miles to Lubec. The Museum is on the most eastern coast of Maine adjacent to the Canadian Province of New Brunswick.
Highlights: Ship models

Robert H. Smith

General Information: A block of shops and displays illustrate the growth of the food-canning industry from the first, primitive hand-formed can of the 1830s to the thriving canneries of the 1930s. Displays include: model ship collections; early nineteenth-century corn cannery; rare model corn cooker and can filler; original double steamer; and early blueberry cannery with original stamping presses and dies.

Admission: Entry fee. Open Wednesday-Friday, 1 P.M.-5 P.M., Saturday, 1 P.M.-4 P.M., Sunday, 1 P.M.-5 P.M. June-September.

PORTLAND, MAINE

Osher Map Library
University of Southern Maine
P.O. Box 9301
Portland, ME 04104-9301
(207) 780-4850 (voice), -5310 (Fax), -5646 (TDD)
E-mail: curator@usm.maine.edu
Location: The Library is on the Portland campus of the University of Southern Maine, at the intersection of Forest Avenue and Bedford Street. ***Highlights:*** Rare map library,
Website: www.usm.maine.edu/maps/library.html

General Information: The Osher Map Library and Smith Center for Cartographic Education is the only separately established rare map library in northern New England. The Smith and Osher collections comprise fine examples of original maps, atlases, geographies, and globes spanning the years from 1475 to the present. They constitute a rich and multifaceted resource for the study and teaching of geography, history, art, and cultural development. For the University, the people of Maine, scholars, students, and visitors, the collections are indeed a treasure.

Activities: The Osher Map Library is committed to sharing its collection with a broad constituency by means of exhibitions, lectures, conferences, and other special events. It encourages collaborative efforts with other institutions including museums, historical societies, and teaching institutions ranging from primary schools to the university level. It serves the University community and residents of Maine and Northern New England, including the general public and local school systems, as well as the global community of scholars and researchers.

Admission: No entry fee. Open Monday: closed Tuesday: 12:30 P.M. - 4:30 P.M.; Wednesday: 12:30 P.M.- 4:30 and 6 P.M. - 8 P.M.; Thursday: 12.30 P.M. - 4.30 P.M. and 6 P.M. - 8 P.M.; Friday: school groups by appointment; Saturday: 9 A.M. - 1 P.M. Because the university schedule changes between the academic year and vacations, it is advisable to call ahead — (207) 780-4850 — to confirm these times.

BRUNSWICK, MAINE

Peary-MacMillan Arctic Museum
9500 College Station, Bowdoin College
Brunswick, ME 04011-8495
(207) 725-3416 Fax: (207) 725-3499 E-mail: nwagner@bowdoin.edu
Location: Brunswick is twenty-five miles north of Portland just off I-95 or Rte. 1 and eight miles from historic Bath. The Museum is located in Hubbard Hall, on the campus of historic Bowdoin College.
Highlights: Arctic exploration, **Website:** www.bowdoin.edu/dept/arctic/
General Information: Named after alumni Robert E. Peary (1877) and Donald B. MacMillan (1898), the museum preserves the long association between Bowdoin College and the Arctic, and features displays of Arctic natural history specimens, exploration equipment and photographs, and Inuit (Eskimo) art and artifacts.

Peary graduated from Bowdoin in 1877 and began his Arctic explorations in 1886 in Greenland. He culminated his Arctic work with his expedition to the North Pole. The Museum's exhibits include a gallery focusing on Perry's 1908-09 North Pole expedition, and introduction to Arctic peoples and environments, and changing exhibits on Arctic themes. Several models of the exploration ships SS *Roosevelt* and the Schooner *Bowdoin* are on display.

The Special Collections of Bowdoin's Hawthorne-Longfellow Library contain the personal papers and photographs of several Arctic explorers and prominent sea captains.

Admission: No entry fee. Open Tuesday-Saturday 10 A.M.-5 P.M., Sunday 2 P.M.-5 P.M., year round. The museum is closed on Mondays and national holidays.

SEARSPORT, MAINE

Penobscot Marine Museum
Church Street
P. O. Box 498
Searsport, ME 04974-0498
(207) 548-2529 Fax: (207) 548-2520
E-mail: museumoffices@penobscotmarinemuseum.org
Location: Searsport is equidistant between Bangor (to the north) and Camden (to the south) on the upper Penobscot Bay. The Museum complex is located on Rte. 1 in downtown Searsport.

Robert H. Smith

Highlights: Eight exhibit buildings that contain the largest collection of marine paintings in Maine, ship models, small craft, historic home, education center, research Library (12,000 volumes) and gift shop.
Website: www.penobscotmarinemuseum.org

General Information: Penobscot Marine Museum, founded in 1936, consists of an historic district of 13 buildings (eight listed on the National Register of Historic Places). Attractions include: Captain Jeremiah Merithew's House (1860), Fowler House (1820), Old Town Hall (1845), Former Church Vestry (1846), Duncan House (1850), modern library and art gallery, two small craft barns and a boat house. The Josiah Dutch House contains the education center.

PMM's Maine Watercraft collection is now centered in multi-level barns and a boat house contains both wooden fishing craft and early 20th century sailing craft. Rotating exhibits in the art gallery, permanent exhibits include "Challenge of the Down Easter" and "Working the Bay." The Stephen Phillips Memorial Library features changing exhibits and an extensive collection of maritime history and genealogy.

The Museum contains 300 paintings, ship models, builders' half-models, and shipbuilders' tools, and American and Oriental furniture. The country's largest collection of marine paintings by Thomas and James Buttersworth in New England are also on display.

Activities: Docent tours at every exhibit. Children's activities: capstan drills, yard-in-the-yard, story time, etc.

Admission: Entry fee. Open Memorial Day-October 15, daily 10 A.M.- 5 P.M., Sunday noon-5 P.M. Winter hours by appointment

SOUTH PORTLAND, MAINE

Portland Harbor Museum
Southern Maine Technical College
Fort Road
South Portland, ME 04106
(207) 799-6337 Fax: (same) E-mail: info@portharbmuseum.org
Location: From I-295 in Portland, take Exit 6A and follow Rte. 77 over the Casco Bay Bridge to South Portland. From the bridge, go straight ahead and follow Broadway until it ends. Follow signs to museum.
Highlights: Annually changing exhibits plus permanent exhibits on the only surviving clipper ship, extreme clipper ship *Snow Squall*, and the lighthouses of Casco Bay, Spring Point Ledge Lighthouse, historic Fort Preble, Willard Beach, and a Signed Shoreline Walkway, **Website:** www.portlandharbormuseum.org

General Information: The Portland Harbor Museum (formerly the Spring Point Museum) was founded in 1985 to interpret the history of the harbor, its islands and surrounding communities. The bow of the extreme clipper ship *Snow*

Squall was brought to the museum from the Falkland Islands in 1987 to form the centerpiece of a major research and preservation project. Built at South Portland in 1851, the 742-ton vessel sailed out of New York for thirteen years to San Francisco and the Far East. In 1864, she sustained severe damage trying to round Cape Horn and lay in Port Stanley, Falkland Islands, for almost a century and a quarter before being recovered to South Portland. At the conclusion of the Snow Squall Project in 1995, sections of the bow were given to three other maritime museums but major pieces were retained by Portland Harbor Museum for exhibition and as a memorial to Maine's role in the greatest age of sail.

In 1998 Portland Harbor Museum was awarded stewardship of the adjacent Spring Point Ledge Light under the Maine Lights Program, with a goal to preserve the century old lighthouse. It is opened for public tours four times each year. The museum also maintains collections of maritime artifacts and archival material.

Activities: The 2001 exhibit is titled, *"They came by Sea: Portland Harbor, A Tourist Destination."*

Admission: Entry fee. Open May-December on weekends, and Friday-Sunday in June, July-August open daily, 10 A.M.-4:30 P.M.

CAPE ELIZABETH, MAINE

Portland Head Light
Fort Williams Park
1000 Shore Road
P. O. Box 6260
Cape Elizabeth, ME 04107
(207) 799-2661 Fax: (207) E-mail: cephl@aol.com
Location: On Casco Bay, Cape Elizabeth is four miles south of South Portland, off Rte. 77. The Light is in Fort Williams Park.
Highlights: Portland Head Light, gift shop,
Website: www.portlandheadlight.com

General Information: After seventy-four ship owners petitioned for a beacon to guide them into Maine's busiest harbor, Portland Head Light was first lit on January 10, 1791. The final funds were authorized by George Washington as the first light authorized by the United States and is one of the oldest lighthouses in continuous use.

Henry Wadsworth Longfellow frequently hiked from Portland to compose under the 72-foot tower. Waves swept away the 2,000-pound fog bell in 1869, deposited the ship *Annie C. McGuire* at the base of the cliffs in 1886, and smashed the whistlehouse wall in 1973 in knocking out the fog horn and temporarily extinguishing the light.

Robert H. Smith

Portland Head Light is one of the most-visited lights on the Atlantic seaboard. The tower's hurricane deck provides a view of more than 200 islands in the sweep of Casco Bay.

Admission: no entry fee to Park; open daily, sunrise-sunset year-round. Entry fee to Light-house and museum open daily 10 A.M.-4 P.M. Memorial Day-October. April, May, November, December weekends, 10 A.M.-4 P.M.

EASTPORT, MAINE

Quoddy Maritime Museum
P.O. Box 98
Corner of Water & Boynton Streets
Eastport, ME 04361
(207) 853-4297 E-mail: charleton@acadia.net
Location: Follow Rte 190 to downtown Eastport, turn right at the Post Office, museum is on the right in the last two buildings of the first block ***Highlights:*** Local maritime history, gift shop,
Website: www.eastport.u104.k12.me.us/quoddy.htm

General Information: The Quoddy Maritime Museum, opened in June of 1998, and its collections contain maps of area, 14' x 15' model of the proposed Passamaquoddy Tidal Power Project, a video oral history display as well as other VHS tapes of maritime interest, and more. Currently on exhibit is "Lewis Hine visits Eastport, 1911." Also, Quoddy Crafts features the work of 20 local crafters. A museum gift shop is on site. A gift shop and visitor center is maintained to answer tourist inquiries.

Admission: No entry fee. Open Memorial Day to Salmon Festival (second Saturday in September), Monday-Saturday, 9 A.M.-5 P.M. Call for additional information.

ISLESBORO, MAINE

Sailor's Memorial Museum and Lighthouse
Grindle Point
P. O. Box 76
Islesboro, ME 04848
(207) 734-2253
Location: Take I-95 to Augusta, exiting onto Rte. 202. Travel east forty-six miles to Belfast, then south on Rte. 1 thirteen miles to Lincolnville. At Linconville Beach, board the auto ferry to Islesboro.
Highlights: Lighthouse, Gift Shop

General Information: Sailor's Memorial Museum, founded in 1936, contains collections that include maritime and other historic coastal artifacts and

Smith's Guide to Maritime Museums of North America

materials, primarily about local heritage. The Grindle Point keeper's house is also open to visitors.

Admission: No entry fee. Open Tuesday-Sunday, 10 A.M.-4 P.M., mid June-Labor Day.

Shore Village Museum, founded in 1977 at Rockland, ME, is known as "Maine's Lighthouse Museum," where visitors can view a fine collection of many Fresnel lighthouse lenses, some seen in this photograph. (Photo R. H. Smith)

Robert H. Smith

Colchester Reef Light-house, which once stood on the shore of Lake Champlain, is one of thirty-seven historic buildings on forty-five park-like acres at the Shelburne Museum, Shelburne, VT. Here, a "collection of collections" has been established on the shores of this magnificent lake. (Photo R. H. Smith)

ROCKLAND, MAINE

Shore Village Museum
104 Limerock Street
Rockland, ME 04841
(207) 594-0311 Fax:(207) 594-9481 E-mail: knb@ime.net
Location: From Portland, follow I-95 twenty-three miles north to Rte. 1. Head east for fifty-five miles into Rockland.
Highlights:, Lighthouse lenses, ship models, *Shore Village Museum* (newsletter), **Website:** www.lighthouse.cc/shorevillage

General Information: Shore Village Museum, also known as "Maine's Lighthouse Museum," founded in 1977, contains a collection of many Fresnel lighthouse lenses. Other collections include lighthouse artifacts; weapons; uniforms; John W. Flint collection of nautical instruments and marine artifacts; related books; marine items from the U.S. Coast Guard, including working foghorns and lights. Also exhibited are thirty-four dolls dressed in historic costumes, lobstering tools, ship models, items of local historic interest, and the

largest collection of lighthouse lenses and artifacts on display in the Americas. A "please touch" museum invites children to come and enjoy.
Activities: Guided tours, lectures, gallery talks, and special programs
Admission: No charge but donations accepted. Open daily, 10 A.M.-4 P.M., June-October 15. Other times by appointment or chance throughout the year.

NEWFIELD, MAINE

Willowbrook at Newfield
68 Elm Street
P. O. Box 28
Newfield, ME 04056
(207) 793-2784 E-mail: director@willowbrookmuseum.org
Location: Willowbrook is 40 miles west of Portland (Rte. 11) and 21 miles north of Sanford via US 202 for 11 miles, then north ten miles to Newfield.
Highlights: Ship models, restored small craft, gift shop
Website: www.willowbrookmuseum.org/
General Information: A nineteenth-century restored village on a ten-acre site with thirty-seven buildings containing over 10,000 artifacts, carefully restored by local Maine artisans and craftsmen and women, make up Willowbrook at Newfield. The Village represents many aspects of rural New England life. Displays in a marine room contain navigational tools, shipbuilders' tools, uniforms, ship models, paintings, maps, and other memorabilia. Several marine engines and about five restored small craft are also on display.
Admission: Entry fee. Open daily, 10 A.M.-5 P.M., mid-May-September 30.

NEW HAMPSHIRE

PORTSMOUTH, NEW HAMPSHIRE

John Paul Jones House (1758)
P.O. Box 728
Portsmouth, NH 03802-0728
(603) 436-8420
Location: The home is located on the corner of State and Middle Streets.
Highlights: The John Paul Jones House
General Information: The house was built by Capt. Gregory Purcell in 1758. After his death his widow operated the house as a genteel guesthouse. Most notable of her guests was John Paul Jones, who lived here in 1777 while supervising the outfitting of the *Ranger* and again in 1781 while the *America* was being built. China, silver, books, portraits, costumes, and a model of the *Ranger* are displayed.

Robert H. Smith

Admission: Entry fee. Open daily, June 1-mid-October.

WOLFEBORO FALLS, NEW HAMPSHIRE

New Hampshire Antique & Classic Boat Museum
397 Center Street, Rte. 28
Wolfeboro Falls, NH 03896-1195
(603) 5690-4554 E-mail: museum@nhacbm.org
Location: The Museum is located on Route 28 two miles east from the junction of Rte. 109 & 28 in Wolfeboro
Highlights: Region's boating heritage, **Website:** www.nhacbm.org
  General Information: The New Hampshire Antique & Classic Boat
Museum, incorporated in 1994, honors the New Hampshire Lakes Region's boating heritage and its role in the cultural and social fabric of the Lakes Region. This Museum collects, preserves, studies and interprets, and displays to the public, objects relating to the boating history of the United States in general and the Lakes Region in particular. Changing exhibits feature fifteen to twenty boats and related memorabilia from a bygone era. Exhibits also include outboards and inboards, runabouts, canoes, kayaks, and launches. The Museum is located in the theatre of the former Allen A Resort. Check calendar on the web to coordinate visits and scheduled events.
  Admission: Entry fee. Open daily Open daily Memorial Day Weekend to Columbus Day (October 12) Weekend, Monday through Saturday, 10 A.M.- 4 P.M., Sunday, Noon to 4 P.M.

PORTSMOUTH, NEW HAMPSHIRE

Port of Portsmouth Maritime Museum
USS *Albacore* (Submarine)
Port of Portsmouth Maritime Museum
600 Market Street
Portsmouth, NH 03801
(603) 436-3680 Fax: (603) 436-3680 E-mail: jbsergeant@aol.com
Location: Travel sixty-five miles north of Boston on I-95. The Museum is at Albacore Park in Portsmouth, one-quarter mile from exit 7 on Market Street.
Highlights: USS *Albacore* (AGSS-569),
Website: www.portsmouthnh.com/visitors/albacore.html
  General Information: The Portsmouth Maritime Museum, established October 1985, features USS *Albacore* (AGSS-569: research submarine). Built at the Portsmouth Naval Shipyard and launched in 1953, *Albacore* served with the US Navy from 1953 to 1972 though it never fired a weapon, and it never went to war.

Primarily, the submarine was used for testing a new teardrop hull design, dive brakes, sonar systems, escape mechanisms, all manner of innovative theories. The *Albacore* was a laboratory afloat. Its teardrop hull design is a triumph and a model for contemporary submarines the world over.

Activities: Tours of the *Albacore* and documentary

Admission: Entry fee. Open daily 9:30 A.M.-5:30 P.M., Memorial Day to Columbus Day; 9:30 A.M.-4 P.M., Thursday-Monday rest of year.

PORTSMOUTH, NEW HAMPSHIRE

Portsmouth Athenaeum
9 Market Square
P.O. Box 848
Portsmouth, NH 03801
(603) 431-2538 E-mail: athenaeum@juno.com
Location: Downtown Portsmouth
Highlights: Library and archives, ship models,
Website: www.tfaoi.com/newsmu/nmus108.htm

General Information: The Portsmouth Athenaeum maintains maritime history collections (manuscripts, log books, book collections, photograph collections). Visits to the Athenaeum's reading room may be made on Thursdays, 1 P.M.-4 P.M., to view half-lift builder's models, fully rigged ship models, and marine paintings. The Athenaeum research library, located at 9 Market Square on the third floor, provides access to the archives, books, maps, and historic photographs relating primarily to the history of the Portsmouth area and to the maritime history of New England.

Activities: Summer and Winter major exhibits on local art and history.

Admission: No entry fee. Open Tuesday and Thursday 1 P.M.-4 P.M., Saturday 10 A.M.- 4 P.M.

PORTSMOUTH, NEW HAMPSHIRE

Strawbery Banke Museum
Marcy Street
P.O. Box 300
Portsmouth, NH 03802-0300
(603) 433-1100 E-mail: hharris@strawberybanke.org
Location: From I-95, take Exit 7 and follow the green "Strawbery Banke" signs down Market Street, left on Bow Street, right on Chapel Street, then left on State Street to Marcy Street where Strawbery Banke (area) is located on the Portsmouth waterfront. Free off-street parking.
Highlights: Maritime history, historic houses, museum ship,

Robert H. Smith

Website: www.strawberybanke.org/

General Information: Strawbery Banke Museum—"a neighborhood where the past is forever present!"—is located on a 10-acre site where the restored buildings are on their original sites near the Piscataqua River Waterfront in Portsmouth, NH. Spend the day exploring the earliest Portsmouth neighborhood known for 400 years as Puddle Dock.

Stroll through the centuries from the 1600s to the 1950s. Visit 10 historic furnished houses, exhibition houses, enjoy conversations with costumed role-players, relax in the shade of award-winning period gardens, and walk the friendly lanes. Of maritime interest, visit the gundalow, the *Captain Edward H. Adams*, berthed across the street at Prescott Park. It is a replica of typical local, early flat working barges.

Other nearby maritime-historically-interesting sites include the submarine *Albacore* at the Port of Portsmouth Maritime Museum on the extension of Market Street, and a boatbuilder's shop. Also the Portsmouth Athenaeum in Market Square, which houses shipping records, ship models, and Store as it appeared in 1943 — all tell the story of the evolution of the neighborhood, and paintings from the nineteenth-century maritime heyday of the city.

Exhibits include archaeological digs, early tools, seventeenth- and eighteenth-century construction techniques. And across the river at Kittery, Maine, is the Portsmouth Naval Shipyard Command Museum.

Activities: A special holiday event, annual candlelight stroll, first two weekends in December. Museum shop, cafe, picnic areas, family activity Center and daily programs are available.

Admission: Entry fee for museum. Open daily May-October, 10 A.M. - 5 P.M.; November-April, Thursday-Sunday, 90 minute guided Winter walking tours, 10 A.M. - 2 P.M. (Museum closed in January; tours subject to weather)

VERMONT

                                                                        BASIN HARBOR, VERMONT

Lake Champlain Maritime Museum
4472 Basin Harbor Road
Basin Harbor, VT 05491
(802) 475-2022 Fax: (802) 475-2953 E-mail: lcmm@lcmm.org

Location: From Burlington: Rte. 7 south twenty miles to Vergennes, follow Rte. 22A through Vergennes and seven miles west to Panton Road, to Basin Harbor Road, follow signs to "Maritime Museum." From Champlain Bridge take Rte. 17 to Lake Road and follow signs.

Highlights: Philadelphia II (54-foot Revolutionary War gunboat replica), Nautical Archaeology Center with artifact conservation lab, operational boatshop, special exhibits on view in 2001: Key to Liberty: The Revolutionary

War in the Champlain Valley; The Champlain Bridge: Where have all the Ferries Gone? The Dawn of Steam Navigation and the Paddle Steamer *Lady Sherbrooke*; Maritime Models and Water Colors of H. Richard Heilman; The Shipyard at Burlington: The building of the replica 1862 Canal Schooner *Lois McClure*, Coast Guard Buoy Tender (CG 52302), Boat building school, research library by appointment, *LCMM news*, **Website:** www.lcmm.org/

General Information: Through nautical exploration, hands-on exhibits and learning adventures for all ages, Lake Champlain Maritime Museum brings to life the stories of Lake Champlain and its people. Discover why Lake Champlain is considered the most historic body of water in North America. Explore vibrant history and characters of the Champlain Valley through its military, commercial, and recreational periods. View a large collection of original small watercraft built over the last 150 years. Learn about the largest collection of wooden shipwrecks in North America and talk to archeological conservators in our Nautical Archeology Center.

Step back in time as you climb aboard the 54-foot square-rigged Revolutionary War gunboat replica *Philadelphia II* and learn about the life of citizen soldiers in the Champlain Valley in 1776. Watch craftsmen continue traditional maritime skills of boatbuilding and blacksmithing in our working shops. Museum store, children's playground, picnic area on site. Red Mill restaurant next door.

Special Exhibits: There are over a dozen exhibit buildings at the Lake Champlain Maritime Museum at Basin Harbor. These present the maritime history and nautical archeology of the Champlain Valley through hands-on interactive learning stations, video and audio displays, historical artifacts and images. Long term exhibitions are enhanced by new research, new acquisitions and special short-term installations each season.

Admission: Entry fee. Open daily, May 1-October 14, 10 A.M.- 5 P.M.

SHELBURNE, VERMONT

Shelburne Museum, Inc.
US Rte. 7
Shelburne, VT 05482
(802) 985-3344 (tape recording); 985-3346 Fax: (802) 985-2331
E-mail: info@shelburnemuseum.org
Location: Shelburne lies seven miles south of Burlington, on Rte. 7.
Highlights: Thirty-seven historic buildings on forty-five park-like acres, The SS *Ticonderoga* (lake paddle-wheeler), Colchester Reef Light-house, canoe exhibit, scrimshaw, canal circus barge models, decoy exhibit, covered bridge, newsletter, research library, gift shop, **Website:** www.shelburnemuseum.org/

Robert H. Smith

General Information: Shelburne Museum, Inc., founded in 1947, exhibits a collection of American fine, folk, and decorative art; utilitarian art; regional architecture; SS *Ticonderoga*, built at Shelburne Harbor, Vermont, in 1906, the last vertical beam passenger and freight sidewheel steamer intact in the United States. Other exhibits include steam train and private car; carriages; horse-drawn vehicles; toys; tools; dolls; weapons; hunting trophies; American Indian artifacts; American paintings; oil paintings of sidewheelers by James Bard, paintings of ships by Fitzhugh Lane and Albert Bierstadt, and French Impressionist paintings, drawings, and sculptures; horticultural and arboreal collection. The Museum is a "collection of collections" well worth seeing.

A scrimshaw exhibit is shown in the Variety Unit Building, and canoes — guide and dugout — are shown in the Beach Lodge. And in the Circus Building, along with a complete miniature circus parade, are two model canal barges. The original barges owned and operated in the late 1800s by Sig Sawtelle, transported a 150-animal-and-people circus along the Erie and Oswego Canals. In the Dorset House, wildfowl decoys, miniature bird carvings, and firearms including two large punt guns used to take ducks and geese for market. A punt gun, with a barrel over 8 feet long, is muzzle-loaded with one-half to two-pounds of bird shot rammed over an equal measure of black powder, and then wadded with pieces of old rope, cork, and paper. Over 100 ducks could be taken, but a good shot would be 30 ducks or ten geese.

Also exhibited is Colchester Reef Lighthouse (1871) from Lake Champlain, containing maritime prints, figureheads, scrimshaw, early maps, and charts. The covered bridge (c.1845) is the only double-lane covered bridge with footpath in Vermont.

The Museum is an assembly of everything that is distinctively characteristic of New England. Each structure is unique, including the 220-foot steam paddlewheeler, SS *Ticonderoga*, hauled from nearby Lake Champlain on railroad tracks laid for that purpose, to its final "port," the Shelburne Museum. A research library is available on the premises.

Activities: Lectures, tours, and research library.

Admission: Entry fee (second consecutive day free). Memberships are available. Open daily, 10 A.M.-5 P.M., mid-May to mid-October.

Open daily, April through mid-May, 1 P.M.-4 P.M. and mid-October to end of December, selected buildings open including The S. S. *Ticonderoga*."

MASSACHUSETTS

FALL RIVER, MASSACHUSETTS

Battleship Cove
Central and Water Streets

Fall River, MA 02721
1 (800) 533-3194 (508) 678-1100 Fax: (508) 674-5597
E-mail: battleship@battleshipcove.com
Location: Battleship Cove is located off Route I-95 (Exit 5) and Route 24 (Exit 7). Follow the signs to Battleship Cove.
Highlights: North Dakota Class battleship USS *Massachusetts*, (BB-59), Gearing Class destroyer USS *Joseph P. Kennedy, Jr.* (DD-850), Balao Class submarine USS *Lionfish* SS-298), Russian Missile Corvette *Hiddensee*, and PT Boats 796 & 617. The world's largest PT Boat Museum and Library, and the Admiral Arleigh A. Burke National Destroyermen's Museum.
Website: www.battleshipcove.com

  General Information: Battleship Cove has grown to become the world's largest fleet of Historic Naval Ships. It is a popular destination for Overnight Camping and school group visits. they offer a wide range of special programs including reunions, memorial services, banquets. birthday parties, facilities for business meetings, and a sailing program. All ex US Navy ships at Battleship Cove are designated by the U.S. Department of the Interior and the National Park Service as National Historic Landmarks to educate the public about the cost of war, the lives sacrificed for the freedom of our country, and are a tribute to those who selflessly served our nation. the public has limited access to library resources. For the kid in everyone, there is a restored Carousel housed in a modern, Victorian-style pavilion (open seasonally. Gift shop. Snack Bar. Free Parking

  Activities: Overnight Camping Program and Educational Programs.

  Admission: Entry fee. Memberships are available. Ships and Museum open daily 9 A.M.-5 P.M.; Summer hours 9 A.M.-6 P.M. Closed Thanksgiving and New Year's Day.

BEVERLY, MASSACHUSETTS

Beverly Historical Society and Museum
117 Cabot Street
Beverly, MA 01915
(978) 922-1186 E-mail: beverlyhistoricalsociety@nii.net
Location: Beverly (established in 1693) is on SR-1A, twenty-five miles northeast of Boston.
Highlights: Library (3,000 volumes) ***Website:*** www.beverlyhistory.org

  General Information: Beverly Historical Society and Museum, founded 1891, includes general maritime history through a 3,000-volume library that includes extensive shipping papers and log books. (Of historical note, George Washington, on September 5, 1775, at Glovers Wharf in Beverly, commissioned the schooner *Hannah*.)

Robert H. Smith

Admission: Entry fee. Memberships are available. Open Wednesday-Friday, 1 A.M.-4 P.M.; and for researchers, Wednesday evenings, 7 P.M.-9 P.M.

BOSTON, MASSACHUSETTS

Boston Marine Society
Boston National Historical Park
Building 32, Charlestown Navy Yard
Boston, MA 02129
(617) 242-0522 Fax: (617) 244-0505
Location: In Boston, take I-93 to Rte. 1 north. Follow the signs to Charlestown Navy Yard across Charlestown Bridge - USS *Constitution* site. *Highlights:* Oil paintings, ship models
General Information: Boston Marine Society, founded in 1742, maintains a collection of artifacts, oil paintings, and ship models at its site in the Charlestown Naval Shipyard.
Admission: No entry fee. Open Monday-Friday, 10 A.M.-3 P.M., year-round.

BOSTON, MASSACHUSETTS

Boston Tea Party Ship and Museum
Congress Street Bridge on Harborwalk
Boston, MA 02210
(617) 338-1773 Fax: (617) 338-1974 E-mail: teapartyship@historictours.com
Location: The Museum is located on the Congress Street Bridge on Harbor Walk, south side of Boston's downtown area.
Highlights: *Beaver II* (brig), live, participatory, humorous reenactments of the Boston Tea Party, gift shop, Protest Room,
Website: www.bostonteapartyship.com/
General Information: On the night of December 16, 1773, a small band of Bostonians climbed aboard three vessels moored at Griffin's Wharf and destroyed 340 chests, each weighing 400 pounds, of dutied tea by dumping them into the harbor. ("Rally, Mohawks/Bring out your axes!/And tell King George/We'll pay no taxes!") This violent protest to Parliament's tax on tea — the Boston Tea Party — shattered a three-year period of relative calm between Great Britain and her colonies. It led, almost without interruption, to the outbreak of war at Lexington and Concord.

The Boston Tea Party Ship and Museum dramatically re-creates the notorious 1773 protest in exhibits and aboard the full-scale working replica of one of the original tea party ships, the brig *Beaver II*. This 110-foot brigantine sailed across the Atlantic with a cargo of tea and is now moored at the Official

Boston Tea Party Site. (When your tour ends, you will be in the Protest Room. "Take a stand" and voice or write your protest. Everyone does!)

Activities: Activities include an interactive, humorous reenactment, the story of the brig *Beaver II*, and audiovisual presentation chronicling the cross-Atlantic voyage of the brig *Beaver II*, tossing tea chests overboard, and talking with Colonial guides. Complimentary tea is served.

Admission: Entry fee. Open daily 9 A.M.- 5 P.M. Spring and Fall, 9 A.M.-6 P.M. Summer. Closed Mid-December, January, and February.

GLOUCESTER, MASSACHUSETTS

Cape Ann Historical Museum
27 Pleasant Street
Gloucester, MA 01930
(978) 283-0455 Fax: (987) 283-4141

Location: The Museum is located in the heart of downtown Gloucester, one block north from Main Street and one short block east of City Hall and the Sawyer Free Library.

Highlights: Permanent exhibition which explores Cape Ann's fisheries and maritime history; vessels: Howard Blackburn's *Great Republic* and Alfred Johnson's *Centennial*; nation's largest collection of paintings and drawings by marine artist Fitz Hugh Lane (1804-1865), Gloucester Fishermen's exhibits, museum collections, library/archives/photograph collections, Museum shop, 1890 Fresnel bulls-eye lens

General Information: The Cape Ann Historical Museum, founded in 1875, celebrates the area's proud fishing and maritime heritage with permanent exhibitions of artifacts and photographs from the continent's most productive nineteenth-century fishing port. Exhibits feature displays of fine arts, American decorative arts and furnishings, and guided tours of the furnished home of Captain Elias Davis, built in 1804 for one of Gloucester's enterprising merchant sea captains. In 1998, many items from the Gloucester Fisherman's Museum's collection were transferred to the Cape Ann Historical Museum.

The Museum exhibits the nation's largest collection of paintings and drawings by Fitz Hugh Lane (1804-1865). A native of Gloucester, Lane is now recognized as one of America's most important nineteenth-century maritime artists.

The Museum's Gloucester 1892 room displays a large model of the Gloucester waterfront with a variety of fishing-related trades and businesses. Here you will find a fully equipped Cape dory, sailmakers bench and tools, schooner half hulls, and other exhibits with the fisheries focus.

The Museum's library, archives, and photograph collections specializing in Cape Ann's art history, fishing history, and genealogy are available for research.

Robert H. Smith

Activities: Special exhibitions on Cape Ann.
Admission: Entry fee. Open Tuesday-Saturday, 10 A.M.-5 P.M., year-round except February. Memberships are available. Group tours arranged by reservation: (978) 283-0455.

BUZZARDS BAY, MASSACHUSETTS

Capt. Charles H. Hurley Library
101 Academy Drive
Buzzards Bay, MA 02532
(508) 830-5000 Ext. 1201 Fax: (508) 830-5074
Location: At beginning of Cape Cod, Buzzards Bay is sixty miles southeast of Boston off I-495. Exit onto Rte. 6, heading east four miles. The Capt. Charles H. Hurley Library is located on the campus of The Massachusetts Maritime Academy.
Highlights: Scale models, library (52,000 volumes on transportation and engineering),
General Information: Capt. Charles H. Hurley Library, founded 1980, has collections, archives, and ninety-five scale models set in a base representing the sea and panoramic background. The Library features books primarily on maritime transportation and engineering. They are available for in-house or inter-library loan. Reading rooms are likewise available.
Activities: Guided tours, lectures, education programs, and library.
Admission: No entry fee. Open daily: Monday-Thursday, 7 A.M.-11 P.M., Friday, 7 A.M.-5 P.M.; Saturday, 12 Noon-6 P.M.; Sunday, 3:30 P.M.- 11 P.M.

MILTON, MASSACHUSETTS

Captain Robert Bennet Forbes House
215 Adams Street
Milton, MA 02186
(617) 696-1815 (phone and Fax) E-mail: fhm@qis.net
Location: Milton is six miles south of Boston. The museum, on top of Milton Hill, has a commanding view of the Neponset River and Boston Harbor.
Highlights: Ship models, China trade memorabilia, *Forbes House Jottings* (newsletter), **Website:** www.key-biz.com/ssn/Milton/forbes.html
General Information: The museum, established in 1984, is a historic house restored to its 1870s condition. It commemorates Captain Robert Bennet Forbes, displaying ship models, marine art prints, drawings, and paintings. The furnishings include Chinese porcelain and furniture.
Admission: Entry fee. Open Wednesdays and Sundays, 1 P.M.-4 P.M. and other week days by appointment. Closed holidays.

CHARLESTOWN, MASSACHUSETTS

Charlestown Navy Yard
Attn.: Superintendent
Boston National Historical Park
Charlestown Navy Yard
Boston, MA 02129-4543
(617) 242-5645 (617) 242-5601 Fax: (617) 242-6006
Location: From points south: I-93 north to North Station Exit (#25). Turn right at end of ramp (Causeway Street), follow this street to first traffic light (N. Washington Street) and take a left over Charlestown Bridge. Turn right at traffic light at end of bridge (Chelsea Street). Follow signs for public parking. Mass Turnpike (I-90): Take Mass Pike to the end. Get on I-93 North and follow directions above. From points north: Route 1: Take Rte. 1 South to Charlestown Exit. Bear right and follow ramp to traffic light. Turn right onto Rutherford Avenue. Move to far left lane and turn left at traffic light onto Chelsea Street. Follow directions above. I-93: Take I-93 South to Sullivan Square Exit. Go straight up ramp and onto Rutherford Avenue. Follow signs for City Square and turn left on to Chelsea Street. Follow directions above. Public transportation: A water shuttle leaves every 30 minutes on the half-hour from Boston's Long Wharf for the Charlestown Navy Yard.
Highlights: USS *Constitution* ("Old Ironsides"), USS *Constitution* Museum, USS *Cassin Young* (World War II Fletcher Class destroyer),
Website: www.nps.gov/bost/
   General Information: The shipyard, in service from 1800-1974, has one of the oldest dry-docks in the United States (1833), officers' quarters, and the Commandant's house (1805). "Old Ironsides," launched in 1797) the oldest fully commissioned warship in the world, was the first ship to use the dry-dock.
   Activities: Self-guided and National Park Service ranger-guided tours.
   Admission: No entry fee. Open daily, 9 A.M.-5 P.M., year-round (except Thanksgiving, Christmas and New Year's Day). Public docking is available at nearby marinas.

COHASSET, MASSACHUSETTS

Cohasset Maritime Museum
4 Elm Street Mail: 14 Summer Street
Cohasset, MA 02025 Cohasset, MA 02025
(781) 381-1434
Location: Cohasset is a suburb of Boston, fifteen miles to the south and east. Head south on Rte. 3 to Rte 228 toward Hingham. Turn south on Rte. 3A and

turn left on Sohier Street to Cohasset center, where the Museum is located midtown in the village. On-street parking.

Highlights: Ship models, 1760 ship chandlery

General Information: Cohasset Maritime Museum was established in 1957 by the Cohasset Historical Society, which also maintains two other historical buildings. Its collections relate to the town's seafaring history: shipwreck relics; lifesaving equipment; nineteenth-century maritime artifacts; sailing ship models; paintings; early tools; Indian stone artifacts; and general historical artifact collections of local origin. (Cohasset was settled around 1670, as the east part of Hingham. Captain John Smith visited here briefly in 1614 to trade with Quonahasset Indians.)

Activities: Guided tours and summer walking tours of Cohasset

Admission: No entry fee. Memberships are available. Open Tuesday-Sunday 1:30 P.M.-4 P.M., mid June 1 through September.

NEWBURYPORT, MASSACHUSETTS

Custom House Maritime Museum
25 Water Street
Newburyport, MA 01950
(978) 462-8681 Fax: (978) 462-8740

Location: Newburyport is situated forty miles north of Boston on the south bank of the Merrimack River. Take I-95 to exit 57. Head east on Rte. 113, which becomes High Street. 2 1/4 miles from the Interstate, at a yellow blinker, turn left onto Green Street. Go three blocks to the foot of Green Street, and turn right on Merrimack Street. In one block this becomes Water Street. One block further on the left is the grey granite Custom House Maritime Museum. *Highlights:* Exhibits, programs, tide-pool touch tank, research library (200 volumes), The Maritime Museum Shop

General Information: At the northeastern corner of Massachusetts, five miles south of the New Hampshire border, the Custom House Maritime Museum of Newburyport, founded in 1969, is located in a Greek Revival custom house built in 1835 by the government architect Robert Mills (also architect of the US Treasury, to which the Custom Services reported, and of the Washington Monument).

Museum collections, spanning a period of 300 years, include: local maritime, nautical, and fishing artifacts, half-hull models (a form believed to have been invented in Newburyport), ship models; sea captains' souvenirs of their travels to Asia, Europe, and the South Seas; shipbuilding and navigation tools and instruments, and Coast Guard artifacts.

Newburyport is the traditional birthplace of the U.S. Revenue Service, which evolved into the modern Coast Guard. The first Revenue Cutter, the *Massachusetts*, was built here.

The library contains books on maritime history, ship types and shipbuilding, the lighthouse service, the Coast Guard, and Newburyport history. Manuscripts include captain's journals, business papers, navigation charts, and local ephemera. Library and manuscripts are available for use on the premises by appointment.

Activities: Tours, lectures, youth programs.

Admission: Nominal. Memberships are available. Open Monday-Saturday 10 A.M.-4 P.M., Sunday 1 P.M.-4 P.M., April-December 24; Closed Jan.-Mar.

NANTUCKET ISLAND, MASSACHUSETTS

Egan Institute of Maritime Studies
The Coffin School
4 Winter Street
Nantucket, MA 02554
508-228-2505 Fax: 508-228-7069 E-mail: eganinst@nantucket.net
Location: On Nantucket Island
Highlights: Nantucket history, art, literature and maritime traditions,
Website: www.marinehomecenter.com/eganinstitute

General information: The Egan Institute of Maritime Studies is housed in the historic Coffin School, a brick Greek Revival style building built in 1854. The school was founded by the American, born Sir Admiral Isaac Coffin in 1827, to benefit his island kin and serve as a memorial. The Egan Institute was founded in 1996 to advance the scholarly study and appreciation of the history, literature, art and maritime traditions of Nantucket Island.

"In addition to sponsoring research, educational programs, the Egan Institute seeks to perpetuate the legacy of the school's founder, Admiral Coffin, through its support of nautical training for the youth of Nantucket. Nantucket Island Community Sailing is housed in the lower level of the Institute.

Activities: Lectures and other educational programs are offered throughout the year along with special exhibitions, and a lecture series. Also, Mill Hill Press, an arm of the Institute, publishes books on topics relating to Nantucket history.

Admission: Entry fee - modest. Open daily from late May through early October, 1 p.m. to 5 p.m.

Robert H. Smith

ESSEX, MASSACHUSETTS

Essex Shipbuilding Museum
28 & 66 Main Street on Route 133
Essex, MA 01929
(978) 768-7541 Fax: (978) 768-2541
E-mail: info@essexshipbuildingmuseum.com
Location: Travel I-95 north from Boston to Rte. 128 north to Gloucester. Take Exit 15 (School Street, Essex-Manchester) and go 3.2 miles to Essex. At a "T" Intersection with Rte. 133, turn left, north toward Ipswich. Look for the Museum and shipyard on the right on Rte. 133. 66 Main Street is Museum entrance and Gift Shop; one and one-half blocks north are the exhibits at 28 Main.
Highlights: Hands-on exhibits of building tools, fully rigged ship models and half-models, photographs and videotape of the *Ste. Rosalie's* (dragger 1947), construction, and schooner *Evelina M. Goulart*, Waterline Center,
Website: www.essexshipbuildingmuseum.com

   General Information: Essex Shipbuilding Museum, founded in 1976, honors the shipbuilders of Essex who built more two-masted vessels than anywhere else in the Western World — over 4,000 two-masted schooners.

   Museum exhibits at the 1835 schoolhouse, at 28 Main Street, portray the evolution of the American fishing schooner from the Chebacco boat to Schooner *Gertrude L. Thebaud.*

   Many shipbuilders are buried in the Ancient Burying Ground adjacent to the schoolhouse. The shipyard site on the scenic Essex River is now the site of small craft activity, including sea-kayaking and boat-building, as well as the Waterline Center of the Museum where education programs are often in progress.

   The Museum maintains an excellent archive of ships' plans, photographs, and original documents of the shipbuilding industry of interest to model builders, historians, and writers. The Museum welcomes those involved in research, restoration, and relaxation.

   Admission: Entry fee (Museum members, children under six, and Essex residents are free). Memberships are available. Open Thursday-Sunday, 11 A.M. -4 P.M. year round. Call to schedule school and other group tours and for research.

Smith's Guide to Maritime Museums of North America
PROVINCETOWN, MASSACHUSETTS

Expedition *Whydah*
Sea Lab and Learning Center
16 MacMillan Wharf, P.O. Box 493
Provincetown, MA 02657
(508) 487-8899 E-mail: whydahweb@whydah.com
Location: The Center is at the seaward end on MacMillan Wharf in Provincetown
Highlights: The Treasure of the Pirate Ship *Whydah*,
Website: www.whydah.com/

General Information: Swashbuckling sea wolves hold our imagination in an iron grip. In 1984, treasure-hunter Barry Clifford led a team that discovered one of the world's unique archaeological sites off the east coast of Cape Cod at Wellfleet—the shipwreck of the *Whydah*.

Commanded by the pirate Sam Bellamy, the *Whydah* (pn. WID—ah) was driven to her grave by a savage storm in 1717. Nearly 280 years later, the world's first sunken pirate treasure — together with such personal remains as clothing, weapons, and jewelry — showcase both the history of the ship and the legendary love story of "Black Sam" and a Cape Cod girl.

The *Whydah* went down with picked booty of over fifty other vessels, thus giving scholars an unprecedented cross-cultural window to the 18th-century. Aside from a sampling of the *Whydah* Collection, the exhibit tells the story of the *Whydah*, together with Barry Clifford's discovery of her treasures. The visitor learns first-hand how these treasures are recovered and preserved.

Described as "a model for private archaeology," this exhibition is a once- in-a-lifetime educational experience: Learn how pieces of eight are wrested from the ocean floor. See for yourself how pirates lived — and died. Speak with our scientists as they unlock "time-capsules" to reveal the mysterious relics hidden within...Explore a sealed cannon with a fiber-optic camera...Help us decipher the pirates' secret riddles...Watch for still-dripping treasures come ashore from our salvage ship as the quest continues for the *Whydah's* untold hoard! And see the videos with Walter Cronkite and the National Geographic Society.

Admission: Entry fee. Open daily 10 A.M. - 5 P.m., May 1-November 1 (extended hours June, July, and August); Saturdays and Sundays only, November 12 - January 1. Closed January 2 - April 31 except by appointment.

Robert H. Smith

FALMOUTH, MASSACHUSETTS

Falmouth Historical Society Museums
Falmouth Historical Society
55-65 Palmer Avenue
P.O. Box 174
Falmouth, MA 02541
(508) 548-4857 E-mail: fhsoc@juno.com
Location: From Boston travel south on I-495. Turn onto SR-25 east for five miles to the junction of SR-28. Falmouth is seventeen miles south on SR-28; the Museums are on the north side of Village Green at Falmouth Center. *Highlights:* Whaling era memorabilia,
Website: www.falmouthhistoricalsociety.org/
   General Information: Falmouth was settled in 1661 and was a center for whaling and shipbuilding. In the former home of a sea captain, the Falmouth Historical Society's Museums (founded in 1900) maintain a small maritime collection with memorabilia from the whaling era.
   Activities: Summer guided tours of a 1790 home (the Julia Wood House), a "museum" building, and a barn with farm equipment.
   Admission: Entry fee. Open Tuesday-Saturday, 10 A..M.-4 P.M., June 15-September 1.

GLOUCESTER, MASSACHUSETTS

The Gloucester *Adventure*
Harbor Loop, P.O. Box 1306
Gloucester, MA 01930
(978) 281-8079 Fax: (978) 281-2393 E-mail: scurry@schooner-adventure.org
Location: Located at Harbor Loop off Rogers Street next to the Coast Guard Station. *Highlights: Adventure* (sailing fishing schooner), Ship's Store, **Website:** www.schooner-adventure.org
   General Information: The society was established in 1988 to preserve the historic Gloucester fishing schooner 121.5-foot *Adventure*. Built in 1926, she is the last American Grand Banks fishing schooner to fish and one of a handful still sailing. She is listed on the National Register of Historic Places and has a permanent place in our national maritime heritage. The Adventure is currently undergoing restoration, and is not sailing but is open to the public for tours and events.
   Bowsprintless, the "knockabout," 121-foot *Adventure* was built in nearby Essex. In twenty-seven years of fishing, she consistently brought in great quantities of codfish and haddock (capacity of 160,000 pounds). Later in her career she carried passengers on pleasure cruises along the Maine Coast. Now

she is a monument to Gloucester's history, and used for education and the pleasure of the public.

Admission: Donations accepted. Open year round, Thursday-Sunday, and Saturdays in the winter.

CAMBRIDGE, MASSACHUSETTS

Hart Nautical Collections
M.I.T. Museum, Hart Nautical Gallery
55 Massachusetts Avenue
Cambridge, MA 02139
(617) 253-5942 Fax: (617) 258-9107 E-mail: kurt@mit.edu
Location: Across the Charles River from Boston in Cambridge, these collections are reached by entering the lobby at 77 Massachusetts Avenue, then turning right down the hall heading in the direction of the Charles River.
Highlights: Ship models, major collections of working drawings,
Website: http://web.mit.edu/museum/collections/hart-nautical.html
General Information: The Francis Russell Hart Nautical Museum (now the Hart Nautical Collections) was founded in 1921 as a part of the Department of Naval Architecture and Marine Engineering at MIT. In 1940 the collection was officially named in honor of Francis R. Hart, former President of the United Fruit Company and Class of 1889, who had worked with the Museum from its founding until his death in 1938.

In 1982, the Hart Nautical Collections joined with the Massachusetts Institute of Technology in Cambridge (MIT). The MIT Museum continues the original commitment of the Hart Nautical Museum by preserving and interpreting the history of one of the oldest engineering fields; namely, marine engineering, ship design and construction. Exhibits include exquisitely crafted model ships built to scale, descriptively labeled so you can wander about on your own. Models range from simple a tiny, plain Norwegian pram to a complex four-foot reproduction of the US frigate *President*, fully rigged, complete with coiled lines, lifeboats, and brass fittings.

For exotica, a Korean warship *Turtle* has a spiked cover to shelter its gunners and crew. The sixteenth-century real ship spouted sulfuric fumes from the *Turtle's* mouth to frighten its superstitious foe and to provide a smoke-screen.

Major Collections:
- Captain Arthur H. Clark Collections — paintings, photographs, prints, plans of vessels, half-models, books
- Allan Forbes Collection — paintings/prints on whales.
- C. H. W. Foster Collection—yachting photographs (1885-1930)
- Haffenreffer-Herreshoff Collection—working drawings
- McInnis-Lawley Collection—working drawings

Robert H. Smith

- Gordon Munro Collection—working drawings and models (1915-1940)
- George Owen Collection—working drawings/models (1902-1958)
- Frank C. Paine Collection—working drawings, models, photographs (1923-39)
- Bethlehem Steel Collection—working drawings and photographs (1851-1940)

Admission: No entry fee. Research by appointment only at 265 Massachusetts Avenue.

WELLFLEET, MASSACHUSETTS

Historical Society Museum
Main Street
Wellfleet, MA 02667
(508) 349-3346

Location: From Boston take SR-3 south to Rte. 6 (forty-one miles).
Travel east to Cape Cod, then an additional forty-one miles to Wellfleet center at Cape Cod's northern tip. The Museum is about 500 feet east of the business district and a few steps from the Town Hall on north side of street at Cape Cod's northern tip.

Highlights: Old Cape Cod history, ship models

General Information: The Historical Society Museum is housed in a building dating from just before the Civil War, when it began as a dry goods store. Displays include marine items, whaling tools, Marconi (radio) memorabilia, needlecraft, and photograph collection. Nearby Rider House is restored and depicts life on Old Cape Cod through displays of early farming, carpentry tools, and a herb garden.

Admission: No entry fee. Open Tuesday-Saturday, 2 P.M.-5 P.M., late June-Labor Day.

Smith's Guide to Maritime Museums of North America

Lowell's Boat Shop, a National Historic Landmark, is the oldest continuously operating manufacturer of wooden boats in the country—since 1793. Dories by the thousands were hand-crafted here—and still are. (Photo R. H. Smith)

Lobster boat model at Penobscot Marine Museum, founded in 1936, in the middle of a 13-building-historic district in Searsport, ME. (Photo R. H. Smith)

Robert H. Smith

YARMOUTH PORT, MASSACHUSETTS

Historical Society of Old Yarmouth
11 Strawberry Lane
P.O. Box 11
Yarmouth Port, MA 02675
(508) 362-3012
Location: Yarmouth Port is 18 miles east of the Borne Bridge (Sagamore) on Cape Cod off Rte. 6 at Exit 8, one mile north to town.
The Captain Bangs Hallet House/Museum is on the Common in Yarmouth Port near to the Post Office on Rte. 6A.
Highlights: Maritime local history
   General Information: The Historical Society of Old Yarmouth was founded in 1953 to develop community interest in and preserve the history of Yarmouth. To achieve this goal, the Society owns and maintains the Captain Bangs Hallet House, Kelley Chapel, and adjoining conservation lands and buildings. It also sponsors special programs throughout the year.
   The lovely Greek Revival style home, built in the 1840s, was donated to the Society by the Thacher family in 1956. Through the efforts of friends and members of the Society, the house was refurbished and furnished and is today arranged in a manner reminiscent of the lifestyle of a prosperous, nineteenth-century sea captain.
   Admission: Entry fee. Open June 1 through mid-October, Thursday, Friday, Saturday, and Sunday. Tours at 1 P.M., 2 P.M., and 3 P.M.

HULL, MASSACHUSETTS

Hull Lifesaving Museum
1117 Nantasket Avenue
P. O. Box 221
Hull, MA 02045
(781) 925-0992 (fax)
E-mail: hullmuse@channel1.com or hullmuse@channel1.com
Location: By land, take Rte 3 South to Exit 14 for Rte. 228 into Hull. Follow Nantasket Avenue and signs for the museum for 5 miles.
Highlights: Exhibits on maritime culture and lifesaving traditions of Boston Harbor and the region, 29 ft. 1888 surfboat *Nantasket*, and rescue apparatus,
Website: www.bostonharborheritage.org
   General Information: The Hull Lifesaving Museum, the museum of Boston Harbor heritage, is situated dramatically at the mouth of Boston Harbor, with breathtaking views of Boston Light. The restored Point Allerton Life Saving

Station (ca. 1889), was the home of Joshua James and his crew, the most celebrated lifesavers of their day.

The Orientation Room traces the history of organized lifesaving from its roots in the 18th century through today's modern Coast Guard. In other galleries, visitors learn about lighthouses, storms, shipwrecks, and rescues. In the Navigation Loft, a special play attic is set up for children, with dress-ups, games, and a climb-on, rigged bow; stairs lead to the Observation Cupola, where you can scan stunning views of Boston Harbor and Islands, life surfmen of old.

From the door of the Museum, you can see for miles out to sea and photograph Boston Light, the oldest lighthouse in the nation. Nearby, you can look out from Fort Revere's Observation Tower on Telegraph Hill to recognize why this site was chosen to scan Boston Harbor. Walk through the well-marked Hull village to see the buildings where Joshua James grew up.

Activities: lecture series, boat-building workshops, school-vacation programs, art shows, group tours; the museum's award-winning open-water rowing program operates year-round in Boston Harbor from a fleet of 14 big, traditional boats – most built by the rowers themselves. Youth and adult programs conducted to boathouses in Hull and Charlestown Navy Yard.

Admission: Entry fee. Open June-Labor Day: Wednesday-Sunday, 10 A.M.; September-May: Friday-Sunday, 10 A.M. – 4 P.M.

NEW BEDFORD, MASSACHUSETTS

"Lightship *New Bedford"* (WAL-536)
c/o Harbor Development Commission Mail: Mayor's Office
Pier 3 133 William Street
New Bedford, MA New Bedford, MA 02740
(508) 993-1770 (508) 979-1410 Fax: (508) 979-6189
Location: Berthed at the town landing.
Highlights: The Lightship *New Bedford*
General Information: The 133-foot steel-hulled lightship, built in 1930, and designated as No. LV-114 (WAL-536), is berthed south of Leonard's Wharf, New Brunswick Harbor. It was among the last built before the U.S. Lighthouse Service became a part of the Coast Guard in 1939. From 1930 to 1942, it was anchored off Fire Island. She guided mariners to New York Harbor and then to Cape Hatteras from 1945-1947, where she replaced a lightship sunk by a German U-Boat during WW II. Then from 1969-1971, she was stationed at Portland, ME. Finally retired in 1971, she was rescued in 1985 and restored to become a floating exhibit.

Admission: Currently — subject to renovation

Robert H. Smith

AMESBURY, MASSACHUSETTS

Lowell's Boat Shop
459 Main Street
Amesbury, MA 01913
(978) 388-0162
Location: Amesbury is one mile west of I-95 on the north bank of the Merrimack River in the northeast corner of Massachusetts.
Highlights: Wooden boat (dory) history, boat building, rowing/sailing, **Website:** www.lowellsboatshop.org

General Information: Lowell's Boat Shop, a National Historic Landmark, is the oldest continuously operating manufacturer of wooden boats in the country—since 1793. The dory shop is owned by the Newburyport Maritime Society which also operates the Custom House Maritime Museum, Newburyport, Massachusetts. The Society operates Lowell's as a museum and working boat-building shop to preserve the knowledge and history of the traditional craft of building small wooden boats. The heart and soul of LBS is continuing to build new boats for customers and repairing boats that were built here.

Activities: Boatbuilding, repair, and restoration; classes for adults and youth (year round); row a hand-crafted traditional wooden boat from the shop's boat livery (seasonal). Group tours by appointment.

Admission: No entry fee; fee for pre-scheduled group tours. Museum open Wednesday-Saturday, 8 A.M. - 4 P.M. year round. The Boat Livery is open Thursday-Friday, 4 P.M.-7 P.M., Saturday-Sunday 1 P.M.-7 P.M. Memorial Day-Labor Day. Rowing/sailing classes Wednesday-Saturday, 8 A.M.- 4 P.M.

MARBLEHEAD, MASSACHUSETTS

Marblehead Historical Society
170 Washington Street
P.O. Box 1048
Marblehead, MA 01945 E-mail: info@essexheritage.org
(781) 631-1069 (Adm. offices) (781) 631-1069 (Events/info, reservations)
Location: From Boston north on I-95 to 128 North. Exit 25A, Rte. 114 East-10 miles to Marblehead.
Highlights: Maritime folk art paintings and models (19th and 20th century), maritime trade (18th and 19th century), fishing history, Gift & Book Shop,
Website: www.essexheritage.org/jeremiah_lee.htm

General Information: The Marblehead Society's collections include ships' logs, marine artifacts, sextants, paintings, and early fishing equipment. Permanent and annual changing exhibits. Gift and Book Shop, including prints of maritime folk art paintings and framed reproductions of watercolor illustrations from an 18th century diary (Ashley Bowen) for sale.

Admission: No entry fee but donations welcome. Galleries open Tuesday-Saturday, 10 A.M. - 4 P.M., Sunday, 1 P.M. - 4 P.M year round. Museum rooms in Lee Mansion open June 1-October 15. Office and archives open Tuesday-Friday, 10 A.M. - 4 P.M. Appointments appreciated.

FALL RIVER, MASSACHUSETTS

Marine Museum at Fall River
70 Water Street
Fall River, MA 02721-1598
(508) 674-3533 E-mail: staff@marinemuseum.org
Location: The Museum is housed in an old mill structure on the waterfront in Battleship Cove just a short walk from the battleship USS *Massachusetts* (BB 59), the Heritage State Park, and a restored vintage carousel; at the junction of I-195 and Rte 138.
Highlights: The *Titanic* exhibit, ship models, *Fall River Line Journal* (quarterly newsletter), library and archives (2,000 volumes), gift shop, **Website:** www.marinemuseum.org/

General Information: The Marine Museum at Fall River, Inc., was founded in 1968 as a repository for the memorabilia of the Fall River Steamship Company's famous Fall River Line (1847-1937) which used Fall River as the New England terminus for its New York to New England run New England, connecting by rail to Boston. The highlight of the Fall River Line exhibit is a 13-foot builder's model of the steamer *Puritan*.. The Line is a particular concern of the Museum in the broader context of the development of steam navigation and coastal blue water shipping. Other special interests include marine archaeology and underwater exploration; the local history of Narragansett Bay and its ports, tributaries, and adjacent waters; and the maritime background of the various ethnic groups in the community.

A centerpiece of the Museum is a twenty-eight-foot-long model of the RMS *Titanic*, created by 20th Century Fox Studios for the 1953 movie of the same name starring Barbara Stanwyck, Clifton Webb, and Robert Wagner. Original *Titanic* newspapers and photographs compliment the exhibit.

A growing collection of china and silver and other artifacts recovered from the wreck of the *Andrea Doria* form a new special exhibit, with accurate scale models of both the *Andrea Doria* and the *Stockholm*, the ship that she collided with. The gift shop features books and prints on the *Titanic* and the old Fall River Line paddle wheel steamers.

The library and archives feature:

Robert H. Smith

- The William King Covel Collection, the Museum's first major acquisition, purchased from this Newport, Rhode Island, native in the mid 1960s. It consists of photographic prints, negatives, glass slides, and paintings, relating primarily to the Fall River Steamship Co.'s great "white palaces" that sailed Long Island Sound carrying passengers, raw cotton bales, and finished cotton;
- The John A Breynaert Collection of 1000+ volumes, accumulated by the late Mr. Breynaert, an executive of General Dynamics Fore River Shipyard of Quincy, Massachusetts;
- The United Fruit Company Collection comprises ship models, logs, journals, books, and photographs relating to the company's steamships operating between New England and its Caribbean banana plantation holdings;
- Other excellent ship models form Seamen's Church Institute of New York and Philadelphia; German prisoner-of-war models *von Tirpitz* and *Admiral Hippe*r, and four highly detailed American warship models built by Dr. Arthur Hickey, including the USS *Missouri* as configured at the time of the surrender of Japan.

Activities: Museum facilities are available for meetings, lectures, etc. The library contains books on maritime history that are available on the premises.

Admission: Entry fee. Memberships are available. Open Monday-Saturday, 9 A.M.-5 P.M., Sunday, and holidays, noon.- 5 P.M. Closed Thanksgiving, Christmas, and New Year's Day.

SCITUATE, MASSACHUSETTS

The Maritime & Irish Mossing Museum
c/o The Scituate Historical Society
P.O. Box 276
Scituate, MA 02066
(781) 545-1083 Fax: 781/544-1249 E-mail: history@ziplink.net
Location: Scituate is located about 30 miles south of Boston. Take Rte. 3 to Exit 13 and head east 1/4 mile. Turn right on Rte. 123 and go several miles through Norwell to Rte. 3A. Cross 3A and bear right at fork, following sign to Scituate Harbor. Museum is on the right hand side just past the nursing home.
Highlights: Shipwrecks, shipbuilding, Irish Mossing, museum store, **Website:** www.ziplink.net/~history/maritime.htm

General Information: The Maritime & Irish Mossing Museum housed in the 1739 home of Captain Benjamin James, contains six exhibit rooms. The Shipwreck Room focuses on four maritime disasters that took place off Scituate including the *Fairfax-Pinthis* collision (1930), and *Etrusco* (1956). The Life-Saving Room remembers the deeds of the lifesavers of the Massachusetts

Humane Society, U.S. Life-Saving Service and the U.S. Coast Guard, as well as the stories of Scituate and Minot's Lighthouses. A Fourth Order Fresnel lens was recently added to the collection. The Shipbuilding Room traces the 250-year history of this industry on the North River.

The Captain's Room presents a glimpse into a sea captain's room in the mid-nineteenth century. The Irish Mossing Room is perhaps the only exhibit of its kind in America. Irish Moss, also known as carageen, is a non-edible North Atlantic seaweed (Chondrus crispus) that yields a mucilaginous substance used medicinally and as an emulsifier in several food products. The Reception Room contains changing exhibits and an orientation video. The museum store has many items of local and historical interest. Nearby is Scituate Lighthouse, Lawson's Tower, the Stockbridge Grist Mill, and other seacoast attractions.

Admission: Entry fee. Open July through Labor Day, Saturday and Sunday 1 P.M. - 5 P.M. Group tours by appointment. Call (781) 545-1083. Please contact the Scituate Historical Society for winter hours.

EDGARTOWN, MASSACHUSETTS

Martha's Vineyard Historical Society and Museum
P. O. Box 1310
Edgartown, MA 02539
(508) 627-4441
Location: Edgartown, on Martha's Vineyard, is six miles from the ferry dock in Vineyard Haven or Oak Bluffs.
Highlights: Lighthouse Fresnel lens, whaleboat, Norman's Land double- ender, whaling information, research library (Francis Foster Museum)

General Information: The Society was founded to preserve the history of Martha's Vineyard and the Elizabeth Islands through Museum's, libraries, publications, and educational programs. The main maritime informational collection is housed at the Francis Foster Museum, which includes a research library containing many whaling logs, coastal vessel records, and customs records.

Admission: Entry fee. Open summer, Tuesday- Saturday, 10 A.M.-4:30 P.M.; rest of the year, Wednesday-Friday 1 P.M.-4 P.M., Saturday 10 A.M.-4 P.M.

Robert H. Smith

MARION, MASSACHUSETTS

***Mary Celeste* Museum**
c/o Sippican Historical Society
Front and Main Streets
Marion, MA 02738
(508) 748-1116 E-mail: outpost@fortogden.com
Location: Center of Marion
Highlights: *Mary Celeste* history,
Website: www.fortogden.com/maryceleste.html
 General Information: The Sippican Historical Society maintains the *Mary Celeste* Museum in memory of Captain Benjamin Briggs, skipper of the famous ship *Mary Celeste* of 1872. He was a native of Marion, where the Museum contains many items of interest concerning the mysterious vessel.

 The Atlantic Financial Insurance Company of Madison, New Jersey, paid the original insurance claim on the loss of the *Mary Celest* and maintains the records in its offices.

 Admission: No entry fee. Open Saturdays during June, July, and August.

MEDFORD, MASSACHUSETTS

Medford Historical Society Museum
10 Governors Avenue Mail: c/o M. F. Bradford
Medford, MA 02155 153 Brooks Street
(781) 391-8739 Medford, MA 02155
Location: The Museum is on Governors Avenue just off High Street. Take Exit 32 (Medford Exit) off Rte. 93, then Rte. 60 to Governors Avenue. The Museum is on the left.
Highlights: Ship models, Civil War prints, Peter Tufts house
 General Information: The Medford Historical Society Museum houses a wide variety of artifacts and records about the city. Even Medford's city seal depicts a ship under construction. From 1803-1873 Medford built 568 ships—her merchant ships and clippers sailed around the globe.

 The Museum contains a number of ship models (both full and half-hull), as well as shipbuilding tools. A diorama of the city just before the Civil War affords visitors an excellent idea of how city might have looked in its shipbuilding days. Medford was also the terminus of the Middlesex Canal (see separate listing) and an important distillery center in the Triangle Trade in rum and slaves. The Museum also holds one of the largest collections of Civil War prints available. The Society also operates the Peter Tufts house which is one of the oldest brick houses in the country.

Activities: The MHS has memberships in several categories. The Society presents programs for its members and the public. It provides educational programs for local schools. The Society works to conserve the many documents and objects in its collections.
Admission: No entry fee. Open Sundays 2 P.M.- 4 P.M.

LOWELL, MASSACHUSETTS

Middlesex Canal Museum & Visitor Center
at the Faulkner Mills
71 Faulkner Street
N. Billerica, MA 01862
(978) 670-2740 E-mail: middlesexcanalcomm.jreardon@juno.com
Location: The Museum lies approximately 20 miles north of Boston, MA or 5 miles south of Lowell, MA at the Concord River Millpond where the canal began.
Highlights: Middlesex Canal, *Canal Routes* (quarterly newsletter)
Websites: www.middlesexcanal.org
General Information: The Middlesex Canal Museum, opened in July 2001, contains some archives of the Middlesex Canal Association and its exhibit artifacts. The Millpond was the highest point in the 27-mile Middlesex Canal, and so was its primary source of water. It is a great setting.
Admission: No entry fee. Open Saturdays 10:00 AM - 4:00 PM and Sundays 12:00- 4:00 from April through September
(See also: Medford Historical Society Museum)

BOSTON, MASSACHUSETTS

Museum of Science
Science Park
Boston, MA 02114
(617) 723-2500 E-mail: information@mos.org
Location: The Museum is located at the Charles River Dam, McGrath and Leverett Circle in Cambridge, adjacent to downtown Boston.
Highlights: Ship models, **Website:** www.mos.org
General Information: The Museum of Science offers several small exhibits to quench your nautical thirst. Visitors can view ship models on the basement level of blue wing in the Museum. There is also a replica of the E.B. McKay shipyard where the famed *Flying Cloud* clipper ship was built. Its located in the Museum's Big Dig exhibit. Ship models, ranging from ancient Egyptian sailing craft to modern power vessels, will be found on the Museum's second floor.

Robert H. Smith

Another exhibit that visitors can see is a model of a yacht *Hi-Esmaro* located on the 3rd floor of the Museum. The first floor contains a full-size replica of a ship's bridge. Visitors can visualize steering their vessel through dangerous waters. And through the window you'll glimpse three typical harbor buoys, once having done service at sea. They are now floating in the Charles River basin. A plaque describes their original uses.

Admission: Entry fee. The Museum is open daily, except Thanksgiving and Christmas. It closes at 2:00 P.M. on Christmas Eve.

NANTUCKET ISLAND, MASSACHUSETTS

Nantucket Life-Saving Museum
Suite 4, 57 Old South Road
Nantucket, MA 02554
(508) 228-1154 E-mail: mo7250@nantucket.net
Location: The Museum is located 2.4 miles from the Rotary or 2.4 miles from the junction of the Sconset and Polpis Road until you come to Folger's Marsh at 158 Polpis Road, a short distance from the town's center. Look for the white rocks with lettering and turn in to ample parking.
Highlights: H. H. Kynett Library and Research Center, two fully restored and operable Beachcarts, with Lyle and Hunt guns, Breeches Buoy and Francis Life Car, Fresnel lighthouse lenses from Brant Point Light (1856) and Great Point Light (1857), *Andrea Doria* artifacts,
Website: www.nantucket.net/museums/lifesaving/
General Information: The Nantucket Life Saving Museum, located at Folger's Marsh on Polpis Road, was established in 1972. It is an authentic re-creation of the original Station on Nantucket Island that was built by the United States Life Saving Service in 1874. The Museum is dedicated to the drama of human efforts against the relentless sea. It focuses on the heroic deeds of the U.S. Life Saving Service, U.S. Revenue Cutter Service founded by Alexander Hamilton, U.S. Lighthouse Service, U.S. Coast Guard, and the Massachusetts Humane Society, whose members all risked their lives — and in some cases lost their lives — rescuing shipwrecked sailors on the shores and shoals of Nantucket. *"You have to go out, but you don't have to come back."*

Also displayed are artifacts from recent wrecks, such as the Italian liner *Andrea Doria*, and memorabilia from the U.S. Coast Guard's heroic contribution to the Battle of the Atlantic. Seasonally, the local Coast Guard Station, in cooperation with the Museum, demonstrates the operation of the fully restored Beachcart and its equipment, plus demonstrating the operation of one of the life boats on the waters of Nantucket Harbor. Books on lifesaving, replica buttons, surfman's devices, shirts, hats, and other memorabilia are for sale in the Museum. You are invited to become a member/supporter.

Admission: Entry fee. Memberships are available. Open June 15 to October, 9:30 A.M. - 4:00 P.M. Open for group tours and members at other times by special arrangement.

NEW BEDFORD, MASSACHUSETTS

New Bedford Free Public Library
613 Pleasant Street
New Bedford, MA 02740
(508) 961-3104 E-mail: tfurtado@sailsinc.org
Location: New Bedford is seventy miles south of Boston on I-195. The library is located at 613 Pleasant Street in center of city.
Highlights: History on whaling, New Bedford Customs House records,
Website: www.ci.new-bedford.ma.us/nbfpl.htm
General Information: The New Bedford Free Public Library, founded in 1852, contains collections of Custom House records for the Port of New Bedford 1796-1920, 526 whaling logbooks (and several merchant) for 526 voyages, whaling agent records including those of C.W. Morgan, William Rotch, George Hussey, C.R. Tucker, and J & W.R. Wing. Also a complete run of the Whalemen's Shipping List and Merchant Transcript newspaper edited by Lindsey beginning in 1843, and extensive rare printed book collection on Whaling and Maritime History.

The library has undertaken it's most recent State grant funded project to create a comprehensive automated database of the Whaling Crew Lists from the earliest to 1850. The resulting database will be searchable on 10 fields and be made available for searching free of charge through the City of New Bedford - New Bedford Free Public Library Homepage.

Admission: No entry fee. Open Monday-Thursday, 9 A.M.-9 P.M., Fridays and Saturdays, 9 A.M.-5 P.M., year-round. Closed national holidays.

NEW BEDFORD, MASSACHUSETTS

New Bedford Whaling Museum
18 Johnny Cake Hill
New Bedford, MA 02740-6398
(508) 997-0046 Library Fax: (508) 997- 994-4350
E-mail: abrengle@whalingmuseum.org
Location: The Museum is nestled in New Bedford's historic district on Johnny Cake Hill (a road).
Highlights: Half-size (eighty-nine-foot) model of whaling bark *Lagoda*, ship models, scrimshaw, *The Bulletin from Johnny Cake Hill* (quarterly newsletter), library (20,000 volumes), 66-foot skeleton of a juvenile blue whale,

Robert H. Smith

Website: www.whalingmuseum.org/

General Information: Under the sponsorship of the Old Dartmouth Historical Society, the New Bedford Whaling Museum was established in 1907 for the purpose of collecting, exhibiting, interpreting, and preserving the history of American whaling and the local area. The Museum is one of the largest museums in America devoted to local history. During the whaling era, New Bedford's local history was world history, and that fact is reflected in its collections as the far- flung whaleships made the city known in every ocean on the globe.

The principal whaling exhibition consists of: the full-rigged half-scale 89-foot model of the New Bedford whaling bark *Lagoda*, which may be boarded; the 100-foot Richard Ellis mural of sperm whales; whaling industry tools and artifacts; and exhibits of waterfront trades that supported the whaling industry; plus interactive exhibits on whales and whale conservation.

The exhibit galleries contain examples from the permanent collections of scrimshaw, painting, prints, ship models; exhibits pertaining to life in New Bedford and Old Dartmouth; "The World of the Whaleman," featuring two sections of the 1848 Russell-Purrington "Panorama of a Whaling Voyage Round the World"; and changing exhibitions of varied nature.

The library contains a permanent collection of well over 15,000 books, pamphlets, maps, charts, broadsides, and periodicals as well as 1800 reels of microfilm and access to 15,000 photographic negatives. There are 750 feet of manuscripts, including over 1,100 logbooks and journals. (Library users may wish to call in advance of visit.)

During the 1820s, when the whaling industry in New Bedford was rising, local citizens organized the Seamen's Bethel dedicated to the moral and religious improvement of seamen. It is right across the street from the Whaling Museum.

Activities: guided tours; lectures; films; gallery talks; education programs. A whaling film is shown daily in a large theatre.

Admission: Entry fee. Open daily 9 A.M.-5 P.M., Closed Thanksgiving, Christmas, and New Year's Day.

SALEM, MASSACHUSETTS

New England Pirate Museum
274 Derby Street
Salem, MA 01970
(978) 741-2800 Fax: (978) 741-2902 E-mail: KTNAN@aol.com
Location: Salem is located 16 miles north of Boston, and is a convenient 30 minute drive. Take Rte. 128 North, Exit 25A and follow Rte. 114 East. In Salem, follow signs to Waterfront, and The New England Pirate Museum which is next

to the Salem Beer Works, across from Pickering Wharf, and a 5 Minute Walk from Salem Train Depot.
Highlights: Pirate history, **Website:** www.piratemuseum.com/pirate.html
General Information: The New England Pirate Museum features exhibits recounting the history of marauding pirates who once plundered merchant ships off the New England Coast. The Museum re-creates a colonial seaport, pirate ship, and treasure-laden cave.
Activities: Guided tours
Admission: Entry fee. Open daily May-October, 10 A.M.- 5 P.M. In November, Saturday and Sunday, 10 A.M.- 5 P.M.

WELLFLEET, MASSACHUSETTS

Old Harbor Life-Saving Station
c/o Cape Cod National Seashore
National Park Service
99 Marconi Site Road
Wellfleet, MA 02667
(508) 349-3785
Location: From Boston, south on Rte. 3. Exit on Rte. 6 east seventy-three miles to Provincetown. Turn right at first traffic light (Race Point Road), then three miles to the end of Race Point Beach. Take boardwalk past the shower/lavatory building to museum.
Highlights: Life-saving equipment,
Website: www.cr.nps.gov/history/maritime/park/oldhbrls.htm
General Information: "You have to go, but you don't have to come back." That was the life-savers' motto, and their work earned them the title, "Guardians of the Ocean Graveyard." Life-Savers were stationed on Cape Cod between 1872 and 1915. The Old Harbor Life-Saving Station, under the auspices of the National Park Service, contains exhibits from the U.S. Life-Saving Service with the historical perspective of those who risked their lives helping those in storm-tossed seas. The Salt Pond Visitor Center, about halfway up the Cape, on Rte. 6 in Eastham, also exhibits Life-Saving Service artifacts.
The Province Lands Visitor Center (508/487-1256) is located one mile from the station and provides orientation to the Provincetown area.
Activities: Every Thursday in summer, re-enactment of Breeches Buoy ship-to-shore rescue; 6 P.M. at station.
Admission: No entry fee but beach parking fee. Station open daily in the summer months only 3 P.M.- 4 P.M., variable hours spring and fall — call ahead.

Robert H. Smith

BOSTON, MASSACHUSETTS

The Old State House - The Bostonian Society
206 Washington Street
Boston, MA 02109
(617) 720-1713
Location: The Old State House is in downtown Boston on the Freedom Trail.
Highlights: Ship models, marine paintings, maritime wood sculpture, scrimshaw, extensive research library (6,000 volumes), gift shop,
Website: www.infonavigate.com/boston/23.htm
   General Information: The Old State House, built in 1713, was the site of many events leading to the American Revolution, such as James Otis' speech protesting the Writs of Assistance, the Stamp Act Debates, and the Boston Massacre.
   From its balcony, the Declaration of Independence was first read to Bostonians in 1776. The building contains a museum maintained by The Bostonian Society, which was founded in 1881 to preserve the Old State House from demolition. The museum's exhibits, including a fine collection of maritime artifacts, illustrate the history of the city of Boston. Among these are: seascapes, ship portraits, views of Boston Harbor, a life-size female figurehead carved by Isaac Fowle, navigational instruments, and scrimshaw.
   The non-circulating library contains over 6,000 books, maps, documents, and broadsides related to Boston history. A reading area is available for researchers. The museum's gift shop sells guidebooks, books on Boston history and marine subjects, reproductions of American Colonial and maritime objects, and a wide variety of souvenirs.
   Activities: Lectures, gallery talks, and guided tours available by appointment
   Admission: Entry fee. Open daily, 9 A.M.-5 P.M. Closed Thanksgiving, Christmas, New Year's Day. Library open Wednesday-Friday, 9:30 A.M.-4:30 P.M., and Saturday, 10 A.M. to 3 P.M. with admission free for members and visitors.

OSTERVILLE, MASSACHUSETTS

Osterville Historical Society and Museum
Parker and West Bay Roads
Osterville, Cape Cod, MA 02655
508-428-5861 E-mail: welcome@osterville.org
Location: Take Hwy. 6, Exit 5 going south 10 miles to Osterville.
Highlights: Cape Cod history, **Website**: www.osterville.org/OHSindex.htm
   General Information: The Osterville Historical Society was first formed in 1931, its collection of historical memorabilia was small and very little space was

required to house and display the items. The Society was able to use the old Osterville Community Center Building, formerly "Dry Swamp Academy", the school for Osterville children.

By 1960, the Society's collection had outgrown the available space and an appeal went out to find a new location. The appeal was soon answered. Through the generosity of Mrs. Gladys Brooks Thayer of Oyster Harbors and New York, the Society was able to acquire its present building, the Captain Jonathan Parker House, at the corner of West Bay and Parker Roads. This historic sea captain's home was built by Parker in 1824 and is one of the oldest houses in Osterville. Little of the original three room house is visible, as rooms, porches and dormers have been added to its basic Cape Cod "half house" form.

Admission: No entry fee. Open mid-June to mid-October, Sunday 1:30 P.M. to 4 P.M.

FALL RIVER, MASSACHUSETTS

The PT Boat Museum and Library
Battleship Cove
Central and Water Streets
Fall River, MA 02721
(508) 678-1100
Location: The Museum and Library are located at Battleship Cove in Fall River, off I-195, at exit 5.
Highlights: World War II PT boats 617 (The only 80-foot Elco Boat on display in the world) and 796, PT Memorial and a 200 volume library, Newsletter: *The PT Boater*
General Information: The collections at the PT Boat Museum include books, diaries, insignia, memorabilia of forty-three operating squadrons of World War II P.T. boats, tenders, and bases, films, photographs, and plans. Also on display is a one-man Japanese suicide demolition boat. See also the listing in Germantown, Tennessee for PT Boats, Inc. Headquarters.
Admission: Entry fee. Memberships are available. Open daily, 9 A.M.- 5 P.M., year-round.

SALEM, MASSACHUSETTS

Peabody Essex Museum
East India Square
Salem, MA 01970
1-800-745-4054, (978) 740-1650 or 9500 E-mail: pem@pem.org
Location: Salem is only nineteen miles northeast of Boston on Rte. 95. The Museum is in the heart of downtown Salem.

Robert H. Smith

Highlights: Maritime paintings and prints, ship models, figureheads, objects related to Nathaniel Bowditch, scrimshaw, *American Neptune* (quarterly), recreated interior of early-nineteenth-century yacht, Phillips Library,
Website: www.pem.org/

General Information: In 1799 Salem's sea captains and merchants of the East India Marine Society founded Peabody Essex Museum, our country's oldest continuing museum. One can study early methods of navigation and the development of navigational instruments, focusing on Nathaniel Bowditch, Salem resident and author of the *American Practical Navigator*.

One of the largest museums in Massachusetts, the Peabody Essex Museum is home to renowned collections of maritime art and history; Asian export art; art from China, Japan, India, and Korea; Oceanic art; Native American art; American decorative art, folk art, costumes, and textiles; and art from Africa. Spread over two city blocks and several off-campus sites, the museum also includes one of the nation's premier ensembles of early American architecture.

The Museum showcases the maritime history of New England, including marine paintings, ship models, figureheads, scrimshaw, nautical tools, and instruments, and an exhibit on an early nineteenth century yacht. The museum's Phillips Library contains maritime history, cultural history of Asia and Oceania, photographs, natural history of Essex County, paintings, prints, ship models, charts, and arts and crafts.

Activities: Changing exhibitions, music, film, guided tours, lectures, gallery talks, and education programs.

Admission: Entry fee. Memberships available. Open seven days a week from April 1 through October 31, Monday-Saturday, 10 A.M.-5 P.M.; Sunday, Noon-5 P.M. Closed Thanksgiving, December 25, New Year's Day, and Mondays from November 1 through March 31.

PLYMOUTH, MASSACHUSETTS

Pilgrim Hall Museum
75 Court Street
Plymouth, MA 02360
(508) 746-1620 E-mail: pegbaker@ici.net
Location: The Museum is at 75 Court Street (Rte. 3A) at Chilton Street, two blocks up the hill west of Water Street.
Highlights: Hull of the *Sparrowhawk*, museum shop,
Website: www.pilgrimhall.org/

General Information: Built in 1824 by the Pilgrim Society of Plymouth, the Museum exhibits and interprets the history of the Pilgrims and the town they founded. Pilgrim Hall is one of the oldest museum in continuous operation in the United States Maritime. A maritime exhibit is in the recovered and preserved lower half of the hull and frame of the *Sparrowhawk*, an ocean-going vessel sunk off Cape Cod in 1626. *Sparrowhawk* was found in May 1863; the timbers were excavated from marsh-mud and sand. P. T. Barnum even took her on tour. Now, *Sparrowhawk* is displayed in the main hall. Also, see the painting of Edward Winslow — the only portrait of a Pilgrim painted from life.

Admission: Entry fee. Open daily, 9:30 A.M.-4:30 P.M., February-December. Closed Christmas Day and the month of January.

Located near Plimoth Plantation is the recreation *Mayflower II*, typical of ships that brought the Pilgrims to the New World in 1620. Costumed interpreters and modern guides describe life aboard the ship in 1620. (Photo R. H. Smith)

Robert H. Smith

The pirateship *Whydah* (pn. WID—ah), driven to her grave by a savage storm in 1717, was found nearly 280 years later, with the sunken pirate treasure — together with such personal remains as clothing, weapons, and jewelry — showcased at the Expedition *Whydah* Pirate Ship Museum. (Photo R. H. Smith)

PLYMOUTH, MASSACHUSETTS

Plimoth Plantation
1627 Pilgrim Village
P. O. Box 1620
Plymouth, MA 02360
(508) 746-1622 Fax: (508) 746-4978 E-mail: mpecoraro@plimoth.org
Location: From Boston, take SR-3 forty-one miles southeast to Plymouth. Follow Rte. 3A to Plimoth Plantation at Mayflower.
Highlights: The living museum of seventeenth-century Plymouth, The *Mayflower II* (replica ship), library (4,000 volumes),
Website: www.plimoth.org/

General Information: Featured are a reproduction of a 1627 Pilgrim Village and Wampanoag Indian Homesite. Village and homesite feature costumed personnel, who re-create life in seventeenth-century Plymouth. Collections include: archaeology with seventeenth-century English and Native American artifacts; house furnishings; tools; arms and armor.

Also located near Plimoth Plantation is the recreation *Mayflower II*, typical of ships that brought the Pilgrims to the New World in 1620. Costumed interpreters and modern guides describe life aboard the ship in 1620 and the 1957 voyage of the *Mayflower* II. Exhibits recount the history of the Mayflower.

Activities: The library contains imprints and manuscripts available for use by appointment. Additionally, theatre, picnic area, lectures, demonstrations, recreation, and first-person interpretation of daily life in seventeenth-century Plymouth are presented. Education programs are available. Visitor Center, cafeteria and museum shops are on-site.

Admission: Entry fee and memberships are available. *Mayflower II*: Open daily, 9 A.M.-5 P.M., March 26-June 15; open daily 9 A.M.-6:30 P.M., mid June-August; open daily, 9 A.M.-5 P.M., September-November. Village: open daily, 9 A.M.-5 P.M., April-November.

NEW BEDFORD, MASSACHUSETTS

SS *Nobska* Steamer
The New England Steamship Foundation
63 Union Street
New Bedford, MA 02740
(508) 999-1925 Fax: (508) 999-0230
Location: The main offices of the Foundation are in the Sundial Building on Union Street in the newly designated National Park in New Bedford and right around the corner from the New Bedford Whaling Museum.
Highlights: S/S *Nobska* (coastal steamer)
General Information: The New England Steamship Foundation, owners of the S/S *Nobska*, have offices located in the Sundial Building (same block as the Whaling Museum). The S/S *Nobska*, launched in 1925 at the Bath (Maine) Iron Works, served the islands of Martha's Vineyard and Nantucket from Woods Hole, Massachusetts, from 1925 until her retirement in 1973.

The Sundial Building provides the Foundation with exhibition and office space where Vocational Technical students and volunteers have restored the building, which experienced a disastrous fire in 1977.

The *Nobska's* external-combustion, triple-expansion steam engine is in excellent condition, and she is now in drydock at the Charlestown Navy Yard, a part of the Boston National Historical Park in Boston being restored to bring her to operational status as a living, operating representative of the coastal steamboat era. Re-launching is scheduled for 2003 when she will be, for the first time, formally christened, will assume the role of a floating museum ship, and will re-establish her runs to Martha's Vineyard and Nantucket.

Admission: Visit the ship's offices for updated reconstruction information. Memberships are available.

Robert H. Smith

SALEM, MASSACHUSETTS

Salem Maritime National Historic Site
Custom House
174 Derby Street
Salem, MA 01970
(978) 740-1660 Fax: (978) 740-1665
Location: Salem is nineteen miles northeast of Boston on Rte. 1A. *Highlights:* Historical waterfront commercial district which includes: Derby, Central, and Hatch's Wharves, Warehouses, the Custom House, the Scale House, the West India Goods Store, Derby House, Hawkes House, Narbonne-Hale House, and the Lighthouse. Gift shop nearby.
Website: www.nps.gov/sama

General Information: Salem Maritime National Historic Site, established in 1938, extends over 9.2 acres from the historic waterfront back into downtown

Salem. There are two visitor centers: Downtown Visitor Center is located on the corner of New Liberty and Essex Streets; Orientation Center is on Derby

Street. The site is operated by the National Park Service. It includes: Derby Wharf — once center of Salem shipping; Derby House — home of Elias Hasket Derby, a Salem merchant and the first U.S. millionaire; U.S. Custom

House; and a commercial and residential village from the days when Salem was a seaport rivaling Boston and New York. A full-scale replica of a 1797 Salem merchant vessel, *Friendship*, is under construction.

The wharves at Salem Maritime National Historic Site stretch out into the salt waters of Salem Harbor, testifying to the city's former dependence on the sea. The once-busy wharves and the buildings facing the harbor are remnants of the shipping industry that prospered in Massachusetts Bay's oldest seaport well into the nineteenth century. In its prime there were fifteen buildings on Derby Wharf.

Admission: No entry fee; fee for tours of buildings. Open daily, 9 A.M.-5 P.M., winter months; 9 A.M.-6 P.M., summer months. Closed Thanksgiving, Christmas, and New Year's Day. Call for current hours of operation and program offerings.

EASTHAM, MASSACHUSETTS

Salt Pond Visitor Center
National Park Service Visitor Center
Rt. 6
Eastham, MA 02642
(508) 255-3421

Location: Eastham, on Cape Cod, is 40 miles from Borne Bridges to the Visitor Center.
Highlights: Local maritime historical displays,
Website: www.nps.gov/caco/places/saltpondvc.html
    General Information: The National Park Service has developed a fine exhibition space in the Visitor Center, where the curator has collected maritime artifacts along with an excellent collection of local flora and fauna, stuffed birds, and other important items, leading the visitor through the past where our forefathers first landed to establish settlements on the coast of Massachusetts.

    When visiting here be sure to see the excellent video presentation on the environmental development of Cape Cod. The Cape is a glacial deposit that is constantly undergoing natural changes as winds and water move sand along the shorelines, tearing away one place and building up another.

    Admission: No entry fee. Open year-round, daily 9 A.M.-4:30 P.M., Columbus Day-Memorial Day.

ROCKPORT, MASSACHUSETTS

Sandy Bay Historical Society and Museums
P. O. Box 63
Rockport, MA 01966
(978) 546-9533 E-mail: deskrcc@rockportusa.com
Location: From I-95 (north or south) some fifteen miles north of Boston, exit onto Rte. 128, then east twenty-two miles to county Rte. 127 four miles to Rockport.
Highlights: Ship models, Rockport history,
Website: www.rockportusa.com/aboutrockport/SBHS.html
    General Information: The Sandy Bay Historical Society and Museums, Inc. maintains two historic houses as its museums; The "Old Castle" (1715) in Pigeon Cove and the Sewall-Scripture House (1832) at 40 King Street. Collected and exhibited are materials about the town of Rockport and its people. Included in the exhibits are ship models, artifacts, and paintings pertaining to local fishing and coastal trade.

    Admission: Entry fee and contributions welcome. Open daily, 2:00 P.M.-5:00 P.M. June 30-Labor Day.

NEW BEDFORD, MASSACHUSETTS

Schooner *Ernestina* Commission
89 North Water Street, P.O. Box 2010
New Bedford, MA 02740
(508) 992-4900 (E-mail on website)

Robert H. Smith

Location: New Bedford is forty miles south of Boston.
Highlights: Schooner *Ernestina Morrissey,* **Website:** www.ernestina.org/
General Information: Launched in Essex, MA in 1894, as the 156-foot *Effie M. Morrissey*, she served three long, distinguished careers as a Grand Banks fishing schooner, U.S. Navy survey and supply vessel in World War II, and finally, as an immigrant packet sailing out of Cape Verde, a West African Republic, where she was renamed *Ernestina* in 1948. A small museum contains research materials on nineteenth-century fishing schooners; Arctic expeditions; World War II; Republic of Cape Verde and Portugal Atlantic packet ships; historic restoration; and information on the African-American contribution to American maritime heritage. She is the "Official Vessel of the Commonwealth of Massachusetts."
Admission: Entry fee. Open Monday-Friday, 10 A.M.-3 P.M., year-round.

SCITUATE, MASSACHUSETTS

Scituate Lighthouse
43 Cudworth Road
P.O. Box 276
Scituate, MA 02066
(781) 545-1083 E-mail: history@ziplink.net
Location: Scituate is south of Boston and south of Cohasset on the Atlantic coast and is accessible from Rte-3A. Go to the harbor, then take Jericho Road north to Lighthouse Road.
Highlights: Lighthouse, historic structures, library (300 volumes), **Website:** www.ziplink.net/~history/litehse.htm
General Information: Illuminated in 1811, Scituate Lighthouse is the sixth oldest active aid to navigation in New England, and the ninth oldest in the United States. It features the story of Abigal and Rebecca Bates, daughters of the keeper, who took up a fife and a drum and frightened away British sailors intent on ransacking the town of Scituate during the War of 1812. The fife is on display during tours.

The Lighthouse now features twenty-five new graphic panels inside the runway between the tower and the keeper's house that detail different aspects of the science and history of American lighthouses. The tower is open to the public four times per year; group tours can be arranged by request. The lighthouse is less than two miles from the Scituate Maritime and Irish Mossing Museum, also operated by the Scituate Historical Society.
Admission: Entry fee. Call for group rates.

MARBLEHEAD, MASSACHUSETTS

1768 Jeremiah Lee Mansion
(Marblehead Historical Society)
161 Washington Street
Marblehead, MA 01945
(781) 631-1768
Location: From Boston north on I-95 to 128 North. Exit 25A, Rte. 114 East-10 miles to Marblehead.
Highlights: Home of Col. Lee with abundant artifacts.
　General Information: Opulent home of Colonel Jeremiah Lee, a wealthy merchant and ship-owner who supported the Revolution in risky undercover capacities. In the home you will find Ceramics and other artifacts from maritime trade (18th and 19th century), fishing history. Architecture (18th century), furnishings, (18th and early 19th century), rare original hand-painted English wallpaper, rich mahogany woodwork, caved rococo interiors. Also be seen are Portraits of sea captains, ships, and foreign ports.
　Admission: Entry fee. Mansion open Tuesday-Saturday, 10 A.M. - 4 P.M., Sunday, 1 P.M.-4 P.M., June 1-October 15.

NORTH TRURO, MASSACHUSETTS

Truro Historical Society Museum
Highland Road
P.O. Box 486
N. Truro, MA 02666
(508) 487-3397
Location: From Boston, take SR-3 south forty-one miles to Rte. 6. Head east to Cape Cod, traveling sixty miles to north tip of Cape Cod.
Highlights: Lighthouse, Cape Cod maritime history, ship models
　General Information: Truro Historical Society Museum is now the operator of the Cape Cod/Highland Lighthouse, which is located some 500 feet from the Museum. In 1996 the lighthouse was moved back from the high bluff overlooking the Atlantic due to continued sloughing off of the bluff into the sea. The attached keeper's cottage is the shop where items sold generate funds to "keep the Cape Cod Lighthouse" in good condition.
　It was here that Captain Miles Standish and party stayed their second night ashore in a strange land and where Indian corn was discovered and used for the Pilgrims' survival.
　The Highland House, a classic turn-of-the-century summer hotel through the late 1960s, now houses the Museum where Henry David Thoreau stayed on his visits to the Cape. The Courtney Allen Room, dedicated as a memorial to the

artist by his friends and neighbors, contains fine examples of his masterful wood carvings, paintings, and models.

The Museum has an exciting collection of artifacts from the town's historical past, including shipwreck mementos, whaling gear, ship models, seventeenth-century firearms, pirates chest and period rooms, and fine art works.

Activities: Lighthouse is open to the public for tour. Children must be 51-inches high to tour the lighthouse.

Admission: No entry fee. Open Monday-Saturday, 10 A.M.-5 P.M., mid-June to mid-September. Entry fee for lighthouse.

CHARLESTOWN, MASSACHUSETTS

USS *Constitution*
USS *Constitution*
Charlestown Navy Yard
Charlestown, MA 02129-2308
(617) 426-1812 Fax: (617) 242-0496 E-mail: sails@navtap.navy.mil
Location: Across the wharf from the USS *Constitution* Museum, the USS *Constitution* is docked at the Charlestown Navy Yard National Park. Follow signs along I-93 to Rte. 1, then turn immediately off onto Constitution Road to the yard, just north of downtown Boston.
Highlights: The USS *Constitution* ("Old Ironsides"),
Website: www.USSconstitution.navy.mil/index.html

General Information: The USS *Constitution*, launched in 1797, is the oldest commissioned warship afloat in the world. The *Constitution* is one of six ships ordered by President George Washington for construction to protect America's growing maritime interests in the 1790s. *Constitution* soon earned widespread renown for her ability to punish French privateers in the Caribbean and thwart Barbary pirates of the Mediterranean. The ship's greatest glory came during the War of 1812 when she defeated four British frigates. During the battle against HMS *Guerriere* in 1812, seamen watched British cannon balls glance off her twenty-one-inch-thick oak hull, and gave her the famous nickname, "Old Ironsides."

In the 1830s, the ship was slated to be broken up, but a public outcry, sparked by a poem by Oliver Wendell Holmes, saved her. Over the following century, the ship undertook many military assignments, including circumnavigating the world and acting as both a barracks and training ship. She was restored in 1927 with contributions from the nation's school children. After a final tour during which she was towed coast-to-coast, in 1934 she was moored in her homeport, the Charlestown Navy Yard. She was again completely restored in 1997 and sailed unassisted for the first time in over 100 years—a remarkable vessel and still fully commissioned in the United States Navy.

As a salute to the nation, every Fourth of July and several other times a year, she is maneuvered into Boston Harbor for an underway sail demonstration. On Independence Day, a twenty-one-gun salute in honor of the Nation's Birthday is presented. Although she has been repaired several times, her basic lines have not been altered nor the ship's symbolic value reduced, and she accurately depicts a U.S. navy ship of the War of 1812, the period of greatest renown for *Constitution*. Nearby, the *Constitution* Museum and the World War II destroyer *Cassin Young*, (operated by the National Park Service), are also open to the public.

USS *Constitution*:
    Rig: Three masted, forty-four-gun frigate.
    Specifications: Sparred length: 308',
    Length overall: 204', beam: 43'6", draft: 22'6", rig height: 185'
    USS *Constitution* Armament:
    Thirty-two: 24-pounder long guns (crew, 9-14 men)
    Twenty: 32-pounder Carronades (crew, 4-9 men)
    Two 24-pounder Bow Chasers
    Crew: 450 Sailors, 44 Marines, and 30 Boys

Activities: The *Constitution* is open year-round, rain or shine, for free public tours guided by U.S. Sailors in historic 1813 uniforms. The visitor center staff will direct you to the self-guided tours.

Admission: No charge. Open daily and holidays 9:30 A.M.-3:30 P.M., year-round.

CHARLESTOWN, MASSACHUSETTS

USS *Constitution* Museum
Boston National Historical Park
Charlestown Navy Yard
P. O. Box 1812
Boston, MA 02129
(617) 426-1812 Fax: (617) 242-0496
Location: Across the wharf from the USS *Constitution* at the Charlestown Navy Yard in Boston is the USS *Constitution* Museum.
Highlights: Computer and hands-on exhibits, video presentation, *Constitution Chronicle* (newsletter), research library, ship models,
Website: www.ussconstitutionmuseum.org/
General Information: USS *Constitution* Museum, founded in 1972, houses objects related to life aboard ship, objects removed during restorations of *Constitution*, examples of sailors' arts, historic memorabilia, and decorative arts related to *Constitution* and the early sailing Navy. Hands-on exhibits examine the construction of "Old Ironsides," her history and preservation, and the lives of her

sailors. Replicas of such components as her keel, yardarms, and sick bay evoke a sense of the complexity of the Ship's design.

Visitors of all ages can fire a cannon, swing in the hammocks, and build a ship model. Two videos include a 10-minute one which will take you on a tour of the Ship which will allow the visitor to see parts of the ship not open to the public. The second video "All Hands on Deck," is a 19-minute video that is part of the Museum's award-winning curriculum. The video follows a 14-year old girl on the day the Ship sailed in 1997 and she meets heroes and heroines from *Constitution's* past.

Visitors can step into the shoes of Captain, Lieutenant, Able-bodied Seaman, Marine, or nine-year-old "Powder Monkey" by playing at the computer exhibit. See what kind of judgment decisions you would make during "The Great Chase" when *Constitution* escaped from five British frigates during the first encounter with the British in the War of 1812.

The entry ramp from the original Museum building to the new wing gives the appearance of shops lining a street in Boston in the 1790s. Looking into the shop windows, the visitor learns about the craftsmen like Benjamin Seward, who supplied small arms of the *Constitution*, Paul Revere who supplied the copper sheathing, and William Bradford, the tailor, who made the crew's uniforms. The second-floor expansion continues the story of her most recent refit (1996).

The newly expanded Samuel Eliot Morison research library, access to which is available by appointment only, contains research materials related to naval and maritime history, originals and microfilm copies of ship logs, personal journals and letters, and plans of the *Constitution*.

Activities: Special programs for school groups by reservation, audiovisual programs, gun drills and performances by the Volunteer Marine Corps Detachment of 1797, and maritime artisan workshops and demonstrations are scheduled periodically.

Admission: No entry fee. Memberships are available. Open daily 9 A.M.- 6 P.M. May-October; 10 A.M.-5 P.M. November-April; Closed Thanksgiving, Christmas, and New Year's Day. The Museum is wheelchair accessible.

QUINCY, MASSACHUSETTS

United States Naval Shipbuilding Museum
739 Washington Street (Wharf Street)
Quincy, MA 02169
(617) 479-7900 Fax: (617) 479-8792 E-mail: jfaheyca139@aol.com
Location: The shipyard and Museum are located at Fore River Yard on Wharf Street just off Rte. 3A. Also, the Harbor Express Boat from Logan Airport or Long Wharf Pier in Boston, right to the USS *Salem*.

Highlights: USS *Salem* (CA 139) (heavy cruiser), archives and historical collection, **Website:** www.uss-salem.org

General Information: The first recorded local vessel constructed at Ship Cove in 1696 was the ketch *Unity*. Shipbuilding continued and surged during the Spanish-American War when Congress authorized Quincy to build the *Lawrence* and *MacDonough* (torpedo boat destroyers) and the armed cruiser *Des Moines*. The 1920s and 1930s saw the USS *Lexington* converted from a battle cruiser to the Navy's first true aircraft carrier. She was sunk in May of 1942 in the Coral Sea.

On September 23, 1941, the battleship *Massachusetts* was launched and delivered some fifteen months ahead of schedule at the yard and served meritoriously in Northern Africa. The USS *Salem's* keel was laid on July 4, 1945 and she was launched on March 27, 1947 and commissioned two years later, May 14, 1949. The cruiser *St. Paul*, launched here, will be memorialized in a special space on the *Salem*. Other spaces will include a special exhibit on Cruiser Sailors, a model room with museum-quality ship models some from the U.S. Navy's vast collection, and a space dedicated to the history of naval small arms, historical correspondence, and artifacts from the land warfare in France in WW I.

The shipyard, called the "greatest shipyard of World War II," is having a new life with the Des Moines class heavy-cruiser *Salem*, one of its fine products to be maintained by the Museum's crew for all to tour and see.

Activities: Guided tours 10 A.M.-6 P.M., overnight camping programs.

Admission: Entry fee. Open daily 10 A.M.-4 P.M. during summer; Friday, Saturday, Sunday (and Monday holidays) 10 A.M.- 4 P.M. during winter.

NANTUCKET ISLAND, MASSACHUSETTS

Whaling Museum
Nantucket Historical Association
Broad Street, P.O. Box 1016
Nantucket Island, MA 02554-1016
(508) 228-1894 Fax: (508) 228-5618 E-mail: cjb@nha.org

Location: Ferry to Nantucket Island from Hyannis. The Museum is at Broad Street at the head of Steamboat Wharf.

Highlights: A finback whale skeleton (forty-three feet long), a lighthouse lens (sixteen feet tall), scrimshaw, library, whaling tools and harpoons

General Information: The Whaling Museum, established in 1846, was built as a candle factory to refine spermaceti oil—a waxlike substance taken from the oil in the head of a sperm whale used to make candles. The building now houses extensive collections of whaling implements used in the pursuit and processing of sperm whales. The huge press, used to extract the wax from the oil, spans the building where a full-size tryworks (large iron cooking pots where whale blubber

Robert H. Smith

is rendered), a whaleboat from the bark *Sunbeam*, and an unparalleled collection of scrimshaw are displayed.

The skeleton of a forty-three-foot finback whale is exhibited, and the original sixteen-foot-tall lens from the Sankaty Lighthouse highlights an area devoted to navigation and exploration. Also displayed are paintings and portraits of those who made Nantucket the third-largest port in the United States.

The Research Center, located on Fair Street, contains 450 rare books, 363 log books and journals, 477 account books, 400 manuscript collections, and 45,000 photographs for use by students, historians, and genealogists.

Activities: Guided tours of twelve historic Nantucket buildings

Admission: Entry fee. Open daily, 10 A.M.-5 P.M., May 28-October 12; Saturdays and Sundays only, 10 A.M.-5 P.M., October 13-December 31, and March 1-May 27. The Research Center is open Monday-Friday, 9 A.M.-4 P.M. Closed Christmas.

WOODS HOLE, MASSACHUSETTS

Woods Hole Historical Collection
Woods Hole Historical Museum
579 Woods Hole Road
P.O. Box 185
Woods Hole, MA 02543
(617) 548-7270 E-mail: woods_hole_historical@hotmail.com
Location: Woods Hole is on the southwest tip of Cape Cod where the ferries are boarded for Martha's Vineyard and Nantucket. The collection archives and exhibit galleries are located in Bradley House (circa 1800), next to the Woods Hole Library and the Woods Hole Small Craft Exhibit building. There is very limited parking.
Highlights: Historical restored smallcraft, Small Craft Museum, Woods Hole spiritsail boat, a Cape Cod Knockabout, and a Herreshoff twelve and one-half, restored; scale model of Woods Hole in 1890s, exhibits, library and archives with photographs, oral history collection, gift shop,
Website: http://woodsholemuseum.org

General Information: The Woods Hole Historical Collection was founded in 1973 as an adjunct of the Woods Hole Library, to establish and preserve a collection of objects and materials of cultural, historical, and artistic value illustrating the history of Woods Hole and to keep the story of its heritage alive.

The Small Boat Museum, opened in 1996, exhibits local small-craft in the Swift Barn, built in 1877. It cost $80.71, labor and materials. Numerous models, other maritime artifacts, and illustrations are displayed. Other exhibits include 1890s Woods Hole spirit sailboat *SPY*, built by the same Mr. Swift who built the barn. Also displayed: the Herreshoff 12 Cod Knock-about *IMP*, a two time national champion. All these sailing craft were raced in local waters. The workshop exhibits the talents, tools, and hobbies of a late-nineteenth- century physician: etching, constructing fishing rods, and tying flies. Other galleries have changing exhibits.

The Small Boat Collection includes a Chamberlain Dory made entirely of local wood and a 1922 Old Town canoe which was the preferred pleasure craft of summer scientists here in the 1920s and 1930s. Also in the barn are boat models. A new shed addition houses the Knock-about Penguin, allowing children to climb aboard and sail away with their imaginations.

The archives contains local business records and personal correspondence, household receipts, postcards, newspaper articles, diaries, ships' logs, maps, and a large photograph collection including photos by Baldwin Coolidge of Woods Hole at the turn of the century. The library contains about one hundred volumes devoted primarily to maritime and Cape Cod History. The artifact collection includes paintings, memorabilia, and tools.

Activities: Semi-annual journal *Spiritsail*, newsletter, lunch-time talks (ten a year); walking tours of the Woods Hold Village (on Tuesday afternoons in July and August), an on-going boat restoration program, special events

Admission: No entry fee. Memberships are available. Open Tuesday-Saturday, 10 A.M.-4 P.M., June 18-September 30. Other times by appointment.

RHODE ISLAND
PROVIDENCE, RHODE ISLAND

Alfred S. Brownell Collection of Atlantic Coast Fishing Craft Models
Providence Public Library
225 Washington Street
Providence, RI 02903-3283
(401) 455-8000/8021
Location: This particular collection is housed in the Providence Public Library on Level A. The Library is in downtown near I-95.
Highlights: Small craft collection, log book collection, scrimshaw, Nicholson Whaling Collection, library,
Website: www.provlib.org/accessinfo/special/special.htm
General Information: The Alfred S. Brownell Collection of Atlantic Coast Fishing Craft Models, comprises eleven ship models of Atlantic Coast Fishing Craft. They were presented to the Library about 1950 by Mr. Brownell, himself a marine historian and one of the most highly regarded model-boat builders. The eleven distinct types of fishing craft were evolved as early as the Colonial times to meet the needs of men fishing in such diverse areas as the sheltered waters of

Robert H. Smith

Long Island Sound, the stormy ocean off the coast of Maine, and the shallow oyster beds of the Chesapeake Bay.

Thousands of hours were required to prepare scale drawings and produce each model. The fishing fleet contained in the Collection includes a Block Island Double Ender, Chesapeake Bay Bugeye and Skipjack, a Colonial Fishing Schooner, an Eastport Pinky, a Friendship Sloop, a Gloucester Sloop, a Maine Pinky, a New Haven Sharpie, a Quoddy, and a Tancook Whaler. The collection may be viewed during regular Library hours.

Most of the collections is displayed on level A of the library. In addition, the Nicholson Whaling Collection of over 1,000 whaling logs, books, and seventy-seven pieces of scrimshaw is in the Special Collections Department.

Activities: Library available for research

Admission: No entry fee. Regular Library hours are: Monday-Thursday 9 A.M. - 8 P.M., Friday-Saturday 9 A.M.-5:30 P.M. and Sunday 1 P.M.-5 P.M. October - May only. Nicholson Whaling Collection logbooks on microfilm are available during regular library hours; also available through interlibrary loan. Nicholson Collections materials in the Special Collections Department librarian only works part-time on Monday-Thursday and is available by appointment only - the Call 401-455-8021 to make an appointment.

JAMESTOWN, RHODE ISLAND

Beavertail Lighthouse & Museum
P.O. Box 83
Jamestown, RI 02835
(401) 423-3270 E-mail: info@beavertaillight.org
Location: Located on Conanicut Island in the middle of Southern Narragansett Bay.
Highlights: Beavertail Lighthouse, **Website:** www.beavertaillight.org
General Information: Since 1749, the Beavertail Lighthouse has guided mariners from its site at the tip of Narragansett Bay on Conanicut Island. The lighthouse is located in a beautiful state park, where the surf crashes on the shore rocks and is just a short drive from Newport.

A small museum was established in the 1898 Assistant Keeper's House. A fourth-order Fresnel lens is on display along with exhibits on Rhode Island lighthouse history. Current efforts have been successful in maintaining this granite tower built in 1856 that rises 64 feet above the bay. It was here that local inventor David Melville demonstrated the first gas-fired lamp for lighthouse use in 1817. He devised a system that burned coal to generate hydrogen that was funneled through copper tubes to the lamp mechanism.

Another "first" for Beavertail was established when it was chosen a as the test facility for new fog signals in the second half of the nineteenth century.

Admission: No entry fee. Open Memorial Day-Mid June, weekends only; open daily 10 A.M.-4 P.M., Mid-June-Labor Day; Labor Day - Columbus Day weekends only.

BLOCK ISLAND, RHODE ISLAND

Block Island Southeast Lighthouse
Old Town Road and Ocean Avenue
P.O. Box 949
Block Island, RI 02807
(401) 466-5009
Location: Block Island is approximately 15-miles south of Narragansett Bay.
Highlights: Lighthouse
General Information: Southeast Light is a restored lighthouse built in 1875. In a tower were its lantern is 240 feet above sea level, sends its light 35 miles out to sea. The Block Island Historical Society provides archival information about the island and lighthouse.
Admission: Entry fee. Open daily, May through Labor Day, 10 A.M.-4 P.M.

WOONSOCKET, RHODE ISLAND

Chafee Blackstone National Corridor
1 Depot Square
Woonsocket, RI 02895
(401) 762-0250 Fax: (401) 762-0530 E-mail: BLAC_Superintendent@nps.gov
Location: Visitor Center and museums: Off State Rte. 146 at Woonsocket, follow signs to visitor center. Slater Mill Visitor Center is off State Rte. 146 on County Rte. 15.
Highlights: Blackstone Canal historical information,
Website: www.nps.gov/blac
General Information: The John H. Chafee Blackstone River Valley National Heritage Corridor was founded in 1986 through legislative act. It was established to create an interworking network of parks and three visitor centers. One, in Woonsocket, one in Uxbridge, MA, and the other in Pawtucket, RI. The centers, and river access, provide historical views through the parks and museums along the Blackstone Canal and Towpath cutting through town limits and south across the state line into Rhode Island in its rush to Narragansett Bay, forty-three miles to the south. Originally, there were 45 locks providing transportation between Providence, RI and Wooster, MA, the 2nd and 3rd largest towns in New England.
Admission: Check at Visitor Centers for information and tours.

Robert H. Smith

BRISTOL, RHODE ISLAND

Herreshoff Marine Museum and America's Cup Hall of Fame
7 Burnside Street
P. O. Box 450
Bristol, RI 02809
(401) 253-5000 and 253-6222 E-mail: herrshoff@ids.net
Location: The Museum and America's Cup Hall of Fame are located on the site of the old family shipyard one-mile south of downtown Bristol (twelve miles southeast of Providence) and one- and one-fourth miles north of Mt. Hope Bridge on Rte. 114. From I-95, take exit 7 (Seekonk/Barrington), follow Rte. 114S through Barrington, Warren, and Bristol; turn left on Burnside Street. From Newport, take the Mount Hope Bridge to Rte. 114 N, turn right at Burnside Street.
Highlights: Exhibits of Herreshoff-built yachts and steam engines, photographs and other memorabilia, ship models, America's Cup Museum, gift shop,
Website: www.herreshoff.org/
General Information: The Herreshoff Marine Museum, founded in 1971, displays yachts, steam engines, fittings, photographs, and memorabilia commemorating the unique accomplishments of the Herreshoff Manufacturing Company, which existed from 1863 to 1946 during the "Golden Age of Yachting." John Brown Herreshoff founded the Company and in 1878 he took his younger brother, Nathanael Greene Herreshoff, into partnership.

After attending Massachusetts Institute of Technology, Nat was employed by the famed Corliss Engine Works in Providence for nine years. Upon joining his brother's firm of boatbuilders, he concentrated initially on designing steam vessels.

In the early 1890s Nat turned to designing sailing yachts; the creation of these vessels — of all sizes and descriptions — occupied most of the rest of his professional career. Yachts of his design, built at the family's yard, defended the America's Cup six times from 1893 to 1920, and the Herreshoff Manufacturing Company also built the Cup Defenders of 1930 and 1934.

Activities: Rendezvous of Herreshoff-designed boats every 2 years (next, 2002), annual summer waterfront clambakes, lectures, and workshops.
Admission: Entry fee. Open 10 A.M.- 5 P.M., May-October 7 days a week.

NEWPORT, RHODE ISLAND

The International Yacht Restoration School
449 Thames Street
Newport, RI 02840
401/848-5777 Fax: 401/842-0669 E-mail: info@iyrs.org

Location: The unique and valuable facility is located on a 2 acre waterfront wharf on Thames Street in downtown Newport. IYRS is on the right at 449 Thames Street with administrative offices across the street at 458 Thames. Parking is available in front of the School.
Highlights: Yacht restoration, **Website:** www.iyrs.org/
General Information: The International Yacht Restoration School is a not-for-profit educational institution in Newport, Rhode Island. A full-time, state licensed vocational program in the restoration and construction of classic watercraft is enhanced by an historic waterfront campus and marina, which is open to the public year-round. IYRS acquired the site in 1995, and immediately began the rehabilitation of the 1905 Newport Electric Company generating plant. This building is now our main restoration facility. An active marina hosts classic restored yachts from around the world.

The second building on the campus, originally built in 1831 as a steam-powered cotton mill, is on the National Register of Historic Places. This building has been stabilized and will later be renovated for use as classrooms, workrooms, offices and student housing.

Our purpose is clear: To teach the skills, history, science and art of restoring, maintaining and building classic yachts; to preserve the knowledge, heritage, craftsmanship and aesthetic genius inherent in these yachts; to maintain a fleet of restored watercraft for the purpose of teaching seamanship, navigation and maintenance skills; to safeguard our site and historic buildings as an important piece of America's working waterfront, and to show that honest work, integrity, and mastery of a craft are among life's greatest achievements.

IYRS is committed to remaining open to the public, and providing access to our waterfront. We are dedicated to preserving and continuing an important local tradition of fine nautical craftsmanship. We believe that preserving the past informs and improves the future.

Admission: No entry fee. Donations suggested. Open Monday - Saturday, 10 A.M. - 5 P.M., Sunday - Seasonal. Open for tours.

JAMESTOWN, RHODE ISLAND

The Jamestown Museum
P.O. Box 156
Jamestown, RI 02835
(401) 434-0784
Location: Located on Conanicut Island at the mouth of Narragansett Bay, Jamestown can be easily reached by following Rte. 138 between Newport and Saunderstown. The Jamestown Museum is located on Narragansett Avenue in the village of Jamestown.
Highlights: Narragansett Bay ferryboat exhibit,

Robert H. Smith

General Information: The Museum (1886) is a repository for Jamestown's past history. Exhibits include ship models, pictures, maps, and operating gear from the ferries that connected the island to neighboring communities (Newport) for over three hundred years until the Newport Bridge was completed in 1969.

Admission: No entry fee, but donations accepted. Open Wednesday-Sunday, 1 P.M.-4 P.M., mid-June-Labor Day.

NEWPORT, RHODE ISLAND

The Museum of Newport History
Newport Historical Society
82 Truro Street
Newport, RI 02840
(401) 841-8770 Fax: (401) 846-1853
Location: The Museum is located at Thames Street at the foot of Washington Square adjacent to the Brick Market just one block from the famous dock area of downtown Newport.
Highlights: Ship models, research library (9,000 volumes), historical photographs (100,000), **Website:** www.newporthistorical.com/museumof.htm

General Information: The rehabilitation of the Historic Brick Market (1772) now houses the Museum of Newport History first opened in 1993. The Museum is a collaborative effort of the Newport Historical Society and the Brick Market (1762) Foundation formed by the city in 1988. The space-intensive Brick Market building span 350 years.

The Museum offers a spectacular multi-dimensional, interactive exhibit highlighting Newport's long and colorful history brings Newport's history to life. Displays include interactive computers, artifacts of everyday life, graphics, thousands of historic photographs, and audiovisual programs on laser discs to tell Newport's story.

The Museum contains fine ship models, brilliant paintings, exquisite Colonial silver, the printing press used by James Franklin, brother of Benjamin, the figurehead from the yacht *Aloha*, and much more.

The Newport Historical Society maintains a research library including ship logs that are especially helpful in genealogical research in Rhode Island. The Society also operates the Wanton-Lyman-Hazard House (1670), the Friends Meeting House (1699), and the Seventh Day Baptist Meeting House (1729).

Activities: Guided walking tours Thursday-Saturday mornings, June-September. Board a reproduction 1890s omnibus to watch a video tour of historic Bellevue Avenue.

Admission: Entry fee. Open Monday, Wednesday-Saturday, 10 A.M.-5 P.M.; Sunday, 1 P.M.-5 P.M.; summer weekend hours. Closed Tuesday.

NEWPORT, RHODE ISLAND

Museum of Yachting
Fort Adams State Park
P. O. Box 129
Newport, RI 02840
(401) 847-1018 Fax: (401) 847-8320 E-mail: museum@moy.org
Location: Newport lies nineteen miles south of Fall River, Massachusetts, on SR-24. The Museum of Yachting is at Fort Adams State Park, the landing for the Newport to Block Island Ferry. Newport may also be reached from south and west by using State Rte. 138, east off I-95 North.
Highlights: 12-Meter yacht *Courageous*, ship models, small-craft collection, Singlehanded Sailors Hall of Fame, America's Cup Gallery, *Spinnaker* (quarterly newsletter), library, gift shop, **Website:** www.moy.org/
General Information: The flagship of the Museum is the 12-Meter yacht *Courageous*, winner of the America's Cup challenges in 1974 and 1977, is berthed at the Museum. She is available for charter and participates in racing on Narragansett Bay in the summer season.

The Museum's developers envisioned a facility where visitors could learn something about yachting history, technology, and the people who have been instrumental in that evolution. Its exhibits include the America's Cup Gallery, the Hall of Fame for Singlehanded Sailors, Phil Weld Library, the Golden Age of Yachting, and The Great Designers. Other craft, such as a Bris "amphibie" sailing craft fifteen feet in length, are also included. And a special Exhibits Gallery has an in water classic boat collection. The Museum's library contains over 2000 volumes of nautical-oriented books and other material available to members or qualified researchers by appointment.

A voluminous America's Cup scrapbook collection, covering the period from 1885 to the present, is available as a research tool.

Activities: An annual classic regatta on Labor Day weekend, an unlimited regatta in August, winter educational program, and a School of Wooden Boat Building is conducted at the Museum. The Museum also sponsors the Sparkman-Stephens Regatta in June. There are thirteen 12-meters in Newport which race in this event under the auspices of the Museum of Yachting.

Admission: Entry fee. Open daily, 10 A.M.-5 P.M., May 15-October 31. Call for hours.

Robert H. Smith

NEWPORT, RHODE ISLAND

Naval War College Museum
686 Cushing Road
Newport, RI 02841-5010
(401) 841-4052/1317
Location: From I-95, exit onto SR-24/114 heading south. After thirteen miles exit west onto Admiral Kalbfus Road to the Naval War College at Coasters Harbor Island, Newport.
Highlights: History of naval warfare, history of the Navy in Narragansett Bay, torpedo development, ship models, library,
Website: www.nwc.navy.mil/museum/
   General Information: Founded in 1978, the Naval War College Museum exhibits a fine collection of art, artifacts, imprints, and prints on the history of naval warfare and the navy in the Narragansett Bay region. The history of the "art and science" of naval warfare, as chiefly studied at the Naval War College through the years, is the principal exhibit theme of the Museum.

Exhibits explain the importance of the sea as a factor in the formulation of national policy objectives and as the arena wherein decisions are wrought through diplomacy and trial by arms. A second exhibit theme is the naval heritage of Narragansett Bay and exhibits tell the story of the long and eventful relationship of the navy with Narragansett Bay and people of Rhode Island, including the development of the torpedo on Newport's Goat Island.

New exhibits focus on Theodore Roosevelt's incredible impact on the Navy, including his writing some 37 important books. One multi-volume treatise on the War of 1812 formed the basis for Congressional action in 1889 authorizing steel ships for the Navy. The exhibits are most informative and educational. A small library of books on museology and naval history is available on the premises, as is the archive and reading room.
   Activities: Guided tours
   Admission: No entry fee. Open Monday-Friday, 10 A.M.-4 P.M., Saturdays and Sundays, noon-4 P.M., June-September.

Smith's Guide to Maritime Museums of North America

Founded in 1978, the Naval War College Museum exhibits a fine collection of art, artifacts, imprints, and prints on the history of naval warfare and the navy in the Narragansett Bay region of Newport, RI. (Photo R. H. Smith)

Robert H. Smith

The Seaman Church Institute, established to house and serve sailors, also houses the Whale Museum and is just across from the important Museum of Newport History in Newport, RI. (Photo R. H. Smith)

PROVIDENCE, RHODE ISLAND

Providence **(Reproduction-18th Century Sloop)**
c/o Providence Maritime Heritage Foundation
P. O. Box 1261
Providence, RI 02906
(401) 274-7447 E-mail: info@sloopprovidence.org
Location: The replica is moored on the Providence River off I-95 in the city.
Highlights: The *Providence* (replica sloop),
Website: www.sloopprovidence.org

General Information: Providence merchant John Brown built sailing ships until 1775, which engaged in highly prosperous trade with ports in the West Indies. Rhode Island, the first colony to organize a navy, commissioned *Katy* (later renamed the *Providence*) to confront British customs ships in Narragansett Bay.

She was the first ship commissioned into the Continental Navy; the first command of John Paul Jones, the first ship to land U.S. Marines on foreign soil, the first ship to fly the U.S. flag on foreign soil, and the most successful ship of the Colonial Navy in the Revolutionary War (over forty captures or sinkings)!

Five months after the first at-sea fight of the Revolution, in May 1775, the *Katy,* renamed *Providence,* was Rhode Island's initial contribution to the Continental Navy. John Paul Jones described her four years of fighting: "Hers is a record unmatched by any other Continental vessel, and her quarter deck served as a proving ground for some of the greatest Revolutionary captains." She was burned by her own crew in Penobscot Bay, Maine, in August 1779 to avoid capture by the British.

Today from Narragansett Bay comes a fully operational 110-foot reproduction of the *Providence,* the ship that sailed in those waters two hundred years ago.

Activities: Available for charter, visits to patriotic or historical events in U.S. seaports. American Sail Training programs, Apprenticeships, school programs, and dockside tours.

Admission: Call or write the Museum for information about sailing on *Providence.*

PROVIDENCE, RHODE ISLAND

The Rhode Island Historical Society Library
121 Hope Street
Providence, RI 02906
(401) 331-8575 Fax: (401) 751-7930 E-mail: aboisvertr@rihs.org
Location: The Library is in the east side area of Providence.
Highlights: Whaling records, photographs, Customs House records, ship's logs,
Website: www.rihs.org/index.shtml

General Information: The Rhode Island Historical Society Library houses the third largest genealogical collection in New England. Manuscript collections date from 1636 to the present. They include maritime records which document Rhode Island's coastal and global trade, as well as Customs House records for Providence and Bristol-Warren, hundreds of ship's logs, and records of many mercantile firms.

The graphics collection houses a quarter-million, architectural drawings, maps, and broadsides. It is equally rich in watercolors, drawings, engravings, etchings, and ephemera. Audiovisual holdings contain 4 million feet of amateur, feature, and news film, and sound recordings. It provides researchers with the best available visual documentation of Rhode Island's landscape and culture.

Admission: No entry fee but donation recommended. Open Tuesday-Saturday, 9 A.M.-5 P.M. Appointment needed for Manuscripts and Graphics Divisions.

Robert H. Smith

NEWPORT, RHODE ISLAND

Rose Island Lighthouse & Museum
P. O. Box 1419
Newport, RI 02840
(401) 847-4242 Fax: (401) 849-3540 E-mail: charlotte@roseisland.org
Location: Rose Island is a 17-acre island located just one mile off Newport in Narragansett Bay between Newport and Conanicut Island and may be reached by ferry from Newport or Jamestown.
Highlights: Lighthouse and keepers' quarters, *Rose Island Lighthouse News* (newsletter), overnight accommodations, clambake and pig roast events,
Website: www.roseislandlighthouse.org/
   General Information: The Rose Island Lighthouse was established in 1870 and kept by civilian families in the U.S. Lighthouse Service until 1941; it remained a part of the U.S. Coast Guard until 1971. Abandoned, it deteriorated, as did the rest of the island which had its initial use as a military base first established during the American Revolution. Much later, during World War I and II, Rose Island was an explosives depot that was part of the Navy's Torpedo Station. The Navy's torpedoes and mines (manufactured at nearby Goat Island) were filled at Rose Island where nearly one and one quarter million pounds of dynamite were stored, making life on the island about as comfortable as living on a powder keg.
   In 1984, local residents, who were concerned about developers' plans for the island, formed the non-profit Rose Island Lighthouse Foundation to restore the lighthouse. The island is divided into two parcels: The smaller — 1.5 acres — contains the lighthouse and was deeded to the City of Newport in 1985 for the Foundation to manage. The other 17 acres was recently purchased by the Foundation and is a protected wildlife refuge. It contains the remains of the nation's first Fort Hamilton, which is 200 years old and includes two circular bastions and a 9-room barracks building with brick-and-stone walls that are 3-4 feet thick and still in good shape. During the earlier wars, other buildings used by the military, including the concrete igloos where ammunition was stored for the defense of Narragansett Bay, are still in place but completely overgrown with the island's natural vegetation. Nary a shot was fired in anger from this fort. This part of the island is privately owned.
   The lighthouse restoration efforts were successful and in 1993 the light was relit by the Foundation as a private aid to navigation for the Bay. Today, the lighthouse is host to four types of visitors: day visitors, school groups, overnight guests, and guests who may become, for a week's stay for a week's stay, "Rose Island Lighthouse Keepers." Such residence requires full agreement to maintain the station, which includes collecting any rain water that falls on the island for

the lighthouse-basement cistern — there is no running water. Also, mowing the lawn and repairing any minor items such as door hinges.

The weekly guests are an important part of the ongoing maintenance of the lighthouse, and reservations are booked years in advance, but you should check the website for cancellations.

Today's visitors can get a glimpse of what keepers' lives were like through photographs and memorabilia provided by the grandchildren of two of the longest-termed keepers, Charles S. Curtis (1887-1918) and Jesse Orton (1921-1936).

Activities: Guided tours. Learn about self-sufficient utilities and island conservation practices. Tour the operating Lighthouse and Fort Hamilton (which is in the process of being restored), picnic tables, shell beaches, public toilets available. Events include an Opening Day Pig Roast over 4th of July, the world's most "trashless" clambake in August, and a rowing/paddling race in September. We encourage visitors to come via the Jamestown-Newport Ferry and get a dollar off their admission when they land at the lighthouse. We have only a small drop-off float where the ferry also comes in and no dockage for people to tie up boats.

Depending on the weather, people can anchor their boats and beach their dinghies near the lighthouse, but nowhere else on the island, since it's private property and a sensitive wildlife refuge — no trespassing while birds are nesting.

NEWPORT, RHODE ISLAND

Singlehanded Sailors Hall of Fame
c/o Museum of Yachting
Fort Adams State Park
P. O. Box 129
Newport, RI 02840
(401) 847-1018 E-mail: museum@moy.org
Location: Newport lies nineteen miles south of Fall River, Massachusetts, on SR-24. The Museum of Yachting is at Fort Adams State Park.
Highlights: Singlehanded Sailors Hall of Fame, **Website:** www.moy.org
General Information: The Singlehanded Sailors Hall of Fame opened in 1986 in the old mule barn at Historic Fort Adams in Newport. The Hall of Fame is filled with charts; a world map showing the records of the twenty-four men and three women now inducted in the Hall of Fame. On exhibit is the eight-foot sloop *Bris* built by Sven Lundin of Sweden. Lundin sailed this very small boat here from Sweden and then donated it to the Museum of Yachting.
Admission: Entry fee. Open seven days a week, 10 A.M.-5 P.M., May 15-October 31.

Robert H. Smith

KINGSTON, RHODE ISLAND

University of Rhode Island Library
Special Collections Department
Kingston, RI 02881
(401) 874-2594 Fax: (401) 876-4608
Location: Kingston is thirty-two miles southwest of Providence on Rte. 138.
Highlights: Ferryboat records, mill, oyster bed, and fishery records,
Website: www.uri.edu/library/
 General Information: The University of Rhode Island Special Collections Department includes 6,075 linear feet of eighteenth- and nineteenth-century material, including ferryboat, mill, oyster bed and fishery records, personal and political papers, store ledgers, journals, and weather statistics. The collection also contains over 137,500 photographs from 1889 to the present.
 Admission: No entry fee. Open Monday-Friday, 9 A.M.-4 P.M.

EAST GREENWICH, RHODE ISLAND

Varnum Memorial Armory
6 Main Street
East Greenwich, RI 02818
(401) 884-4110 or 6158 E-mail: k8bcm@home.com
Location: East Greenwich is twenty miles south of Providence.
Highlights: Limited maritime exhibits,
 General Information: The Varnum Memorial Armory, in the medieval castle style armory, was built by the Varnum Continentals in 1913. A variety of collections focus on naval and marine items and artifacts, military weapons and artifacts from the 16th-century to present. Various military artifacts are displayed from WW I including uniforms, 1883 Gatling Gun and Limber, and several artillery pieces form the Civil War and WW I. Other collections housed here contain Home of Revolutionary officer and lawyer. The General Varnum House Museum displays a few marine exhibits in a fine mansion furnished with period furniture, magnificent paneling, Colonial and Victorian Children's Playrooms, and Colonial garden.
 Admission: Entry fee. Open Memorial Day-Labor Day, Tuesday-Saturday, 1 P.M.-4 P.M. and by appointment.

CONNECTICUT

ESSEX, CONNECTICUT

The Connecticut River Museum
Steamboat Dock
67 Main Street
Essex, CT 06426
(860) 767-8269 E-mail: crm@ctrivermuseum.org.
Location: The Museum is located at the foot of Main Street on the Connecticut River in Essex. From the west: Take I-95 to Exit 69, then Essex/Rte. 9 north three miles to Exit 3 (Essex). From the east: Take I-95, then take Route 9 north to Exit 3 and follow signs to the Museum. From I-91, get off at Exit 22S to Rte 9 to south to Exit 3 and follow signs to the Museum. *Highlights:* The *American Turtle* (first submarine), ship models, small craft (seasonal), *Steamboat Log* (newsletter), Thomas A. Steven Library (a research facility), gift shop, changing exhibits, **Website:** www.ctrivermuseum.org

General Information: The Connecticut River Foundation, founded in 1974, and located in a warehouse building on the 1879 Steamboat Dock, at the foot of Main Street. The dock served as a port of call for steamboat service from New York City to Hartford, Connecticut. The Museum displays a working reproduction of *American Turtle*, the first submarine, invented by David Bushness in 1775. Permanent exhibits include Lay's Wharf (c.1650), small craft exhibits on river hunting, fishing, yachting; steamboating; brownstone schooners; models and paintings on Revolutionary War, the 1812 burning of fleet at Essex and valley archaeology. The Museum offers seasonal in-water exhibitions of antique and classic boats as well as hosting the Traditional Vessels Weekend in September.

Activities: Guided tours, lecture series, films, formally organized education programs, Traditional Vessel Weekend, changing exhibitions, and a permanent collection

Admission: Entry fee. Memberships are available, which may include docking privileges. Open Tuesday-Sunday 10 A.M.- 5 P.M., April-December. Closed national holidays.

NEW LONDON, CONNECTICUT

Custom House Museum
New London Maritime Society
150 Bank Street
New London, CT 06320
(860) 447-2501 Fax: (860) 447-2501 E-mail: maritime.society@snet.net
Location: Town center

Robert H. Smith

Highlights: Maritime history
General Information: The Custom House Museum was created to collect and show maritime history and artifacts are displayed that are especially relevant to southeast Connecticut. The Custom House, constructed in 1833 of granite in Greek Revival style, now serves as a museum. It is a major restoration of the oldest operated Custom House in America, designed by Robert Mills, the nation's first Federal architect, who also modified the building.
Admission: Entry fee. Call for information on times open.

BRIDGEPORT, CONNECTICUT

The *Glacier* Society Museum
P.O. Box 1419
Bridgeport, CT 06601
(203) 375-6638 Fax: (203) 386-0416 E-mail: welcome@glaciersociety.org
Location: Bridgeport, Connecticut
Highlights: The *Glacier* Icebreaker, Newsletter: *The Icebreaking News*,
Website: www.glaciersociety.org
General Information: The *Glacier* Society, an Education Foundation, is dedicated to the restoration and operation of the icebreaker USS/USCGC *Glacier* in honor of all who served in the exploration of the North and South Poles. Historically, she holds the honor of serving as Admiral Richard Byrd's flagship In addition to her record-breaking deployments, the *Glacier* is one of only a few United States ships to serve under the control of both the US Navy and the US Coast Guard.

The USS/USCGC *Glacier* will be placed back into service as a marine science, research, and education platform providing hands-on training to children, students, and adults while teaching the history of Pole exploration. Contact The *Glacier* Society for information.

BRIDGEPORT, CONNECTICUT

HMS *Rose* (Replica Ship)
Homeport: Newport, RI
P.O. Box 207
Newport, RI 02840
(203) 335-1433 Fax: (203) 335-6793 E-mail: info@tallshiprose.org
Location: Newport, Rhode Island
Highlights: HMS *Rose* (world's largest active wooden sail-sailing vessel),
Website: www.tallshiprose.org/

General Information: Built in Nova Scotia in 1970, the HMS*Rose* is the replica of the 1757 British frigate that played a prominent part in the Seven Years War and the American Revolutionary War patrolling Long Island Sound.

The modern *Rose* was built essentially from the same plans as her predecessor, which was launched from the renowned Smith and Rhuland Shipyard, Lunenburg, Nova Scotia.

The Rose recently moved her home port from Bridgeport, CT, back to Newport, RI where she spent the first part of her career. There she is undergoing substantial improvements in preparation for her role in an upcoming film project. Although she won't be available for public tours or sail training in 2001, it's expected she will return to her mission when the film is completed sometime before the 2002 sail training season.

When she opens for tours again, experienced crew will conduct guided tours of the ship and her exhibits illustrating the rich maritime history of Colonial New England. In 1990, Rose became U.S. Coast Guard-certified as the largest sailing school vessel in America.

Activities: Dockside tours when Rose is in port, daily, noon-5 P.M., beginning early 2002.

Admission: Entry fee. See www.tallshiprose.org for more information.

NORWALK, CONNECTICUT

The Maritime Aquarium
10 North Water Street
Norwalk, CT 06854
(203) 852-0700, ext. 206 Fax: (203) 838-5416
Location: Norwalk is just six miles east of Stamford. The Aquarium is in historic "SoNo," a revitalized area of South Norwalk along the waterfront of the Norwalk River and Long Island Sound. It is a short distance from I-95 and a brief walk from the AMTRAK/Metro North railroad station.
Highlights: Connecticut's only IMAX Theatre New gift shop and cafeteria, research vessel *Oceanic* and *The Glory Days*, boatbuilding school,
Website: www.maritimeaquarium.org/
General Information: The Maritime Aquarium at Norwalk, founded in 1988, is devoted to the maritime history and marine life of Long Island Sound. In the Maritime Hall: boatbuilding, touch tank with live rays, animal adaptation exhibits, main and gallery exhibit area. Falconer Hall: Historic and contemporary vessels and several historic replicas. The Maritime Aquarium is home to the research vessel *Oceanic*, the historic Hope oystering sloop, and *The Glory Days*, an elegant steam tender. In the Aquarium: sharks, seals, river otters, and over 1000 marine animals indigenous to Long Island Sound. A permanent sea turtle exhibit has been established.

Robert H. Smith

Activities: Boatbuilding, marine science programs, teacher enrichment, field studies, IMAX films, parties, member events and group tours.

MYSTIC, CONNECTICUT

Mystic Seaport Museum
50 Greenmanville Avenue
P.O. Box 6000
Mystic, CT 06355-0990
(860) 572-5315 Fax: (860) 572-5324 Toll Free: 888-9SEAPORT
E-mail: info@mysticseaport.org
Location: Mystic is seven miles east of New London along the Mystic River on SR 27. ***Highlights:*** Boardable 19th- and 20th-century vessels, ship models, scrimshaw, boatbuilding, G. W. Blunt White Library, Whale Library, 60,000 ship/boat plans, *The Log* (quarterly), *The Windrose* (newsletter), Rosenfeld photograph collection, 60,000 (±), boating), ship/boat plans, library (research and archives of American yachting and gift shop, **Website:** www.mysticseaport.org

General Information: Founded in 1929, Mystic Seaport is the nation's leading maritime museum, housing the largest collection of boats and maritime photography in the world. Renowned for its village area of historic buildings and tall ships, Mystic Seaport includes exhibit galleries and a working shipyard where the art of wooden shipbuilding endures.

In the village are of historic buildings, trade shops and homes that give the visitor an understanding of life in a seaport during the mid-nineteenth century.

The last of the wooden whaling ships, the *Charles W. Morgan*, the 1882 training ship *Joseph Conrad*, and the fishing schooner *L. A. Dunton* may be boarded by visitors. More than 100 other ships and boats are on display in the Museum.

Exhibit galleries offer ship models, scrimshaw, figureheads, paintings, artifacts, small boats, and other relics that trace the history of ships, shipbuilding, and maritime activities. Don't miss Voyages: Stories of America and the Sea, the country's first exhibit to offer a national perspective of the sea's profound role in defining our national identity. Visitors may watch skilled ship-wrights restore historic vessels in the seaport's preservation shipyard. Sea chantey concerts, as well as demonstrations of fireplace cooking, boat building, sail setting, and maritime arts, are given seasonally. Craftspeople may be seen working in some shops. A planetarium offers daily shows. There is also a children's museum where youngsters may play with toys, clothing, and games popular in the 1800s.

The Museum has purchased the entire Rosenfeld Collection of photographs. The collection, which comprises more than one million images, documents more than 100 years of maritime and yachting history, and is the single largest collection of marine photographs in the world.

Mystic Seaport provides opportunities for college-level maritime studies. The Munson Institute conducts graduate-level courses during the summer months while undergraduate maritime studies courses are offered through the Williams College/Mystic Seaport Program during the academic year.
Admission: Entry fee. Memberships are available. Museum open daily, 9 A.M.-5 P.M., to 6 P.M. in summer. Closed Christmas, but open limited hours on Thanksgiving, Christmas Eve, and New Year's Day.

GROTON, CONNECTICUT

Nautilus **and Submarine Force Museum**
Naval Submarine Base New London
1 Crystal Lake Road
Groton, CT 06349-5571
(860) 694-3558 Fax: (860) 694-4150 Toll Free: 1-800-343-0079
E-mail: nautilus@subasenlon.navy.mil
Location: Groton is forty-five miles east of New Haven at exit 86 on I-95. The submarine and Museum are off Rte. 12 near the entrance to the Naval Submarine Base.
Highlights: The USS *Nautilus* (1954), first nuclear-powered submarine in the U.S. Navy, also captured Italian, German, and Japanese mini-submarines, submarine periscopes, **Website:** www.ussnautilus.org/
General Information: The Historic Ship *Nautilus* and Submarine Force Museum (founded in 1964) are located outside the main gate of the naval base. The Museum is a repository for the records and history of the U.S. Submarine Force, from its humble beginnings at the turn of the century to the modern Navy.

In the Museum entrance is an eleven-foot model of the fictional Captain Nemo's *Nautilus* from Jules Verne's "20,000 Leagues Under the Sea." The Museum displays working periscopes, an authentic submarine control room, an extensive wall of ship models that depict the development of the U.S. Submarine Force.

The collection of historic submarines includes the first nuclear-powered submarine *Nautilus* (launched June 14, 1952 and commissioned in 1954). This submarine, and the *Albacore* at the Port of Portsmouth Maritime Museum, were both designed for specific purposes — the *Nautilus* for the newly designed propulsion system (nuclear) and the *Albacore* for a new hull design. Other exterior exhibits include: the Japanese HA-8; Italian *Maiale*; a German *Seehund*; and an early American research submarine; Simon Lake's *Explorer*.

Interior collections include pictures, models, battle flags, paintings, brow canvases, submarine parts, medals, and personal memorabilia from submariners. 20,000 photographs of submarines and related subjects are available for perusal

Robert H. Smith

in the adjoining research library. The Museum has been expanded to include a larger museum store, a 70-seat theater, and extensive cold war era exhibits.

Activities: Self-guided tours of the world's first nuclear- powered vessel, the *Nautilus*; working models of navy periscopes; submarine control room and two mini-theatres with twenty-five-minute films depicting the growth and history of the Submarine Force and the United States Ship *Nautilus*.

Admission: No entry fee. Museum, summer hours: open Wednesday-Monday, 9 A.M.-5 P.M., Tuesdays 1 P.M. to 5 P.M. Winter hours: Wednesday-Monday, 9 A.M. to 4 P.M.

Library: Open Monday, Wednesday, Thursday, and Friday, 8:30 A.M.- 3:30 P.M., by appointment only. Closed Thanksgiving, Christmas, and New Year's day.

(The *Nautilus* is closed the first two weeks in May and the last two weeks in October for maintenance.)

STONINGTON, CONNECTICUT

Old Lighthouse Museum
7 Water Street
Stonington, CT 06378
(860) 535-1440

Location: Stonington is fifteen miles east of New London. From I- 95, take exit 91 South (N. Main Street) to the stop sign. Turn left and take the next right over the bridge to Water Street. The Museum is at the south end of Water Street.

Highlights: Lighthouse, ship models, local history of maritime interest, **Website:** www.stoningtonhistory.org/light.htm

General Information: The Old Lighthouse Museum, founded in 1925, is housed in a stone lighthouse built in 1823. The lighthouse was moved back from the seashore several hundred feet north to the present location where the keeper's house was added. The lighthouse was important to the captains whose steamships transported thousands from New York City to the harbor in Stonington, where they transferred to railroad trains for the balance of the trip to New England areas.

The Museum's exhibits include ship models, whaling gear, firearms, stoneware, and early maritime portraits. Also displayed are furniture; silver and pewter; utensils at Whitehall; seventeenth- and eighteenth-century historical treasures of the town including whaling and War of 1812 relics; manuscript collections. The Pequot Indians, until their defeat in 1637, were dominant in the area. Then the first white settlement was established.

Activities: Guided tours; lectures; formally organized education programs, permanent and temporary exhibits.

Admission: Entry fee. Memberships available. Open Tuesday-Sunday, 11 A.M.-5 P.M., May-November. In July, the Museum is open daily.

PLAINVILLE, CONNECTICUT

Plainville Historic Center
29 Pierce Street
Plainville, CT 06062,
(860) 747-6577 or 0081 Fax: 860/747-6577
Location: The Center is in Plainville via I-84, take exit 34.
Highlights: Farmington Canal, library
  General Information: The Plainville Historic Center is in the former town hall (1890). The museum focuses on Plainville's early days, including the era of the Farmington Canal (1827-47). The museum displays toys, period costumes, tools, clocks, bakery wagon, museum shop, and a large diorama of Center of Plainville in 1830 with bridges, three boats, and dry dock. Extensive canal research material available by appointment.
  Admission: Open May-December, Wednesday and Saturday, noon-3:30 P.M.

DEEP RIVER, CONNECTICUT

Stone House
245 South Main St. (Rte. 154)
P.O. Box 151
Deep River, CT 06417
(860) 526-5811
Location: Via I-95 exit at Old Saybrook north on to Rte. 9 seven miles to the Deep River Exit 5.
Highlights: Local maritime history
  General Information: The Stone House Marine Room contains oil paintings of ships commanded by local shipmasters, rare early photographs of shipyards, navigation instruments, rare documents, and other nautical material. In addition, the Mather Collection of town memorabilia includes scrap books, pictures, and other town history notes, and provides an invaluable reference source of local history. Most of the articles in the museum relate to vessels with local ties: built, owned, captained, or manned by local people.
  Admission: By donations. Open Saturday and Sunday, 2:00 P.M.-4:00 P.M., July-August. Other times by appointment.

Robert H. Smith

MIDDLETOWN, CONNECTICUT

Submarine Library Museum
440 Washington Street (Rte. 66)
Middletown, CT 06457
(860) 346-0388 E-mail: bbastura@webtv.net
Location: Middletown is on the Connecticut River ten miles south of Hartford. The Museum is on Washington Street approximately two miles west of the Connecticut River.
Highlights: Boat models, submarine models, library,
Website: www.ohwy.com/ct/s/sublibmu.htm
 General Information: The Submarine Library Museum exhibits World War I and II submarine memorabilia, artifacts, models of subs, historical files on U.S. and foreign subs, related subjects. Complete set of World War II submarine models.
 Admission: No entry fee. Open Saturday and Sunday, 10 A.M.-5 P.M.

NEW LONDON, CONNECTICUT

U.S. Coast Guard Museum
U.S. Coast Guard Academy
15 Mohegan Avenue
New London, CT 06320-4195
(860) 444-8511
Location: New London is fifty miles east of New Haven. In town, follow signs on Rte. 32 to the U.S. Coast Guard Academy.
Highlights: The *Eagle* (training barque), library (150,000 volumes), gift shop in Visitor's Center,
Website: www.uscg.mil/hq/g-cp/museum/muse_info.html
 General Information: The U.S. Coast Guard Museum in Waesche Hall was founded in 1967. Collections include ship and airplane models; paintings and artifacts; flags and figureheads relating to the U.S. Coast Guard and its predecessors — the Revenue-Cutter Service, Lighthouse Service, Life-Saving Service — and the barque *Eagle*.
 The Museum tells the story of the unique services the U.S. Coast Guard provides and has provided for the two hundred years of our nation's history. Since the Coast Guard provides the infrastructure services for the maritime industries, a visit to the museum adds an important dimension to anyone's tour through maritime and military museums around the country. Only here can one explore all the aspects of marine law enforcement, aids to navigation, search and rescue, and marine safety that make the sea lanes and waterways of America save for mariners the world over.

One of the most distinctive landmarks at the Academy, when it is in port, is America's Tall Ship, the training barque *Eagle*. This beautiful, 295-foot vessel came to the Academy as a reparation prize from Germany after World War II. Perhaps the finest training ship afloat for young sailors, it is on Eagle's decks and aloft in the rigging where future officers get their first tastes of the challenges of life at sea. The *Eagle* celebrated her sixtieth anniversary in 1996.

The Museum's collection of some 6,000 works of art and artifacts depicts the service's diverse and proud history—U.S. Coast Guard (1915 to present), Lighthouse service (1870s - 1939), Life Saving Service (1870s - 1915), and Revenue Cutter Service (1870s-1915).

Admission: No entry fee. Pavilion and Museum open, Monday-Friday, 10 A.M.-5 P.M., May 1-October 31; Museum open daily 8 A.M.-4 P.M. the rest of year. Closed national holidays. If the training barque *Eagle* is in port, she may be boarded.

NEW YORK

BLUE MOUNTAIN LAKE, NEW YORK

Adirondack Museum
Attn.: Maritime Section
P. O. Box 99, Rte. 28N & 30
Blue Mountain Lake, NY 12812-0099
(518) 352-7311 Fax: (518) 352-7653 E-mail: acarroll@adkmuseum.org
Location: Blue Mountain Lake is 103 miles north of Albany (forty-four-miles west of I-87) near junction of Rtes. 28 and 30.
Highlights: Collection of over 200 non-powered freshwater craft, gift shop
General Information: Adirondack Museum, founded in 1957, is a regional Museum of history and art whose specialties are its maritime collections. A 12,000 square-foot exhibit on boats and boating in the region includes over sixty craft on display from the Museum's collection of 205. Some of these are the ten- and one-half pound Rushton canoes, *Sairy Gamp*. Rushton sailing canoes, sixty Adirondack guideboats, and an 32-foot Idem-class sailboat built in 1900 are also displayed. Power craft include the gold cup boats *El Lagarto* (1922) and *Skeeter* (1905). Still other exhibits include small boats, canoes, row boats, and the Adirondack Guide Boat (circa 1800).
Activities: Craft workshops, No-Octane Regatta, Toy Boat Workshop, and special events.
Admission: Entry fee. Open daily 9:30 A.M.-5:30 P.M., Memorial Day through mid-October; closed September 21 for Antiques Show set-up and preview.

Robert H. Smith

KINGS POINT, NEW YORK

American Merchant Marine Museum
US Merchant Marine Academy
Steamboat Road
Kings Point, NY 11024-1699
(516) 773-5515 Fax: (516) 482-5340 E-mail: ammmuseum@aol.com
Location: Kings Point is in northwest Long Island, three miles north of the Long Island Expressway, Exit 33 Bronx, facing Long Island Sound.
Highlights: Thirty-five ship models, steam engine working model, National Maritime Hall of Fame, *The Manifest* (newsletter),
Website: www.usmma.edu/
General Information: The United States is blessed with a rich maritime heritage. From coastal trade vessels of the American colonists to the swift nineteenth-century clipper ships to today's impressive supertankers and containerships, one message is clear — ships made America! This is the theme of the American Merchant Marine Museum (established in 1979), a national repository and exhibition center for the artifacts, art work, ship models, and nautical memorabilia depicting America's maritime past.

Many unique and noteworthy items are included in the Museum's inventory. Among the some thirty-five ship models regularly on display is a highly-valued, eighteen-foot-long model of the famous passenger ship, SS *Washington*. A new exhibit is the re-creation of a 1945 Victory Ship radio room. The highlight of the Museum's collection, however, is the Hales Blue Riband Trophy, a magnificent gilt award last won in 1952 by the SS *United States* for the fastest transatlantic crossing ever by a passenger liner.

The Museum's National Maritime Hall of Fame is the only such exhibition in the nation dedicated to the great people and great ships of our maritime history. Each year, an individual and a vessel which have made outstanding contributions to the maritime industry are inducted in the Hall.

The Academy trains and educates officers for the merchant marine and naval reserve. The seventy-six-acre grounds include the estate of the late Walter Chrysler and the U.S. Merchant Marine Memorial Chapel.

The academy's primary responsibility, as stated in Federal law, is to train midshipmen (the term applies to the 58 women there as well as the 817 men) to navigate and operate ships. The training leads to licensing as deck officers or engineers. The Museum's archives and photograph collection are open by appointment to the public.

Admission: No entry fee. Open Tuesday-Friday, 10 A.M.-3 P.M., Saturday-Sunday 1 P.M.- 4:30 P.M., year-round. Closed during July and federal holidays.

CLAYTON, NEW YORK

The Antique Boat Museum
750 Mary Street
Clayton, NY 13624
(315) 686-4104 Fax: (315) 686-2775 E-mail: abm@gisco.net
Location: The Museum is located at 750 Mary Street. Take I-81 north from Syracuse, New York, to Exit 47. Follow Rte. 12 to Clayton, approximately 20 miles. At Mary Street turn left for two blocks to the Museum.
Highlights: Wooden Boat Collection — over 20 antique boats including the *Dixie II* and *Miss Canada* III (Gold Cup racers), a library (500 volumes), and The River Memories Gift Shop, Boat building school, **Website:** www.abm.org

General Information: The Antique Boat Museum, initially founded in 1964 and more formally organized in 1980, "is America's largest freshwater boating museum with an impressive collection of inland recreational boats. The Museum is housed in a former lumberyard on the Clayton waterfront and is a mixed bag of sheds and buildings full of surprises, and for visitors who grew up on a lake or river — full of nostalgia."

The Museum is a treasure of freshwater boating history, housing a collection of wooden boats that includes native American dugout and birchbark canoes, St. Lawrence skiffs, early twentieth-century speed-boats, launches, dispros (a small fishing boat with a disappearing propeller, hence the nickname dispro), skiffputts, sailing craft, rowing craft, and pleasure boats. Collections also include duckboats; outboards; outboard and inboard engines; launches; runabouts; ice boats; photography collection; and tools.

Featured are the *Dixie II*, winner of the 1908-10 Gold Cup power-boat races, The *Miss Canada III* and other Gold Cup boats; personal boat used by Presidents Grant and Garfield; and other historic craft. Also featured is the *Pardon Me*, one of the largest and most elegant runabouts ever built, and George Boldt's runabout, the *PDQ*. The Cleveland E. Dodge Memorial Launch Building is the largest single exhibit hall of the Museum. Here you will walk among some of the Museum's more than 200 antique boats plus 300 outboard motors, engines, and an extensive collection of nautical memorabilia. Eight boats from the Museum are on loan to the nearby Boldt Castle Yacht House, a short boat tour ride from Alexandria Bay, NY.

Activities: Guided tours, hobby workshops, speedboat rides and skiff rentals are available. Small craft boatbuilding. The Museum hosts a festival of oar, paddle, and sail in mid-July, and the Antique Boat Show & Auction the first weekend in August with more than 125 boats on display. Also, the Antique Raceboat Regatta is a biennial event held on even years.

Admission: Entry fee. Open daily, 9 A.M.- 5 P.M., mid-May through mid-October.

BELLPORT, NEW YORK

Barn Museum
31 Bell Street
Bellport, NY 11713
(631) 286-0888
Location: Bellport, on south side of Long Island, via I-495 sixty-two miles east from New York City to Medford, then south seven miles to Bellport. The Museum is reached through the right-of-way at 12 Bell Street.
Highlights: Whaling history, ship models, scrimshaw, Museum Shop, waterfowl decoys, Sperry navigation instruments
   General Information: Founded in 1972, the Barn Museum contains early American artifacts and a gallery devoted to whaling and fishing in the seventeenth and eighteenth centuries. Exhibits include Tangier Smith's whaling, scrimshaw, nautical implements, Gil Smith Boatyard artifacts, duck hunter batteries, Wilbur Corwin scooter, and gyroscopic instruments of Dr. Elmer A. Sperry.
   Admission: No entry fee. Open Memorial Day-Labor Day, Friday-Saturday, 1 P.M.-4:30 P.M.

BUFFALO, NEW YORK

Buffalo and Erie County Naval and Military Park
1 Naval Park Cove
Buffalo, NY 14202
(716) 847-1773 Fax: (716) 847-6405
E-mail: npark@ci.buffalo.ny.us
Location: Buffalo lies at the west end of upper New York state on Lake Erie. The Park is immediately east of junction of I-190 and Rte. 5, south of the city's center. Take I-190 to downtown Buffalo — from the south take the Church Street exit, go right onto Lower Terrace (first intersection) and right again onto Pearl Street — from the north and Niagara Falls take the Niagara Street exit, go right on Niagara, and turn right onto S. Elmwood, which turns into Lower Terrace after the Church Street intersection. Or take the Kensington Expressway to downtown and the Goodell Street exit, bear left onto Pearl Street and continue to the Park.
Highlights: The *USS The Sullivans* (DD 537) (destroyer), The USS *Little Rock* (CLG 4) (guided-missile light cruiser), The USS *Croaker* (submarine), ship models, **Website:** www.buffalonavalpark.org/
   General Information: The Buffalo and Erie County Naval and Military Park, opened in 1979, is on a six-acre waterfront site, the largest inland park of its kind in the nation and one of the few inland naval parks in the country. Visitors may

board two front-line fighting ships — the guided-missile cruiser USS *Little Rock* and the destroyer USS *The Sullivans*— and see on-shore, a PT boat. *The Sullivans* is a lasting memorial to the five Sullivan brothers that gave their lives with the sinking of USS *Juneau* during WW II. Just forward of the 610-foot *Little Rock* is the 311-foot USS *Croaker* which made six war patrols during WW II. The Museum displays include a model of the *Wolverine*, a sidewheeler converted into an aircraft carrier for flight training during World War II.

Snooks 2nd, one of the 9,500 P-39 airacobras built in Buffalo and Niagara Falls, NY, is on display. After WW II, the plane was abandoned in the jungles of New Guinea and was later salvaged and donated to the Park.

Activities: Guided tours, audiovisual programs, overnight encampment program, and social engagements aboard USS *Little Rock*

Admission: Entry fee. Open daily, 10 A.M.-dusk, April 1-October 31; Saturdays and Sundays only, 10 A.M.-5 P.M., in November.

SYRACUSE, NEW YORK

Canal Society of New York State
311 Montgomery Street
Syracuse, NY 13202
(315) 428-1862 Fax: (315) 478-0103
Location: Take I-690 into Syracuse. Exit onto Erie Boulevard, which intersects with Montgomery.
Highlights: Library (300 volumes),
Website: www.ggw.org/ErieCanal/canal_system.html
General Information: Canal Society of New York State, founded in 1956, is a historical museum with a collection of graphics on the history of the New York State canals. A library is available for research on the premises.

Activities: Guided tours lectures, research on New York State canals

Admission: No entry fee. Memberships are available. Open by appointment only.

CANASTOTA, NEW YORK

Canastota Canal Town Museum
122 Canal Street
Canastota, NY 13032
(315) 697-3451 E-mail: canalmus@dreamscape.com
Location: Canastota is forty-eight miles east of Syracuse off I-90. *Highlights:* Erie Canal history

General Information: Canastota Canal Town Museum, founded in 1970, was established to preserve the Erie Canal's heritage. Construction of the Erie

Robert H. Smith

Canal was hailed as the greatest engineering accomplishment up to that time. Under the leadership of De Witt Clinton, then governor of the state, construction began in 1817 and was completed in 1825. The canal connected Albany, on the east, to Buffalo, on the west, and became the main route between the Atlantic Ocean and the Great Lakes.

The 1860 canal-era museum building is filled with authentic memorabilia as well as exhibits of local businesses.

Admission: No entry fee. Open April-October, Summer: Monday-Friday, 10 A.M.-4 P.M., Saturday, 11 A.M.-4 P.M. Fall, Monday-Friday, 11 A.M.-3 P.M. Closed Saturday/Sunday.

MAYVILLE, NEW YORK

Chautauqua Lake Historic Vessels Co.
15 Water Street
Mayville, NY 14757
(716) 753-2403

Location: Mayville is in the southwest corner of upstate New York and on the north end of the Chautauqua Lake waterfront seven miles south I-86 and on Rte. 394.

Highlights: *Chautauqua Belle* (sternwheeler) and the Bemus Point-Stow Ferry (cable-drawn)

General Information: Chautauqua Lake Historic Vessels Co. owns and operates historic vessels, carrying passengers exactly as was done in the past. Once a secret, strategic water link between French Canada, the Mississippi River, and French Louisiana, Chautauqua Lake has been witness to a wide variety of vessels in her recorded history.

The Chautauqua Lake Historic Vessels include: (1) *Chautauqua Belle*, an old-fashioned, steam-powered sternwheeler, which pays homage to that magnificent fleet of great steamboats that carried cargo and passengers to summer resorts a century ago. With a soft puff of steam and gentle splash of her paddlewheel, it quietly glides across an historic and scenic inland lake.

(2) Bemus Point-Stow Ferry, perhaps the last of a truly American pioneer transport. This cable-drawn ferry has been in operation for over 189 years at a place where one can cross the "Narrows" of Chautauqua Lake by car or on foot.

Activities: The *Chautauqua Belle* — one and one-half hour cruises in the summer. Bemus Point-Stow Ferry — Ferry rides Saturdays and Sundays in June, every day July and August, 11 A.M.-7 P.M.

Admission: Nominal fees.

Smith's Guide to Maritime Museums of North America

The Old Lighthouse at Stonington was important to the captains whose steamships transported thousands from New York City to the harbor where passengers transferred to railroad trains for trip to New England areas. (Photo R. H. Smith)

The Buffalo and Erie County Naval and Military Park, is on a six-acre waterfront site, the largest inland park of its kind and where the museum, with naval vessels, also contains ship models like these. (Photo R. H. Smith)

Robert H. Smith

CHITTENANGO, NEW YORK

Chittenango Landing Canal Boat Museum
7010 Lakeport Road
Chittenango, NY 13037
(315) 687-3801 Fax: same number
Location: Located on the enlarged Erie Canal
Highlights: Library and on-site research center, unique three-bay canal barge dry-dock, **Website:** www.ocmboces.org/cnyregion/chitthome.html

General Information: The Chittenango Landing Canal Boat Museum is a historic preservation site. The site features the original three-bay dry dock with reconstructed miter and drop gates. Along the famous Erie canal, it was here where canal boats were built and repaired in the nineteenth and early twentieth centuries. Also on site are a blacksmith shop, wood-working shop and saw mill, remains of a sunken canal boat, and an interpretive center.

Activities: The Museum offers self-guided tours, day-long school group programs, archaeology instruction and digs, presentations to organizations, towpath walks, and a picnic area.

Admission: No entry fee. Open Saturdays and Sundays 1 P.M.- 4 P.M., May through June; daily 10 A.M. - 4 P.M., Saturday-Sunday, July-August, 1 P.M.-4 P.M.; September-October, Saturday-Sunday, 1 P.M.-4 P.M.; or by appointment.

CITY ISLAND, NEW YORK

City Island Nautical Museum
190 Fordham Street
City Island, NY 10464
(718) 885-0008
Location: The Museum is on City Island, near Pellham Bay Park.
Highlights: Yachting and boatbuilding exhibits, City Island History from 1800, library (500 volumes)

General Information: City Island Historical Society, founded in 1976, operates the nautical historical Museum housed in the former public school (P.S. 17), one of the first schools built in Greater New York City (1887). The Museum building is listed on the National Historic Trust.

Collections include paintings, photographs, artifacts, documents, boats and models, and memorabilia from pre-Plymouth landing times to the present. The part played by City Island in building defenders in the America's Cup Races and in supplying Hell Gate Pilots is emphasized. The library contains information on local history, available for use on the premises.

Activities: Guided tours, lectures, videotapes, and educational programs

Smith's Guide to Maritime Museums of North America

Admission: No entry fee. Memberships are available. Open Sunday 1 P.M.-5 P.M or by appointment only.

PLATTSBURG, NEW YORK

Clinton County Historical Museum
48 Court Street
Plattsburg, NY 12901-2831
(518) 561-0340 E-mail: clintoncohist@westelcom.com
Location: Plattsburg is located on the west shore of Lake Champlain. Exit I-87 at Rte 37. Go east on Rte 3, continuing straight ahead on Cornelia Street. When the road forks, bear left and follow Cornelia Street to Catherine Street, then on Oak for two blocks to Court Street. Oak Street is one way north — go to next street east, then south two blocks to Court Street returning to Oak Street. The Museum is at the corner of Oak and Court Streets with parking off Oak Street behind the building.
Highlights: Lake Champlain battles in the War of 1812, Valcour Island Lighthouse, gift shop.
General Information: The Clinton County Historical Museum exhibits and interprets the area's history from the earliest recorded times (1600) to the present through its collections of paintings, maps, furniture, and decorative arts. The decisive Battle of Plattsburg in 1814 was the culminating event in a century of naval warfare on Lake Champlain among the French, British, and the fledgling American nation. Underwater archaeological discoveries highlight this period. The Museum is also the steward of the Bluff Point Lighthouse on Valcour Island.

The Museum's collections include artifacts from the Battle in 1776 near Valcour Island and the Battle of Plattsburg through dioramas. Other maritime exhibits include artifacts relating to the exploration of the lake by Samuel de Champlain and its later use as an important trade and transportation route.

Admission: Entry fee. Open: Tuesday-Friday, noon-4 P.M.; Saturday, 1 P.M.-4 P.M., year round. Closed public holidays. For lighthouse, call for dates/time open.

Robert H. Smith

COLD SPRING HARBOR, L.I., NEW YORK

Cold Spring Harbor Whaling Museum
Main Street
P. O. Box 25
Cold Spring Harbor, L.I., NY 11724
(631) 367-3418 Fax: (631) 692-7037
Location: Take I-95 east from New York City forty-five miles to SR-110. Travel north six miles to Huntington (just two miles east of Cold Spring Harbor on Rte. 25A).
Highlights: Wonder of Whales gallery, nineteenth-century whaleboat *Daisy*, 700 pieces of scrimshaw, and changing-exhibit gallery, *A Whaling Account* (newsletter), museum store, **Website:** www.cshwhalingmuseum.org
General Information: Between the years 1836 and 1862, the town of Cold Spring Harbor supported a fleet of nine whaling vessels. Their voyages lasted between one and five years, sometimes taking them as far away as the Pacific Arctic. The oil secured by these stout vessels helped to keep American homes illuminated and her industrial machinery running smoothly.

The Cold Spring Harbor Whaling Museum, founded in 1936 displays a fully equipped whaleboat from the brig *Daisy*. Also displayed are whaling implements, marine paintings, ship models, a diorama of Cold Spring Harbor as a whaling port in 1850, and a permanent exhibition on Long Island's whaling industry, called "Mark Well the Whale!" The single largest group of objects consists of 700 scrimshawed items produced by whalers of the nineteenth century. The Museum also supports marine mammal conservation through its education programs and exhibits.

In 1989, a new changing-exhibit gallery opened that features displays on whaling history and traces Cold Spring Harbor's illustrious maritime past. The Museum also supports marine mammal conservation through its education programs and exhibits.
Activities: In-service workshops, adult tours, outreach lectures, and films
Admission: Entry Fee. Open Tuesday-Sunday, 11 A.M.-5 P.M., year-round. Closed Thanksgiving, Christmas, and New Year's Day.

CROWN POINT, NEW YORK

**Crown Point State Historic Site/
Crown Point Reservation Campsite**
RD #1, Box 219
Crown Point, NY 12928
(518) 597-3666

Location: To reach the Crown Point State Take I-87 to exit 28 (Ticonderoga/Crown Point Bridge) and follow NYS Route 74 East to Ticonderoga. At its intersection with NYS Routes 22 & 9N, turn left (north). Continue north through the village of Crown Point to the intersection of NYS Routes 22 & 9N with Bridge Road (NYS Route 910). Turn right (east) and the Crown Point State Historic Site and Crown Point Reservation are four miles up the road (before the bridge to Vermont)

Highlights: Champlain Memorial Light House with the Rodin sculpture "la France" on the Crown Point Reservation; across the road are preserved ruins of le fort St. Frédéric (1734-1759) and His Majesty's Fort at Crown Point (1759-1773); ruins of the Smith & Bullis Lime Kiln; and Prehistoric fossils throughout the Crown Point State Historic Site.

General Information: Crown Point State Historic Site Visitor Center, where your visit was preceded in 1609 by that of Samuel De Champlain, contains exhibits of artifacts found on site of the French and British occupation (1734-1783) and the American occupation (1775-1777). At the Crown Point Reservation stands the Champlain Memorial Light House, originally erected in 1858 and reconstructed in 1909 by the states of Vermont and New York to commemorate the 300th anniversary of the exploration of the lake in 1609 by Samuel de Champlain.

The light house was erected on the site of the Grenadier Redoubt (A small defensive fortification) built by the British in 1759 on the ruins of the French fortified Wind Mill. This site was used by the French as a "staging" area for raids into New England and New York and later by the Americans for their attack on Montreal in 1775.

Lake Champlain was an integral part of the eighteenth century highway linking Dutch and later British New York and French Canada. Crown Point is the narrowest part of Lake Champlain and is located approximately mid-way between Albany, New York and Montreal.

The ruins of le fort St. Frédéric and His Majesty's Fort at Crown Point are preserved by the NYS Office of Parks, Restoration and Historic Preservation, which also operates the Visitor Center/Museum. The Champlain Memorial Light House is maintained by the NYS Department of Environmental Conservation and is open by appointment.

Admission: Entry fee to Visitor Center. The Visitor Center is open May-October, Wednesday - Sunday, 9:00 AM to 5:00 PM. The Crown Point State Historic Site is open until dusk at no charge.

Robert H. Smith

HIGH FALLS, NEW YORK

Delaware and Hudson Canal Museum
Mohonk Road
P.O. Box 23
High Falls, NY 12440
(914) 687-9311
Location: High Falls is twenty-five miles west of Poughkeepsie. Coming from the north on the New York Thruway, take exit 19, then south 9 miles on Rte. 209. Turn east onto Rte. 213 to High Falls. Coming from the south on the New York Thruway, take exit 18 onto Rte. 299. At New Paltz turn north onto Rte. 32 6 miles to Rosendale. At Rosendale, turn west onto Rte. 213 into High Falls, then turn left on Mohonk Road.
Highlights: Exhibits of canal artifacts and detailed dioramas, canal history, working-scale-model of canal lock, Five Locks Walk — self-guided outdoor walking tour of canal and Roebling Aqueduct remains, library and archives.
Website: www.canalmuseum.org/
General Information: In the hamlet of High Falls, where a flight of five locks compensated for a drop of 70 feet in elevation, the Delaware and Hudson (D and H) Canal Museum is located. Founded in 1966, the Museum seeks to inform the public of the great significance of the canal and its related communities; to provide a library and archival facility on the canal and its affiliated industries; and to promote the maintenance and restoration of the extant parts of the canal.

The D and H Canal Historical Society is actively engaged in restoration projects.

Through the efforts of the Society, locks 16, 17, 18, 19, and 20 and the abutments of the two aqueducts in High Falls, plus the waterfilled section of the canal between Alligerville and Accord, have been designated National Historic Landmarks. The locks and the Five Locks Walk are being restored with a major grant.

The canal operated from 1828 to 1898, transporting newly-found anthracite coal on a 108-mile journey from Hanesdale, Pennsylvania, to the Hudson River at Kingston, New York. It was then shipped down river to New York City. The Museum offers a revealing glimpse of what life was like during the canal era, when horses and mules pulled canal boats along the D and H canal route and through its 108 locks.

When other canal companies ceased to exist because of the advent of railroads, the directors the D and H Canal converted their company into a railroad, becoming America's oldest continuously operating transportation company.

Admission: Entry fee. Memberships available. Open Thursday-Monday, 11 A.M.-5 P.M., Sunday, 1 P.M.-5 P.M., May 30 - Labor Day; Saturday, 11 A.M.-5 P.M., Sunday, 1 P.M.-5 P.M. May, September, and October.

DUNKIRK, NEW YORK

Dunkirk Historical Lighthouse and Veteran's Park
1 Lighthouse Point
P.O. Box 69
Dunkirk, NY 14048
(716) 366-5050 E-mail: dklight@mymailstation.com - or - lst551@juno.com
Location: Dunkirk is both forty-miles southwest of Buffalo and forty- miles northeast of Erie, Pennsylvania off Route 5 to Point Drive North. The Lighthouse is privately owned and is near a public park on the west side of the harbor.
Highlights: Historical lighthouse, Veterans Museum,
Website: www.netsync.net/users/skipper

General Information: Dunkirk Light Station, sometimes called Dunkirk Lighthouse was established in 1875. The light acted in tandem with a pierhead beacon to guide ships to the safety of Dunkirk Harbor. This active lighthouse operated with a Third Order Fresnel Lens bought from France in 1875 for $10,000. The Lighthouse consists of the downstairs with displays on how the Keeper lived and pictures and history of the Lighthouse, the upstairs is the Veterans Museum with displays for the Marines, Navy, Vietnam, Army and Airforce. A tour of the tower is available. A separate building has Coast Guard and Submarine Service displays with a third building, maritime history. Many artifacts are also displayed on the grounds along with a 45-foot Buoy Tender, lifeboat, 21-foot Coast Guard Rescue Boat and more.

Admission: Entry fee. Open third Monday in April to June, Monday, Tuesday, Thursday, Friday, Saturday, Closed Sunday and Wednesday, 10 A.M.-2 P.M., Last tour 1 P.M. Open July-August daily except Sunday and Wednesday 10 A.M.-4 P.M., (last tour 2:30 P.M.); Open September-October, 10 A.M. - 2 P.M. (last tour 1 P.M.), daily except Sunday and Wednesday. Closed November-March. Prices and hours are subject to change without notice.

Robert H. Smith

MASSENA, NEW YORK

Dwight D. Eisenhower Lock
c/o Massena Chamber of Commerce
P. O. Box 387
Massena, NY 13662
(315) 769-2422
Location: Between Lake Ontario and the St. Lawrence Seaway two miles off Rte. 37, 160-miles northeast of Syracuse on the St. Lawrence River.
Highlights: Viewing deck for lock operation
   General Information: Although not a canal lock museum, the Dwight D. Eisenhower Lock, built on the St. Lawrence Seaway near Massena, New York, is included to allow comparison to the locks of the 1800s. The Eisenhower Lock is the first lock east of Lake Ontario whose bottom lies below sea level but whose water surface is 246-feet above sea level.
   Admission: Open May-October, daily 7 A.M.-11 P.M., November-April (viewing only).

GREENPORT, NEW YORK

East End Seaport Maritime Museum
Third Street at Ferry Dock
P.O. Box 624
Greenport, NY 11944
(631) 477-0004 or 477-2100 Fax: (631) 477-3422
E-mail: eseaport@aol.com
Location: Greenport is on the east end of Long Island (north side) via I-495 from New York City to Rte. 25 through Riverhead. Then twenty-two miles to Greenport turnoff. It is an easy stroll from downtown Greenport to the Museum.
Highlights: Wooden boatbuilding, oyster harvesting, WW II war-patrol-by-sailboats exhibit, USS *Holland* submarine replica
Website: www.eastendseaport.org
   General Information: The East End Seaport Maritime Museum, overlooks the village and Shelter Island Ferry. The nearby Bug Island Lighthouse burned in 1963, and in 1990 volunteers completely rebuilt it in 60 days. The lighthouse, near Greenport, is the only all-season navigational aid between Plum Gut and Greenport, where the Coast Guard maintains the light. Greenport was an important part of transportation linkage from New York City via railroad to Greenport, then by ferry to Stonington, Connecticut, where passengers transferred to the railroad, which took them on to the New England area.
   Among the exhibits displayed are: the Plum Island Lighthouse Fresnel lens; a model of "Bug Light" (the lighthouse looks like a bug because of its screw-pile

legs); navigational artifacts; and aquarium displays of local fish. Also displayed are photographs showing the "Whisper Patrol," yachts donated to the Navy during World War II for U-Boat patrols off Long Island. In addition, the Museum has a full-size reproduction of a cross-section of the USS *Holland*, the U.S. Navy's first submarine. Also on display is a 22-foot hand-crafted submarine.

Tools, drawings, and models from local shipyards that document the shipbuilding industry are displayed. More than 500 vessels — whaling ships to minesweepers and patrol boats — were built in Greenport yards between 1830 and 1950.

Activities: Community maritime events and ship visits; summer program for children

Admission: No entry fee but donations requested. Open May-December, Saturday-Sunday, 10 A.M.-5 P.M., summer, Mondays and Wednesday-Sunday, 10 A.M.-5 P.M.

EAST HAMPTON, NEW YORK

East Hampton Town Marine Museum
101 Main Street
East Hampton, NY 11937
(631) 267-6544 or Boat Shop at (631) 324-6850 Fax: (631) 324-9885
Location: From New York City take I-495 east on Long Island to SR-46. Follow that Rte. south three miles to SR-27. Head east on it to Atlantic Avenue in Amagansett (East Hampton's neighbor to the north.)
Highlights: Shore whaling, farmers, fishermen and commercial fishing of the area, Edwards whaleboat and Dominy whaleboat, Boat Shop on Three Mile Harbor, boat models
General Information: East Hampton Town Marine Museum, founded in 1966, is located high on Bluff Road in Amagansett, in a former World War II navy barracks that overlook the Atlantic. From its vantage point you can see the off-shore dragger fleet from Montauk, seiners working their dories through the surf, yachts sailing up the coast, wildlife roaming the dunes, and, of course, people walking the beach, swimming, or just looking out to the sea.

The Town Marine Museum tells the story of a town and its 300-year relationship to the sea. Its unique perspective is not that of the historian or scholar, although its exhibits are characterized by thoughtful interpretation of historical research. Rather, it looks at the people who work on the water every day of their lives, to feed their families and their nation. When you visit the Museum's dioramas, which depict early whaling and modern fishing, you will see the east end of Long Island through the eyes of the commercial fisherman.

Activities: Main floor galleries, top-floor galleries, plus stairwell photography.

Robert H. Smith

Admission: Entry fee. Open Tuesday-Sunday 10:30-5, July 1-Labor Day; Saturday-Sunday only, June 1-30 and after Labor Day-September 30; by appointment year-round.

SYRACUSE, NEW YORK

Erie Canal Museum
Weighlock Building
318 Erie Blvd. East at Montgomery Street
Syracuse, NY 13202
(315) 471-0593 Fax: (315) 471-7220 E-mail: contactus@eriecanalmuseum.org
Location: Take either east-west I-90 or north-south I-81 into Syracuse. The Museum is located near the downtown area in the Weighlock Building on the corner of Erie Boulevard East and Montgomery Street.
Highlights: Full-size canal boat, nation's leading Erie Canal collection, Children's hands-on activity area, *Canal Currents* (newsletter), gift shop, **Website:** www.eriecanalmuseum.org/index.asp

General Information: "Fifteen Miles on the Erie Canal..." The Erie Canal is a symbol of American ingenuity; it captures the spirit of a young nation striving to achieve its dreams. The construction of this inland waterway is a story of determination and innovation, unheard of engineering feats and, ultimately, the triumph of man over nature. Erie Canal Museum, founded in 1962, is housed in the Weighlock Building, the last administrative structure in use on the Erie Canal. Visitors may explore the beginnings, construction, use, life, and effects of this great symbol.

A thirty-five-mile stretch of the canal is preserved in Old Erie Canal State Park. Starting near Syracuse in DeWitt and extending to New London near Rome, the park provides an excellent hiking and biking trail on the original towpath trod by mules and horses in the 1800s.

Activities: Group tours, weekend workshops, and special events, slide shows, and exhibitions. Visitors may board the canal boat to experience canal life and work.

Admission: No entry fee. Open daily, 10 A.M.-5 P.M., year-round. Closed Thanksgiving, Christmas, New Year's Day, Easter, and Independence Day.

ROME, NEW YORK

Erie Canal Village
5789 New London Road
Rome, NY 13440
(315) 337-3999 E-mail: ecv@ntcnet.com

Location: The Village is located about eighty miles northwest of Albany, on Rtes. 46 and 49 with three access exits from thruway I-90.

Highlights: Chief Engineer of Rome (horse-drawn canal packet-boat), restored canal village, gift shop,

General Information: The Erie Canal Village was begun in 1973 in Rome.

The 1840s reconstructed village is in a rustic setting near the spot where the first shovel full of dirt was turned for the old Erie Canal on July 4, 1817; a number of nineteenth-century buildings have been restored to recreate a canal-side village. A historical slide presentation gives background of the site from the days of the Durham boats on Wood Creek to the barge canal. The full-size packet boat *Chief Engineer of Rome,* named for Benjamin Wright who became the original Erie Canal chief engineer from Rome, offers horse-drawn rides along a three-mile section of the canal. Also on the site is a stone marker showing where the canal's construction called spitefully by some, "Clinton's Ditch."

Admission: Entry Fee. Open Memorial Day-Labor Day, every day 10 A.M.-5 P.M.

CAPTREE ISLAND, NEW YORK

Fire Island Lighthouse Preservation Society
4640 Captree Island
Captree Island, NY 11702-4601
(516) 321-7028 Fax: (516) 321-7033

Location: The Lighthouse is located along the south shore of Long Island on Fire Island and is accessible via Robert Moses Causeway. Pay parking at Field 5, follow nature walkway to lighthouse.

Highlights: Fire Island Lighthouse

General Information: The Fire Island Lighthouse will give you the opportunity to experience maritime history, wildlife, and a magnificent beach. A nautical Gift Shop and Exhibit Area are located in the Keepers Quarters/Visitors Center.

Activities: Guided tower tours (192-step climb with panoramic view), fall-spring-weekends, July and August, 7 days. Children must be at least 42" tall, closed-toed shoes and reservations are suggested. must be worn for tower tours. Guided and self-guiding nature trail. School groups in spring and fall by reservation only: (516) 661-4876

Admission: Tower tour-entry fee. Open January through March, major holidays officially closed, unofficially open subject to availability of volunteers and weather permitting. Call for further information.

Robert H. Smith

FORT HUNTER, NEW YORK

Fort Hunter - Schoharie Crossing State Historic Site
P. O. Box 140
Fort Hunter, NY 12069
(518) 829-7516
Location: Amsterdam is 34-miles northwest of Albany, Exit 27 off New York State Thruway onto 5S and then to Fort Hunter.
Highlights: Erie Canal Locks, Schoharie aqueduct, restored 1850's canal store building.
General Information: At Schoharie Crossing State Historic Site, visitors can view the remains from all three phases of the Erie Canal, the most dramatic engineering achievement of its time. In addition to the original canal (1825), the Enlarged Canal (1840s), and the Barge Canal (1917), one can see many of the engineering structures which contributed to the canal's success. These include the Schoharie Aqueduct, several canal locks, culverts, and a canal basin.

The site also encompasses a Visitor Center, Putman's Store (a restored canal store dating from the 1850s) and a two- and one-half-mile nature and bike trail along the towpath.

Admission: No entry fee for tours and rides. Grounds are open dawn to dusk year-round. Visitor Center hours: Open Wednesday-Saturday, 10 A.M.-5 P.M., Sunday, 1 P.M.-5 P.M., May 1-October 31. Walking tours available in advance.

Please call for details of special events. P.M. July 1-Labor Day. Walking tours: Open Wednesday-Friday, 11 A.M.-2 P.M., May-October. Special groups may reserve in advance.

HYDE PARK, NEW YORK

Franklin D. Roosevelt Library and Museum
4079 Albany Post Road
Hyde Park, NY 12538
(845) 229-8114 Fax: (845) 229-0872 E-mail: library@roosevelt.nara.gov
Location: Hyde Park is just four miles north of Poughkeepsie on Rte. 9 (approximately 100 miles north of New York City).
Highlights: Library (45,000 volumes) and archives (16 million pages of manuscripts), ship models, museum store,
Website: www.fdrlibrary.marist.edu/
General Information: Franklin D. Roosevelt Library and Museum, founded in 1939 by a joint resolution of Congress, was the first of several presidential libraries. The Museum, open to the public, contains displays on the lives, careers, and interests of both President and Mrs. Franklin D. Roosevelt. The President's naval/marine collections include ship models, books, artifacts, memorabilia,

prints, paintings, photos, letters, logs, and state documents. (The library section is open only to researchers.)

Admission: Entry fee (includes admission to the Roosevelt Home). Open daily, 9 A.M.-5 P.M. Closed Thanksgiving, Christmas, and New Year's Day.

OSWEGO, NEW YORK

H. Lee White Marine Museum
Foot of West First Street
P.O. Box 101
Oswego, NY 13126
(315) 343-0480 Fax: (315) 343-5778

Location: From Rte. 3 in mid-town Oswego, turn north on 1st Street several blocks to the end of the west pier at the mouth of the Oswego River; the pier extends into the middle of the harbor.

Highlights: Oswego Canal exhibits, shipbuilding exhibits, canoes, epic paintings, World War II tugboat (LT-5) National Historic Landmark, Derrick Barge No. 8, ship models, library

General Information: The H. Lee White Marine Museum is located at one of the most historic sites of the United States. Ever since Père Simon LeMoyne first entered the river in 1654 to the present day, events which have shaped our destiny as a nation have taken place here.

Exhibits touch on the 17th century down through 300 years to the present. And explore Lake Ontario with the Iroquois — the American Indian-master boat builder and navigator. March with Rogers Rangers and the leaders of colonial America, and hunt for treasure in the "Lost Treasures of Lake Ontario" exhibit. A fine group of paintings include the Van Cleve Collection, and others depict the Oswego Canal which connects to the Erie Canal near Syracuse, New York. The canal is still an important commercial enterprise.

James Fenimore Cooper, noted American writer, hailed from this port city, and several exhibits present history on his participation in the community.

The Museum holdings include the National Historic Landmark U.S. Army Tug (LT-5) used in the D-Day landings on Normandy, France. And on the pier is the last steampowered derrick barge, the *Lance Knapp*. Other exhibits include documents, artifacts, models, shipwreck information, photographs, maps, reconstructed rooms, and an extensive collection of artifacts acquired through underwater archaeology, and audiovisual experiences.

Admission: Entry fee. Open daily, Memorial Day-June 30 and September, 1 P.M.-5 P.M.; open daily, July-August, 10 A.M.-5 P.M. Group tours by appointment, year round.

Robert H. Smith

ALBANY, NEW YORK

Half Moon **Visitor Center/New Netherland Museum**
P.O. Box 10609
Albany, NY 12201-5609
(518) 443-1609 (914) 413-9924 E-mail: webmaster@newnetherland.org
Highlights: *Halve Maen* (*Half Moon*) (replica ship),
Website: www.newnetherland.org
 General Information: The Museum interprets the history of New Netherland and the Dutch contribution to the development of the United States of America. The *Half Moon* is a full-scale replica of the Dutch East India Company ship that Henry Hudson sailed in 1609. The ship is open for tours seasonally, and winters at King Marine in Verplanck, New York. It sails to ports in the Mid-Atlantic region.
 Admission: Call for information. The *Half Moon* winters at King Marine in Verplanck, NY.

KINGSTON, NEW YORK

Hudson River Maritime Museum
One Rondout Landing
Kingston, NY 12401
(845) 338-0071 Fax: (9845 338-0583 E-mail: hrmm@ulster.net
Location: Kingston is situated on the west side of the Hudson River twenty-five miles north of Poughkeepsie. NYS Thruway to Exit 19: Kingston. Exit Thruway toll gate turning east to roundabout to third spoke off circle to Broadway (I-587). Follow Broadway east through seven stoplights; at eighth stoplight, turn left— Broadway continues. At the foot of Broadway follow road to left. The Museum is on your right at Rondout Landing.
Highlights: The *Mathilda* (an 1898 steam tug), *Focs'le News* (newsletter), Rondout Lighthouse, library (150 volumes), Gift Shop,
Website: www.ulster.net/~hrmm/
 General Information: Rondout Waterfront was a thriving port on the Hudson River for over 300 years. The D & H Canal (see separate entry) brought coal from the mountains of Pennsylvania to Rondout. Today, this bulkhead looks quite different. At the Hudson River Maritime Museum, founded in 1980, the waterfront is home to historic vessels which dock for a few days or a few years, for restoration, repairs, or rest. Museum members can also find dockage available for an overnight stay.
 The Museum preserves the crafts, ships, and exhibits illustrating the maritime history of the Hudson River Region. Over the years, a number of specialized vessels were developed here to fill the transport needs of New York

industry, including the steamboats which raced each other up and down the Hudson in a battle for passengers and cargo.

Exhibits include collections containing over 4,000 items, from various boats used in Hudson River traffic as well as paintings depicting the early era of river use. The library collection pertains to steam and sail on the Hudson River and is available to the public.

As caretakers of Rondout Lighthouse, the Museum offers scheduled and charter boat rides to the lighthouse, located where the Rondout Creek joins the Hudson River. Built in 1913, it is the last and largest lighthouse built along the River.

Activities: Shad Festival in May, other festivals, visiting vessels, Guided tours, lectures, school trips, concerts, Rondout Light visits, and library.

Admission: Entry fee. Memberships are available. Open daily May-October 11 A.M.-5 P.M.

POUGHKEEPSIE, NEW YORK

Hudson River Sloop *Clearwater*
112 Little Market Street
Poughkeepsie, NY 12601
(845) 454-7673 E-mail: Office@Clearwater.Org
Location: Poughkeepsie is seventy-five miles north of New York City. From I-87 exit at New Paltz, travel twelve miles east across the Hudson River.
Highlights: Hudson River Sloop *Clearwater*, **Website:** www.clearwater.org

General Information: The 106-foot Hudson River Sloop *Clearwater* is part of a growing fleet of historic replica wooden vessels on the Hudson River. The *Clearwater*, with a mission to educate the public about the river's heritage and the natural environment, promotes efforts to clean up pollution on the river. The *Clearwater* travels to some 45 docking locations on tidewater Hudson, New York harbors, and Long Island Sound.

Admission: Free when in your port on the Hudson River. Fee for program sails.

NEW YORK CITY, NEW YORK

***Intrepid* Sea-Air-Space Museum**
1 Intrepid Plaza
Pier 86, 46th Street & 12th Avenue
New York, NY 10036
(212) 245-0072 or 245-2533 Fax: (212) 245-7289
E-mail: cjhughes@intrepidmuseum.org
Location: The USS *Intrepid* is docked at New York City's Pier 86, located at 46th Street and 12th Avenue.

Robert H. Smith

Highlights: The USS *Intrepid* (aircraft carrier), The USS *Growler* (guided missile submarine), The USS *Edson* (destroyer), forty-one aircraft ranging from pre-World War I through modern-day aviation on display on flight/hangar decks, library (5,000 volumes), **Website:** www.uss-intrepid.com

General Information: Perhaps no ship in the annals of the US Navy has done more to live up to her name than the USS *Intrepid*. After a gallant thirty-one-years of service, the historic ship is now the *Intrepid* Sea-Air-Space Museum, founded in 1982. The USS *Growler* may also be toured. She is a guided-missile submarine that served the country for six years armed with Regulus missiles, patrolling the western Pacific Ocean as a strategic nuclear defense deterrent during the Bay of Pigs and the Cuban Missile Crisis of the Cold War period.

The USS *Edson*, a Vietnam-era destroyer with the motto "Three Guns, No Waiting," served the country for thirty years. Named for USMC Major General and Congressional Medal of Honor recipient Merritt Austin ("Red Mike") Edson, this ship provided gunfire support during wartime and a training platform for officers and enlisted personnel during times of peace.

Collections include open flight deck with displays; World War II aircraft; Grumman Avenger; Grumman Hellcat; tools; suspended aircraft; vertical flight vehicles; space flight vehicles; ballistic missiles; and forty-one planes and helicopters, ranging from pre-World War I through modern-day aviation.

A Congressional Medal of Honor Museum is housed here also.

The 710-foot-long hangar deck contains well-crafted exhibits, displays, and photographs, along with the Carrier Operations presentations: U.S. Navy Hall, which features the modern, peace-keeping Navy; *Intrepid* Hall, focusing on the *Intrepid* during World War II; Pioneer Hall, a tribute to early aviation; Technologies Hall, where exhibits and displays presenting some of the greatest advances in sea, air, and space technology can be found. Other notable exhibit areas include Combat Information Center; Air Traffic Control; and Undersea Frontier. The library has information pertaining to sea, air, and space, history, and technology.

Activities: Films, educational programs, and special event halls

Admission: Entry fee. Memberships are available. Open Wednesday-Sunday, 10 A.M.-5 P.M., year-round (last admission at 4 P.M.).

LOCKPORT, NEW YORK

Lockport Canal Museum
Richmond Avenue
Lockport, NY 14126
(716) 434-3140

Location: Lockport is some 20 miles northeast of Buffalo on Hwy 78 North/South or 31 East/West in upstate New York.
Highlights: Original flight of five locks and newer barge canal locks 34 & 35
General Information: Nestled at the base of a historic flight of five locks, the Lockport Canal Museum offers an historical view of the original Erie Canal.

Completed in eight years (1817-1825), the canal is considered to be one of the greatest engineering feats in the world. The canal expanded travel from towpaths to tugboats, opening the corridor of travel to the West by connecting the Hudson River with Lake Erie.

Since 1825, the world-famous locks of the old Erie Canal in Lockport, hewn mostly out of solid rock, have attracted poets, engineers, historians, and artists. Upon seeing the locks, General Marquis de Lafayette proclaimed them to be one of the greatest engineering feats of the world. The stonework of these famous five-twin locks is a monument to the skill and ingenuity of the canal builders. And they were not fully finished until 1847. By then, the south-side twin locks had been substantially enlarged and enlarged again to present large canal size in 1916/18. Today, only the north-side five-flight locks exist. The New York State Barge System is 524 miles in length, including the Erie Canal, the Lake Champlain Canal, and the Oswego Canal.

The small Museum at the lower end of the locks, between the five-flight locks and the newer Locks 34 and 35, contains a wealth of photographic history of the building of the canal in its three stages: 1825, the first full opening of the canal; 1835, the construction and widening of the canal; and 1918, the opening of two much larger locks at Lockport with a rise of over 50 feet to the Lake Erie level. The stone work of the original flight of five locks still exists but the lock gates have been removed creating a five-step waterfall as a spillway for the canal.

Admission: No entry fee. Open daily May-October, 9 A.M.- 5 P.M.

WEST SAYVILLE, NEW YORK

Long Island Maritime Museum
Montauk Hwy, Rte. 27A
P. O. Box 184
West Sayville, NY 11796-0184
(631) 854-4974 854-4979 E-mail: limaritimemuseum@aol.com
Location: West Sayville is on the south-central shore of Long Island. From New York City, take I-495 east to exit 59 south (Lakeland Avenue). Follow Lakeland Ave. south for 6 miles into the village of Sayville. Make a right on Main Street, follow for 1 mile to West Avenue South.
Highlights: *Priscilla* (1888 oyster vessel), *Modesty* (1920 oyster dredger), *Charlotte* (1880 tugboat), ship models, *The Dolphin* (newspaper), U.S. Lifesaving Service Exhibit, Penny Boatshop library,

Robert H. Smith

Website: www.limaritime.org

General Information: Long Island Maritime Museum, formerly Suffolk Marine Museum, was founded in 1966 to preserve Long Island's unique maritime heritage for educational purposes. The Museum features a significant small craft collection, with boats ranging from a six-foot sharpie to the sixty- five foot *Priscilla*, a 1888 oyster sloop. Permanent exhibits include the history of the south shore oyster industry, a restored Bayman' Cottage residence, over sixty small craft and a working 19th century boatshop.

The Elward Smith III Library and Archive are available to researchers by appointment.

Activities: Ongoing Boatbuilding programs, lectures, and workshops. Major events include antique boat show, Seafood Festival and Maritime Folklife Festival.

Admission: Entry fee. Open Monday-Saturday 10 A.M.-4 P.M., Sunday, noon-4 P.M.; closed major holidays.

BUFFALO, NEW YORK

Lower Lakes Marine Historical Society
66 Erie Street
Buffalo, NY 14202
(716) 849-0914 E-mail: info@llmhs.org

Location: The museum is located in downtown Buffalo within walking distance of Erie Basin.

Highlights: Library, photo collection, **Website:** www.llmhs.org

General Information: The Lower Lakes Marine Historical Society, founded in 1987, maintains and displays authentic objects, documents, and art relating to a vital period in Buffalo's maritime history.

"Queen City of the Lakes," Buffalo was for generations the gateway to westward expansion, and the region was the focus of French and British Colonial expansion and the flashpoint for major conflicts involving the great colonial powers of the world.

The museum now maintains a library and photo archive with over 300,000 photo images of Buffalo history. At Lower Lakes Marine Historical Society we have made a an effort to collect the history of the individuals that came to the Great Lakes as well as information on those of the vessels which they owned, or sailed. Other artifacts and historical items are finding their way into the exhibits, and displays making this museum a major repository of maritime history.

Admission: Contact for days and times open.

BRONX, NEW YORK

Maritime Industry Museum at Fort Schuyler
New York State Maritime College
Fort Schuyler, Throggs Neck
6 Pennyfield Ave.
Bronx, NY 10465-4198
(718) 409-7218 or 6130 E-mail: maritimemuseum@juno.com
Location: The Museum is on the campus of the State University of New York's Maritime College in the Throggs Neck section of the Bronx under the Throggs Neck Bridge. Take the Ft. Schuyler exit off I-295.
Highlights: Maritime Library, ship models, and training vessel Empire State, marine artifacts, historic Fort Schuyler (1844)
Website: www.maritimeindustrymuseum.org/
General Information: Founded in 1985, the Maritime Industry Museum at Fort Schuyler has various exhibits, including displays depicting the development and history of the international merchant marine, related shoreside industries, and ports. The history of the Maritime College is also a part of the Museum. Exhibits include marine paintings, water colors, photographs, and artifacts. There is also a unique collection of 175 ship models from early sailing vessels to modern freighters and tankers and ocean liners. The Promenade Wing contains a collection of ocean liner models. Also displayed is a diorama of the Brooklyn Navy Yard during WWII and the new Victory Hall dedicated to WWII sailors.

The 565-foot training ship *Empire State* (formerly USNS *Barrett,* then the *Oregon,* then the *Moremoctide*) is the seventh training ship used by the Maritime College since its founding in 1874. Visitors may tour the ship when in port (nine months of the year) where high up on the aft loading stanchion are inscribed the words: "Student Driver.

Activities: Visitors may tour the fort and campus grounds
Admission: No entry fee abut donations accepted. Open Monday-Friday, 8:30 A.M.-4:30 P.M.; Closed Thanksgiving, Christmas, and New Year's Day.

PORT JEFFERSON, NEW YORK

Mather House Museum
115 Prospect Street
P. O. Box 586
Port Jefferson, NY 11777
(631) 473-2665
Location: From New York City take I-495 east sixty-four miles to exit for SR-112. Follow north six miles to SR-25A, heading west to Port Jefferson on north

Robert H. Smith

shore of Long Island (just eighteen miles south of Bridgeport, Connecticut, across Long Island Sound).
Highlights: Maritime history of the region
   General Information: Historical Society of Greater Port Jefferson maintains a small maritime museum with general artifacts and displays, and clock museum.
   Admission: Open Memorial Day through Labor Day. Call for hours.

MONTAUK, NEW YORK

Montauk Point Lighthouse Museum
2000 Montauk Highway
Montauk, NY 11954
(631) 668-2544 Ext. 23 E-mail: keeper@montauklighthouse.com
Location: The lighthouse and Museum are on Montauk Road six miles east of the town of Montauk on the south shore of the eastern tip of Long Island.
Highlights: Lighthouse,
Website: www.montauklighthouse.com/
   General Information: The Montauk Point Lighthouse is one of the oldest active lighthouses in the U.S. The 1796 lighthouse was commissioned, as were many others, by George Washington. There are 137 steps visitors may climb to the top of the tower. The Museum exhibits include displays about maritime history.
   Admission: Entry fee. Open as follows: January 15, 16, Saturday-Sunday, 11 A.M.-4 P.M.; February 12, 13, Saturday-Sunday, 11 A.M.-4 P.M.; March 18-April 23, 11 A.M.-4:30 P.M.; April 24-28, daily 10:30 A.M.-4:30 P.M.; April 29-May 14, weekends 10:30 A.M.-4:30 P.M.; May 15-June 18, daily, 10:30-5 P.M., weekends, 10:30 A.M.-6 P.M.; May 27-28, Saturday-Sunday, 10:30 A.M.-7:30 P.M., Monday, 10:30 A.M.-6 P.M.; June 19-June 30, daily, 10:30 A.M. -6 P.M., weekends, 10:30 A.M.-6 P.M.; July 1,2, Saturday-Sunday, 10:30 A.M.-7 P.M.; July 3- September 1, daily, 10:30 A.M.-6 P.M., Saturday, 10:30 A.M.-7:30 P.M., Sunday, 10:30-6 P.M.

NEW YORK, NEW YORK

Museum of the City of New York
1220 Fifth Avenue, at 103rd Street
New York, NY 10029
(212) 534-1672 Fax: (212) 423-0758
Highlights: Statue of Robert Fulton, ship models, Edward Moran's famous painting of "The Unveiling of the Statue of Liberty,"
Website: www.mcny.org/

General Information: The Museum is a repository of Port of New York maritime artifacts and paintings related to the Port, which are on permanent display in the Marine Gallery on the second floor. Exhibits include the larger-than-life statue of Robert Fulton taken from the old East River ferry terminal, and a figure head of Andrew Jackson from the frigate U.S. *Constitution* ("Old Ironsides").

Admission: No entry fee, but donations accepted. Open Wednesday-Saturday, 10 A.M.-5 P.M.; Sunday, 1 P.M.-5 P.M. Open for tours only on Tuesday by appointment — call (212) 534-1672, Ext. 206

SOUTHOLD, NEW YORK

Nautical Museum at Horton Point Lighthouse
Lighthouse Road
Box 1
Southold, NY 11971
(631) 765-5500
Location: On Long Island follow I-495 approximately seventy-five miles to Riverhead. At the traffic circle, bear east on S.R. 25 twenty-three miles to Southold. The Museum is at Horton Point north off SR-25 on Lighthouse road.
Highlights: A National Historic Register. Working lighthouse, oil house, lower accessibility, **Website:** www.longislandlighthouses.com/hortonpt.htm

General Information: Southold Historical Society's Nautical Museum was established to preserve artifacts including paintings, logs, scrimshaw, tools, letters of maritime interest and the 1857 lighthouse. Horton's Point rises 110 feet above the sea level. Thus, it provides navigational aid in an area characterized by many shipwrecks.

Admission: No entry fee but donations suggested. Open Saturdays and Sundays only, 11:30 A.M.-4 P.M., Memorial Day-Columbus Day.

CUDDEBACKVILLE, NEW YORK

Neversink Valley Area Museum/D and H Canal Park
P. O. Box 263
Cuddebackville, NY 12729
(845) 754-8870 E-mail: nvam@magiccarpet.com
Location: The Delaware and Hudson (D and H) Canal is on Rte. 209 about ten miles north of Port Jervis, which is on I-84 at the juncture of New York, Pennsylvania, and New Jersey.
Highlights: One mile of D & H Canal, six canal-era structures, John A. Roebling's Neversink Aqueduct, guided towpath tours, gift shop, exhibits on local history, **Website:** www.neversinkmuseum.org/

Robert H. Smith

General Information: Neversink Valley Area Museum, D and H Canal Park, founded in 1963, was established to acquire and restore historical sites within the area and to preserve in them artifacts and memorabilia on a 300-acre site. Within the D and H Canal Park is a one-mile section of the canal, a national historic landmark.

Along this one-mile section are the stone abutments for a canal aqueduct built by John Roebling, builder of the Brooklyn Bridge; remains of a lock; and many canal-era structures including a lock keeper's house, canal store, blacksmith's house, carpenter's house, and a full-size canal barge replica. The early days are being re-created by the Museum, in whose collections are examples of the tools and household needs used by the families that lived on and along the waterway. In the early 1800s the United States was facing an energy shortage. To transport anthracite coal (an important fuel), the D and H canal was opened in 1828. It spanned the 108 miles on the Hudson River from Honesdale, Pennsylvania, to an area near Kingston, New York. The trip took ten days by barge and included 108 locks.

Activities: Educational programs for children, guided hikes, picnicking, cross-country skiing, and a self-guided nature trail.

Admission: Entry fee. Open Thursday-Sunday, noon- 4 P.M., March - December or by special appointment.

NEW YORK, NEW YORK

The New-York Historical Society
2 West 77th Street
New York, NY 10024
(212) 873-3400 E-mail: webmaster@nyhistory.org
Location: 77th Street and Central Park West.
Highlights: Library, Henry Luce III Center for the Study of American Culture,
Website: www.nyhistory.org/
General Information: The New-York Historical Society, founded in 1804, maintains a variety of records on maritime history including archives, ship logs, and other library and research information and paintings, drawings, prints, and ephemera related to maritime history.

Admission: Entry fee. Open all year: Tuesday-Sunday, 11 A.M. - 5 P.M.; library hours, Tuesday-Saturday, 11 A.M.- 5 P.M.

Smith's Guide to Maritime Museums of North America

Looking from southeast to northwest near the Hudson River at Cohoes, New York, are 1825 Erie Canal Locks 1, 2, and 3 where freight and passengers moved up the locks for their 363-mile trip to Buffalo, NY. (Photo R. H. Smith)

The Suffolk Historical Museum exhibits collections from the time of the first settlements of 1640, including exhibits on Eastern Long Island Native Americans.
(Photo R. H. Smith)

Robert H. Smith

ALBANY, NEW YORK

New York State Canal System
New York State Canal Corporation
Director of Canals
P.O. Box 189
Albany, NY 12201-0189
(518) 471-5010 Fax: (518) 471-5023 1-800-253-6244
E-mail: PublicInfo@canals.state.ny.us
Highlights: Historic vessels, **Website:** www.canals.state.ny.us/

General Information: The New York State Canal System is a linear park and living museum unto itself. Celebrating 175 years of continuous navigation during the year 2000, this historical water way is filled with representative examples of times past. The New York State Canal Corporation possesses numerous historical vessels, including a 1920s fleet of dredges and tugs, the majority of which are operational and working. The flagship and educational ambassador of the Canal Corporation, tug *Urger* is one of two remaining bell boats in the United States and remains operational after almost 100 years!

The New York Canal System is comprised of four canals, fifty-seven locks—technological marvels, spanning the 525-mile Canal System.: the Erie, Oswego, Champlain, and Cayuga-Seneca Canals. Unique structures across the Canals include the imposing Water Flight of Five, a series of locks which circumvent the Cohoes Falls, providing navigation from the Hudson River to the Mohawk River and forming the entrance way into the legendary the Erie Canal. The Flight of Five possesses the highest vertical lift anywhere in the world, lifting and lowering boats 169 feet in the shortest distance. In the west at Lockport, there is another historical flight of five locks where one can see the original set next to the "more modern" 1918 version of two locks. When passing through, be sure to stop at one of the historical locks and examine the original brass used to operate and maintain these immense historical structures.

Several locks still maintain hydroelectric powerhouses. Originally there were nearly forty of these pagoda-like structures, but today, only six remain. Lock 17 is the highest lock on the system at Little Falls and is breathtaking to behold. The lock is dramatically situated between high rocky cliffs.

In addition, the New York State Canal System possesses lighthouses. Three lighthouses were constructed in the 1900s on Oneida Lake as part of the Erie Canal improvements.

Smith's Guide to Maritime Museums of North America
STATEN ISLAND, NEW YORK

The Noble Maritime Collection
1000 Richmond Terrace
Staten Island, NY 10301
(718) 447-6490 Fax: (718) 447-6056
E-mail: barbarastanwick@noblemaritime.org
Location: Staten Island is accessed from the Battery in Manhattan via Staten Island Ferry Terminal and is easily reached by S-40 Bus. By car from Brooklyn, Queens, Long Island via Verrazano Bridge and to Staten Island Expressway (I-278) to Clove Rd. /Richmond Rd. Exit. At third intersection, bear right onto Clove Rd., continue to Bement Ave., turn right to Snug Harbor; from Staten Island via Expressway (I-278) to Clove Rd./Richmond Rd. exit. At traffic light, turn left onto Clove Rd., continue to Bement Avenue, follow as above.
Highlights: Noble Maritime Art, library, Sailors' Snug Harbor Exhibition,
Website: www.noblemaritime.org/

General Information: The Noble Maritime Collection is located in a Greek Revival building at the Snug Harbor Cultural Center. The Collection is housed in Building D, a former dormitory of Sailors' Snug Harbor, the famous old retirement home for sailors. The *Noble Crew* of volunteers and the Navy are transforming the old dormitory into a modern museum and a maritime study center. What was solely a collection of the works of John A. Noble, one of America's foremost maritime artists, has grown significantly since his death in 1983.

The Collection includes Noble's series of 79 lithographs depicting twentieth-century maritime endeavor; his oil paintings; his "rowboat drawings"; and his over 6,000 historical marine photographs. Inside the Collection's new home the museum is rebuilding Noble's houseboat studio, where his works were "breech berthed" for 40 years at the dilapidated piers of the old Atlas Yacht Club at Port Johnston, where he spent his life in observation of the old ships' graveyards, watching them slowly decay. He worked sporadically from 1936- 1943 as a watchman and "pumpman accursed" for the abandoned ships. Noble fought to keep Sailor's Snug Harbor for the sailors. Now the Collection and its volunteers are restoring the seamen's heritage with an oral history project —

Haunting, new education programs in printmaking, history, and music for school children include boat trips on the Kill van Kull (Kill in Dutch, means creek). By preserving the community's memories and establishing a maritime study center, we "bring the sailors back to Snug Harbor."

Admission: Entry fee. Open Monday-Friday, 9 A.M. - 2 P.M. and by appointment.

Robert H. Smith

NORTHPORT, L.I., NEW YORK

Northport Historical Museum
215 Main Street
P.O. Box 545
Northport (Long Island), NY 11768
(631) 757-9859 Fax: (631) 757-9398 E-mail: info@northporthistorical.org
Location: On Long Island, Northport is thirty-eight miles east of New York City via I-495 to Rte. 110, north six miles to Rte. 25A. Then east six miles to Woodbine Avenue. Left on Woodbine to Main Street and turn right.
Highlights: Permanent exhibit of Northport history from pre 1656 to the present and five rotating exhibits annually, maritime history and tools, museum shop,
Website: www.northporthistorical.org
   General Information: Housed in the 1914 Carnegie Library, the Northport Historical Museum presents permanent and changing exhibits on history of 300-year-old village, shipbuilding tools, photographs, cultural, historical, and geographical features of Northport, Northport Harbor, Eaton's Neck, East Northport, and Fort Salonga, Long Island.
   Admission: No entry fee, but donations accepted. Open Tuesday-Sunday, 1 P.M.-4:30 P.M., year-round.

NEW YORK, NEW YORK

Ocean Liner Museum
P.O. Box 1479
New York, New York 10021
(212) 717-6251 E-mail: OLMinNYC@aol.com
Location: There is no permanent museum facility. The Museum's displays are shown at various locations including on QE2.
Highlights: Ocean liner artifacts and memorabilia,
Website: www.oceanliner.org
   General Information: From the Ocean Liner Museum brochure: "They were the biggest things created by man that moved, capable of carrying thousands across the Atlantic. On board were rooms that recreated the grandeur of a Newport mansion, a Pompeiian pool or the ballroom of a Versailles. Their very names — *Imperator, Rex, Amerika, Normandie, Majestic* — conjure up an image when travel was more than transportation. Liners offered adventure, dreams, or life in a New World. But now, these magnificent ships and the era they represent have gone.
   "The Ocean Liner Museum presently finds, preserves, and, when possible, displays memorabilia, ephemera, and artifacts of artistic, engineering, and historical value connected with these great vessels. The only museum of its kind

in the world, the Ocean Liner Museum is devoted exclusively to the study of passenger ships. Objects of wonder, the liners can still amaze and enchant." The Museum holds lectures, sponsors cruises, organizes an annual ocean liner bazaar, and is involved with other liner-related events. Exhibits are held in different locations.

Admission: Contact by writing, e-mailing, or phoning for information on membership and location of current displays.

OSWEGO, NEW YORK

Oswego Maritime Foundation
McCrobie Building
41 Lake Street
Oswego, NY 13126
(315) 342-5753 (Main office) (315) 342-0882 (Education Center)
E-mail: osmarfnd@Oswego.edu
Location: The Museum is located at the harbor end of West First Street in Oswego (waterfront buildings).
Highlights: Schooner *OMF Ontario*, *Maritimes* (newsletter), boating education, Goble Dry Dock, library, **Website:** www.oswegomaritime.org

General Information: While the cargo of the original lake schooner may have been grain, coal, lumber, or travelers to a new land, the new schooner's cargo will be people of all ages eager to understand something of their maritime heritage, lake history, lake resources, and aquatic ecology. The "Education Through Involvement Program," made possible by the Oswego Maritime Foundation (OMF), is provided aboard the classic gaff-rigged 85-foot schooner OMF *Ontario* of the type that in the not-too-distant past sailed and served as a means of transportation, shipping, and communications on the Great Lakes. The program is operated as a public service project by OMF.

The OMF sponsors and/or helps facilitate research projects by accredited colleges or universities. Volunteer SCUBA divers locate and identify shipwrecks and other submerged cultural resources at such dive sites as "Mary Kay" and "David W. Mills," in order to document them before they are destroyed or obscured by Zebra mussels, using the information secured for educational materials, presentations to community and school groups, and providing it to historical and tourism agencies.

George Goble who, on May 6, 1856, in his just-completed Ontario Dry Dock, later to be known as the Goble Dry Dock, blasted from solid rock, launched his first ship, the schooner *Titan*. The dry-dock is now a part of the OMF facilities at the end of 1st Street next to the pier. OMF used the watered area for its sailing, boating, sport fishing, and SCUBA diving instructional courses.

Robert H. Smith

Admission: The OMF office, library, classroom facilities are open year-round.

The educational is open May - September and located at harbor end of W First Street immediately east of the U.S. Coast Guard Station. Call for times/locations.

SACKETS HARBOR, NEW YORK

Sackets Harbor Battlefield State Historic Site
505 W. Washington Street
P.O. Box 27
Sackets Harbor, NY 13685
(315) 646-3634 Fax: (315) 646-1203
Location: From Syracuse take I-81 north to exit 45 to SR-3. Follow it west eight miles to Sackets Harbor on Lake Ontario. The site is located at 505 West Washington Street at the west end of the village on Lake Ontario.
Highlights: U.S. Navy shipyard; "A Sailor's Life Aboard the Jefferson"; War of 1812 historical information; Battlefield of May 29, 1813, in which 1200 British, Canadian, and Indian troops from Canada failed in a four-hour battle to destroy this American shipyard on Lake Ontario; 1814 Fort Kentucky; Library (1000 volumes); an original War of 1812 32-pounder carronade cannon mounted on a rock adjacent to Washington Street near the Sacket Mansion; and an original carronade cannon flintlock.
Website: www.sacketsharborny.com/battlefield.html
General Information: Sackets Harbor Battlefield State Historic Site, founded in 1933 as a historical navy yard and battlefield complex, is housed in five buildings: The restored 1849 Commandant's and Master's houses; the 1848 Stable; and the 1850 Ice House; and the 1840 Farmhouse. All of these are located on site of a nineteenth-century naval base, which played an important part in the War of 1812. Nearby Seaway Trails Foundation operates a visitor center in the 1818 Union Hotel. Sackets Harbor Battlefield maintains an exhibit room in this facility featuring part of our archaeological collection, War of 1812 personal weapons, an artillery caisson and uniform accouterments.

Sackets Harbor was settled in 1801 and quickly became a flourishing Lake Ontario community. During the War of 1812 it was the center of U.S. Naval and military activity along the upper St. Lawrence River and into distant Lake Erie. The unfinished first-rate-ship-of-the-line, USS *New Orleans*, designed to carry a crew of 1,000, was enclosed in a huge wooden shiphouse to protect it for future use. In 1883, the Navy decided to scrap the vessel. By doing so, together with the improved Canadian-American relations, the need for a naval base at Sackets Harbor ended. The Navy maintained the facility until the 1960s, and was seldom used except by the State's naval militia.

Collections include restored 13-room 1850-61 Navy commandant's house complete with nineteenth century household furniture and accessories. In the 1948 Stable building, naval exhibits focus on the War of 1812 and its weapons, armament and accessories, including an original flintlock used to fire a carronade cannon, and military clothing. and outbuildings.

Activities: Guided and self-guided tours during the summer season, military encampments, picnic area, lectures, special summer programs, parking, and handicapped parking.

Admission: No charge for grounds admittance. Entry fee for Commandant's house. Open Memorial Day to Labor Day, Wednesday-Saturday, 10 A.M.-5 P.M.; Sundays, 1 P.M.- 5 P.M.; Grounds open year-round.

SAG HARBOR, NEW YORK

Sag Harbor Whaling Museum
200 Main Street
P. O. Box 1327
Sag Harbor, NY 11963
(631) 725-0770

Location: On Long Island, take the Long Island Expressway East to Exit 70, Manorville. Follow Manorville Road to the end, picking up Rte. 27 East. Follow Rte. 27 fifteen miles to Bridgehampton. At the end of the business district, turn left at the traffic light onto the Bridgehampton/Sag Harbor Turnpike. The Museum is located on this road just before the business district, on the left, across the street from the John Jermain Library.

Highlights: Whaleboat, whale tryworks, tools, and artifacts, ship models, scrimshaw, nautical gift shop, **Website:** www.sagharborwhalingmuseum.org/

General Information: Sag Harbor Whaling Museum, founded in 1936, is housed in the 1845 Benjamin Huntting home, an owner of whale ships. As you approach the building, you will know it by its beautiful Corinthian columns. A whaleboat is outside at the left of the Museum. At the right in front of the Museum are tryworks — three large kettles used on board whale boats for boiling the blubber to render whale oil.

As you enter the Museum you will pass through the genuine jaw-bones of a right whale. These were brought back to Sag Harbor by a whaler and have been on display for almost one hundred years. Exhibits feature whaling equipment, scrimshaw, oil paintings, ship models, fishing equipment, logbooks, and other Colonial pieces connected with eastern Long Island.

Admission: Entry fee. Open Monday-Saturday, 10 A.M.-5 P.M., Sundays 1 P.M.-5 P.M., May 17th -October. Open October weekends only. Tours by appointment.

Robert H. Smith

SAUGERTIES, NEW YORK

Saugerties Lighthouse Museum
P.O. BOX 564
Saugerties, NY 12477
(914) 247-0656 E-mail: info@saugertieslighthouse.com
Location: The lighthouse is only 100 miles north of the George Washington bridge and 42 miles south of Albany NY. Leave the Thruway (I-87) at exit 20 turn right at the traffic light onto route 212 and follow it into the center of the village of Saugerties where you will intersect with Route 9W. Proceed straight on route 9W North for four blocks. You will arrive at a T where 9W turns left. Turn right onto Mynderse Street. A sign for the lighthouse is there too. Follow this road and bear left at the stop sign. Proceed down the hill and out to the lighthouse parking lot which is just beyond the Coast Guard Station.
Highlights: Lighthouse, Bed & Breakfast all year, store,
Website: www.saugertieslighthouse.com/

General Information: The present Saugerties Lighthouse was built in 1869 and sits on a massive circular stone base sixty feet in diameter with a sixth-order Fresnel lens that used kerosene lamps for illumination.

Nearby, the first lighthouse at the mouth of the Esopus Creek at Saugerties was built in 1838 with funds appropriated from Congress. It was constructed to guide ships away from nearby shallows and into the Esopus Creek when Saugerties was a major port with daily commercial and passenger transportation. The first light was lit with 5 whale oil lamps with parabolic reflectors.

Automation of the light in 1954 made lightkeepers obsolete. The building was closed up and fell into disrepair and decay. Efforts of a local historian and architect succeeded in placing the lighthouse on the National Register in 1978 stimulating local citizens to restore the building. In 1986 the newly formed Saugerties Lighthouse Conservancy acquired the lighthouse and the adjacent wetlands and after extensive fundraising and restoration work the building was completely reconstructed. After 36 years the light was restored to operation in the light tower on August 4, 1990.

Admission: Entry fee: Open weekends and holidays, Memorial Day through Columbus Day, 2 P.M. to 5 P.M. and by appointment or chance. It contains a small museum, keepers quarters, two bedrooms, kitchen and living room. The lighthouse operates as a Bed & Breakfast all year — weekdays most available.

CAMILLUS, NEW YORK

Sims' Store Museum
c/o Town of Camillus
109 East Way
Camillus, NY 13031
(315) 672-5110 or 488-3409
Location: Camillus-Erie Canal Seven Mile Park (300 acres).
Highlights: Canal, Gere Lock #50, original lock gates, historical canal boat tours, "Clinton's Ditch," Nine Mile Creek Aqueduct, Lock Shanty, Sims' Store Museum, replica of an 1856 canal store
General Information: The Sims' Store Museum contains exhibits, early photos and models reflecting canal life and history, rooms depict boat building, digging the canal, structures on the canal, and an 1800's Room. The park includes seven miles of navigable canal and thirteen miles of hiking and biking trails. Within the park, consisting of 300 acres, you can visit the 1844 Nine Mile Creek Aqueduct.
Admission: No entry fee for Museum. Open Saturdays, 9 A.M.-1 P.M., Sundays, 1 P.M.-5 P.M., year-round. Admission fee for boat rides Sundays, May-October.

WHITEHALL, NEW YORK

Skenesborough Museum
Box 238
Whitehall, NY 12887
(518) 499-1155/0716
Location: Take I-87 north from Albany fifty-four miles to Glen Falls. Exit east to SR-149 13-miles to Fort Ann and then 11-miles on Rte. 4, northeast to Whitehall. In Whitehall follow Rte. 4 just over the railroad bridge turning at the first left street to the Museum on right just past park buildings along the Champlain Canal.
Highlights: Dioramas of 1776 shipyard, nineteenth-century canal lock system (Champlain Canal), ship models, gift shop,
Website: www.cyhaus.com/usroute4/whitehall/museum.htm
General Information: Nestled in a wooded valley at the head of Lake Champlain, Whitehall's Skenesborough Museum, founded in 1959, is located in a building constructed by the New York State Canal System in 1917. In 1759, British Captain Philip Skene settled here, building saw and grist mills and an iron foundry and raised horses for the West Indies trade. In the first months of the American Revolution in 1775, Britisher Skene's trading schooner *Katherine* was captured from the Skene estate on a Green Mountain Boys' foray. Benedict

Arnold, using this vessel, led a small band of volunteers down the lake to raid the British Fort in St. Johns, Quebec.

Two days later Benedict Arnold's men sailed it to Crown Point, where he armed it for a definite act of war capturing a British naval ship and renamed it *Enterprise*. In the summer of 1776, the Americans learned that the British were building ships to take back the lake.

George Washington sent Benedict Arnold and Philip Schuyler to Sekenesborough to direct shipwrights who raced to build the American fleet, the first naval boats for the newly developing country, that fought in the decisive Battle of Valcour Island in Lake Champlain just south of present-day Plattsburgh. Of Arnold's gunboats built over two hundred years ago, the *Philadelphia*, now in the Smithsonian, and the *Providence* found in 1997, still under water there, are the only remaining evidence of the ships built at Whitehall.

Skenesborough Museum sits beside the Champlain Canal, completed in 1819, which is still in use today. In the Museum, are displays that explain the Whitehall's place in history in relation to navy, lake, canal, and railroad. The visitor finds photographs, artifacts, and models of the ships of the American Revolution and War of 1812 and the Lake-boat period of 1811-1873. Outside, under cover, is found the hulk of the *Ticonderoga* that fought in the Battle of Plattsburg.

Boaters may tie up along the newly rebuilt canal wall while visiting the Museum. Nearby is Lock 12 of the Champlain Canal System.

Admission: No entry fee, but donations accepted. Open mid-June to Labor Day, Monday-Saturday, 10 A.M.-4 P.M.; Labor Day to mid-October, Saturday, 10 A.M. -3 P.M.; Sunday, noon-3 P.M. Other times by appointment.

SODUS POINT, NEW YORK

Sodus Bay Lighthouse Museum
Sodus Bay Historical Society
P.O. Box 94
Sodus Point, NY 14555
(315) 483-4936 E-mail: sodusbay@ix.netcom.com
Location: East from Rochester, New York, thirty miles to Rte. 88. North two miles to Rte. 14, then east four miles to Sodus Point.
Highlights: Lighthouse, Great Lakes history,
Website: http://peachey.com/soduslight

General Information: Sodus Bay Lighthouse Museum, relates to cultural history and the seafaring activity carried on in the Sodus Bay region. Over the years the Bay has been known for its lumber trade, commercial fishing, grain exports, ice industry, shipbuilding, and summertime recreation.

From the time of the first settlers in the late 1700s, Sodus Bay was considered an ideal harbor for exporting farm products and other commodities.

Commercial captains from Sodus Bay were engaged in transporting cargoes aboard schooners and steamers to ports on Lake Ontario.

In 1824 Congress appropriated $4,500 to construct a lighthouse tower and keeper's residence at Sodus Bay. By 1869 both structures had deteriorated to the extent that Congress appropriated $14,000 to build a second lighthouse to replace the original buildings. The new station was completed in 1871 and was in use until its closing in 1901.

Today, the lighthouse situated on the west side of Sodus Bay is a sought-out recreation area next to Lake Ontario providing summer-time boating and sailing pleasure. The Museum's docents are well versed in local maritime and lighthouse history and will make your visit worthwhile.

Admission: No entry fee but donations appreciated. Open Tuesday-Sunday, 10 A.M. to 5 P.M., May 1 through October 31. In May and October, close at 4 P.M. Open on legal holidays if on Mondays. Other times by appointment.

NEW YORK, NEW YORK

South Street Seaport Museum
207 Front Street
New York, NY 10038
(212) 748-8600 E-mail: sssmmr@rcn.com
Location: The Museum is situated on the lower east side of Manhattan on the East River in an area bounded by South, Front, Pearl, Dover Streets.
Highlights: Boardable historic vessels, The *Titanic* Memorial, special tours of historic district, maritime library, **Website:** www.SouthStSeaport.org/

General Information: South Street Seaport Museum, founded in 1967, is an twelve-block historic area created as a landfill starting in the late eighteenth century and was the city's bustling seaport in the nineteenth century. The brick and granite buildings that line the Belgian block streets were built as shops, warehouses, and counting houses in the early 1800s with a hastiness attested to today by the crooked angles of the windowsills as the landfill continues to settle.

Although many of the buildings are still being restored, the renovation of those along Fulton Street (its name is taken from Robert Fulton, who once docked his famous steamboat here) is complete. The first building of the Fulton Market was constructed by the city in 1869; today's building at the water's edge has been in use since 1907. The adjacent Fulton Market is the third market building to stand on its site since 1822.

Across Fulton Street from market is Schermerhorn Row, a row of early-nineteenth-century buildings housing more shops and restaurants. The upper floors, which normally house museum galleries, are currently closed for construction as the museum prepares the interior spaces for the installation of a 30,000-square-foot permanent exhibit on the Port of New York. The exhibit is expected to open in 2003. In the meantime, the museum maintains three galleries of changing exhibits at 209 and 213 Water Street.

Information on the seaport area is available at the Visitor's Center at 209 Water Street during renovation of Schermerhorn Row) and the Pier 16 Ticket Booth. Abundant parking is available in the Historic District.

Museum ships are docked at the foot of Fulton Street at Piers 15 and 16. Vessels that may be boarded include the *Peking*, a 347-foot four-masted bark built in 1911; the *Wavertree*, 293-foot full-rigged ship built in 1885; schooner *Pioneer* built in 1885; original *Ambrose* lightship; and others.

Activities: Maritime skills activities for on ships and piers during summer months, ship restorations and gallery exhibitions, craft demonstrations, guided tours, lectures, films, summer concerts and sailing on the schooner *Pioneer* and 1930 tug *W.O. Decker*, and excursions on Circle Line vessels.

Admission: Entry fee. Memberships are available. Museum ships are open: April-September daily, 10 A.M.-6 P.M.; October-March, daily, 10 A.M.-5 P.M. Closed Tuesdays.

SOUTHAMPTON, NEW YORK

Southampton Historical Museum
Captain Rogers' Homestead
17 Meeting House Lane
Southampton, NY 11969
(631) 283-2494 Fax:(631) 283-4540 E-mail: hismusdir@hamptons.com
Location: The Museum is located at 17 Meeting House Lane, just off Main street.
Highlights: Southampton Town whaling, library, information in a historic 1843 whaling captain" Greek Revival home.
General Information: The Historical Museum was set up in 1951 in 1843 the house built by Captain Albert Rogers, a whaling captain, The home was owned by Rogers' ancestors from 1648. The home has period rooms, changing exhibition galleries, and a research library with log books and material relating to local whaling culture.

On the grounds are a number of historic structures that have been moved here to preserve them. There is an 1880s carriage barn that displays a large collection of whaling tools, a whaling boat and other memorabilia, a one-room school house, a blacksmith shop, and several other late 19th century buildings that help create the look of a coastal town.

Admission: Entry fee. Open Tuesday-Saturday, 11 A.M.- 5 P.M., Sunday, 1 P.M.-5 P.M.; May-December; winter: Tuesday-Saturday, 11 A.M.- 5 P.M., January-April.

RIVERHEAD, NEW YORK

Suffolk Historical Museum
300 W. Main Street
Riverhead, NY 11901
(631) 727-2881 Fax: (631) 727-3467
E-mail: histsoc@suffolk.lib.ny.us
Location: East end of Long Island off Sunrise Highway: Exit 61 via Riverhead-Moriches Road. (Rte. 51) or: Exit 72 onto Rte. 25. Then 3- miles east on Long Island Expressway. The Museum is on West Main Street. *Highlights:* Ship models, The Weathervane Gift Shop, library (history and genealogical)

General Information: The Suffolk Historical Museum, founded in 1886 to collect, preserve, and interpret the ongoing history of Suffolk County. The County story is told in terms of the people themselves through craft and trade tools, ceramics, agriculture, and whaling. Here are the things they made and used and collected from the time of the first settlements of 1640 including exhibits on Eastern Long Island Native Americans. Tools, textiles, flags, firearms, and pictures are part of the exhibits.

Activities: Educational services and activities.

Admission: No entry Fee but donations accepted. Open Tuesday- Saturday, 12:30 P.M.-4:30 P.M.; Library, Thursday-Saturday, 12:30 P.M.- 4:30 P.M. Closed Sundays and holidays. Library use requires a small donation.

WATERFORD, NEW YORK

Tugboat *Urger*
New York State Canal Corporation
Waterford, NY 12188
(518) 233-8488 Fax: (518) 237-4452
Highlights: Tugboat *Urger*

General Information: The *Urger*, flagship of New York's Canal System. She was launched in Michigan in 1901 working in the Great Lakes before she began working for the State of New York in 1922.

The tug leaves wistful smiles on the faces of people wherever she goes and the year 2001 marks the *Urger's* centennial. Share the *Urger* experience and let your imagination wander back to the far away rollers of Lake Michigan and to the glorious heyday of tugboats and barges on the New York State Canal System. She makes appearances at various festivities. Contact the New York State Canal Corporation for further information.

Robert H. Smith

ALBANY, NEW YORK

USS *Slater* Museum Ship
P.O. Box 1926
Albany, NY 12201-1926
(518) 431-1943 Fax: (518) 423-1123 E-mail: shipsde766@aol.com
Location: The *Slater* is exhibited on the Hudson River in downtown Albany at the Slater Wharf, formerly Snow Dock.
Highlights: USS *Slater* (DE-766), gift shop, overnight camping for youths, *Slater Signals* Newsletter, **Website:** www.ussslater.org
   General Information: The USS *Slater* Museum Ship represents the 565 Destroyer Escorts built during World War II. Only five survive. In 1951, the *Slater* was transferred to the Hellenic Navy where she served with distinction for more than 40 years. Ultimately, the Destroyer Escort Historical Foundation received the *Slater* as a donation and she joined the *Intrepid* Sea: Air: Space Museum in New York City in 1994 on a temporary basis. The *Slater* has now been moved up the Hudson River to Albany, where she has been restored to her WW II configuration by volunteers.
   Admission: Entry fee. Open daily, 9 A.M.-4:30 P.M. April through October.

CENTERPORT, NEW YORK

Vanderbilt Mansion, Marine Museum, Planetarium
180 Little Neck Road
P.O. Box 0605
Centerport, NY 11721-0605
(631) 854-5550
Location: Centerport, on the north side of Long Island, is 38 miles east of New York City via I-495 to Rte. 110 north six miles to Rte. 25A, then east six miles to Centerport overlooking Northport Harbor.
Highlights: Ship models, gift shop, forty-three-acre grounds with gardens and museum, 24-room mansion and a state-of-the-art planetarium.
   General Information: Marine museum with 2,000 marine specimens located in the Hall of Fishes. The mansion contains a collection of fine and decorative arts as well as a natural history and ethnographic collection.
   Admission: Entry fee. Open every Tuesday-Sunday, closed Mondays except for holidays. Hours change with seasons, call the above number for information.

BROOKLYN, NEW YORK

Waterfront Museum and Showboat Barge
290 Conover Street, Pier 45
Brooklyn, NY 11231
(718) 624-4719 E-mail: dsharps@waterfrontmuseum.org
Location: The Museum barge is located at the Red Hook Garden Pier #45 at the foot of Conover Street in the Red Hook section of Brooklyn.
Highlights: Lehigh Valley Railroad Barge 79 (home of Museum), Garden Pier, views of working New York Harbor, cultural arts programming, near-by Trolley Museum, **Website:** www.waterfrontmuseum.org

General Information: Established in 1989, the 1914 Lehigh Valley Railroad Barge #79, listed in the National Register of Historic Places as the only surviving wooden example of the Lighterage Age (1860-1960) afloat today and ready to receive visitors. Aboard the 79 is the Museum's permanent collection of "Railroad Navy" photos, a riptide dinghy, a Peterboro sailing canoe, hawsers, tools, tugboat fenders, and much more.

Hand-crafted wooden vessels of American origin were once nestled along the shores of the Port of New York. Prior to tunnel and bridge construction, cargo had to be transported by water across the Hudson River. To perform this function, various railroad companies maintained large fleets of barges (lighters) and tugs. This "Lighterage System" uses many types of craft including scows, hold barges, sticklighters, car floats, and covered barges — all called lighters.

There were also excursion barges, immigrant barges, produce barges, ice barges, livestock barges, and steel-covered barges. The Museum provides information on this historical past.

Activities: Try your hand with a heaving line, throwing the eye of the line, and making up a Flemish coil. See a continuous video display "Tales of the Waterfront," and attend informational lectures and showboat entertainment. Call for current events schedule, rental, or appointments. Free and low-cost cultural programs, including "Circus Sundays" in June, Sunset Music Service evenings, July-August and more.

Admission: Entry fee. Memberships are encouraged. Call for rental availability for corporate and special events. The Red Hook Pier #45 is open during daylight hours.

NEW JERSEY

ATLANTIC CITY, NEW JERSEY

Absecon Lighthouse
31 South Rhode Island Avenue
Atlantic City, NJ 08470
(609) 449-1360 Fax: (609) 449-1919
Location: Absecon Lighthouse is located in the Inlet Section of Atlantic City.
Highlights: Lighthouse,
General Information: She's had 144 birthdays. She's seen a Civil War and two World Wars. She's weathered hundreds of storms. And she's never looked better. On January 15, 1857, the First-Order Fresnel lens in Absecon Lighthouse shone over the infamous "Graveyard Inlet" in Atlantic City for the first time. By 1912, word of the stately beacon had spread, and she became the most visited lighthouse in the United States. At 171 feet high, with 228 steps, she remains the third tallest lighthouse in the country, and the tallest in New Jersey. Absecon Lighthouse has now been painstakingly restored to her original glory, complete with the First-Order Fresnel lens that first shone over 140 years ago. Come and visit Atlantic City's historic Absecon Lighthouse. After you visit, the phrase "respect your elders" will take on a whole new meaning. (Note: The newly reconstructed Keeper's House is expected to open late summer 2001.)
Admission: Museum: no charge. Lighthouse: entry fee. Operating Hours: July & August: Open Daily, 11 A.M.-4 P.M. Twilight Tours offered Saturday evenings from 7 P.M.-9 P.M., July 1-Labor Day. September-December and March-June: Open Thursday-Monday, 11 A.M.- 4 P.M.. Winter hours in effect for January and February. Please call for details.

SOMERS POINT, NEW JERSEY

Atlantic County Historical Society Museum
907 Shore Road
P. O. Box 301
Somers Point, NJ 08244
(609) 927-5218
Location: Via the Garden State Parkway, take exit 30 South at Somers Point; travel approximately twelve miles south of Atlantic City.
Highlights: Ship models, half models, shipwright tools, ship building history, library
General Information: In the 1700s and 1800s, sailing craft were used to transport cargo all over the world. They also functioned as workboats in bay and coastal waters. Many large and small shipyards existed on the Great Egg Harbor

and Tuckahoe River and its tributaries from Mays Landing down to Somers Point, which was then an official port of entry. The Museum displays a wide variety of ship models and shipbuilding tools. Especially important are the twenty-five boat and ship models carved by Charles Woolbert of Mays Landing, including a bugeye, cutter, barquentine, and many others. A research library contains ships' logs and documents. Next door is the Somers mansion, also open to the public.

Admission: No entry fee. Open Wednesday - Saturday, 10 A.M.-3:30 P.M. Fee for non-member research. Closed holidays.

TUCKERTON, NEW JERSEY

Barnegat Bay Decoy and Baymen's Museum
P.O. Box 52
Tuckerton, NJ 08087-0052
(609) 296-8868 E-mail: baymens@internetMCI.com
Location: Tuckerton is a backwater town about twenty-four miles north of Atlantic City. Take Exit 58 on the Garden State Parkway then south on Rte. 539. Turn right at traffic light.
Highlights: Carved decoys, small-craft display: sneakboxes and garveys, gift shop, photographs (4,000),
General Information: The Barnegat Bay Decoy and Baymen's Museum opened its doors July 17, 1993 "...where one 80-year old decoy was a folk art masterpiece, but (where) a wall full of (decoys) was a monument." Loaned or owned, the Museum has access to a large number of decoys and artifacts which will be housed and be the subject of changing displays. The decoys, intricately carved and impeccably colored, have become respected and valued works of wood sculpture.

Barnegat Bay is embraced by broad reaches and creeks, marshes, and wetlands where small boats — called sneakboxes and garvey boats—and grizzled baymen and market gunners of yesteryear once prowled in pursuit of their feathered, scaled, and skinned prey.

The Museum houses hundreds of exhibits and photographs detailing the lives of the nineteenth- and twentieth-century baymen and water fowl hunters. Once dubbed "Clam Town U.S.A.," Tuckerton was a major supplier in the oyster and clamming industries. "Around the turn of the century, a box car left here every day with 60,000 clams."

The Museum's plans to re-create Tuckerton Seaport in the upland of Tuckerton Creek has begun. It's all about the rich heritage and traditions of the life of the bayman. The maritime museum is one piece of a maritime-oriented bayside village.

Activities: Each year the Barnegat Bay Decoy & Gunning Show is held in September. And the Seaport is a part of the New Jersey Coastal Heritage Trail Route—Barnegat Region.

Admission: Entry fee. Memberships are available. Open Wednesday-Sunday, 10 A.M.-4:30 P.M. year-round.

BARNEGAT LIGHT, NEW JERSEY

Barnegat Lighthouse
Division of Parks and Forestry
State Park Service CN 404
P. O. Box 167
Barnegat Light, NJ 08006
(609) 494-2016

Location: Barnegat Light lies twenty-five miles north of Atlantic City on the northern tip of Long Beach Island in Ocean County. It can be reached from Garden State Parkway by exiting onto Rte. 72 (exit 63) to North Long Beach Island Boulevard. Then travel north some 10 miles to north end of Long Island to lighthouse.

Highlights: Barnegat Lighthouse

General Information: This "Grand Old Champion of the Tides" is a great piece of American sculpture, with the power to move minds and seize hearts. The lighthouse was built in Barnegat Inlet, Barnegat City, in 1834. It cost $6,000, which was appropriated by Congress on June 30, 1834, for that purpose. The tower, fifty feet high, was built of brick and whitewashed from top to bottom. The light, which was the fourth placed on the coast of New Jersey, was white and "fixed" and did not flash. All of the exposed metal parts were painted a dead black, and whale oil was used for the illuminate.

The original structure fell into the water in the early part of 1856. At that time a temporary wooden tower was hastily constructed farther inland and lighted with lamps salvaged from the wreck of the old one. General George G. Meade had Barnegat reconstructed in 1857-58.

The red and white marvel rises 165 feet above the tides — with 217 steps — that mark Barnegat Shoals, the scene of more than 200 shipwrecks. An excellent view is available from the base. The great Fresnel lens was dismantled and stored in the Tomkinsville Lighthouse Depot on Staten Island for possible reuse and future service.

Although it was decommissioned in 1927, the Coast Guard used the lighthouse as a lookout tower during WW II. With the conclusion of the war, the lighthouse and its property were turned over to the state of New Jersey and opened as a park in 1958. When the town of Barnegat Light established a museum of local history in 1954, the lens was returned and is now on display.

The lighthouse contains informational exhibits that can be read along the climb to the top.

Activities: Visitors are invited to enjoy the lighthouse and the coastal panorama view from the lightkeeper's catwalk.

Admission: Entry fee. Open daily, May through October, 9 A.M.-4:30 P.M., and selected evenings during the summer. Also open weekends November through April, 10 A.M. - 3:30 P.M.

CAMDEN, NEW JERSEY

Battleship *New Jersey* Historical Museum Society
Box BB-62
Camden, NJ 07748
(732) 592-1223 E-mail: battleshipnj@quuxuum.org
Location: Proposed site is to be Camden, New Jersey across the river from Philadelphia.
Highlights: Battleship *New Jersey,* **Website:** www.quuxuum.org/bnj/

General Information: USS Battleship *New Jersey* (BB-62) is one of the four battleships of the 45,000-ton Iowa class, the latest, largest, fastest, and most powerful ever built in the U.S. The "Big J" has an unmatched record of service to her country and was, at the conclusion of the Vietnam conflict, the only battleship ever to have served in three wars. The Battleship *Texas* served in both WW I and WW II.

Patriotic New Jersey citizens, ex-Navy people everywhere, battleship fans, naval history followers, and many others want to see this ship preserved. Progress is being made. The USS *New Jersey* Battleship Commission has been formed to carry out the state's functions in the acquisition of the ship and have chosen Camden, New Jersey as the permanent site. Here the ship would be displayed in the populous Philadelphia, Pennsylvania and Camden, New Jersey metropolitan area.

Admission: Contact by phone for update information.

EDGEWATER, NEW JERSEY

Binghamton **(ferry)**
725 River Road
Edgewater, NJ 07020
(201) 941-2300.
Location: Located on the Hudson River three miles south of the George Washington Bridge.
Highlights: Modified but authentic Hoboken-Manhattan ferry

Robert H. Smith

General Information: The 231-foot-long *Binghamton* carried 125 million passengers over a 62-year career and traveled over 200,000 miles on this short route. Beginning service in March 1905, she accommodated twenty-four automobiles and 986 passengers. Now, she serves as a restaurant with tables set even in the space occupied by the intact double-compound marine steam engines.

MORRISTOWN, NEW JERSEY

Canal Society of New Jersey Museum at Waterloo Village
P. O. Box 737
Morristown, NJ 07963-0737
(908) 722-9556 (Phone/Fax) E-mail: info@waterloovillage.org
Location: The Village is located near the junction of Rtes. 80 and 206. Follow signs to Waterloo Village.
Highlights: Morris Canal, Delaware and Raritan Canal, Waterloo Village, **Website:** www.canalsocietynj.org
General Information: Waterloo Village was a nineteenth-century port on the Morris Canal. The Canal Museum was founded in 1975. It exhibits artifacts, documents, photographs, and memorabilia on New Jersey's two towpath canals. Canal works include: a watered section of the canal; the remains of a combined lock and aqueduct; the site of an inclined plane — a unique inclined plane where canal boats were carried up hills in cradles running on tracks; a canal store; a blacksmith shop; and two mule bridges. There is a thirteen-minute video presentation and two half-hour videos: Morris Canal and Delaware & Raritan Canal.
Admission: Entry fee for Waterloo Village. Call Waterloo Village at (973) 347-0900 for schedule.

CAPE MAY, NEW JERSEY

Cape May County Historical and Genealogical Society Museum in the John Holmes House and Barn
504 Route 9 - North
Cape May Court House,
Cape May, NJ 08210-3070
(609) 465-3535 E-mail: museum@co-cape-may.nj.us
Location: Cape May County Court House is the southern terminus of the Garden State Parkway and forty-two miles south of Atlantic City. The Museum, on U.S. Rte. 9 (Shore Road) between Rte. 675 on south and Rte. 609 on the north.
Highlights: Lighthouse lens, John Holmes House, gift shop, library, **Website:** www.cmcmuseum.org

General Information: The Cape May County Historical & Genealogical Society, housed in the vintage 1800's barn, displays a hand-carved duck decoy collection and the original Fresnel lens from the 1859 Cape May Point Lighthouse. The barn also has a maritime and whaling exhibit and a natural history display. In addition, tools and gadgets for the home, farm and business are exhibited including examples of carriages include a stage coach, a peddler's wagon and a handsomely restored doctor's sulky.

Admission: Entry fee. Open mid April through October 31st, Tuesday through Saturday; Open November 1st through mid April, Saturdays only 9 A.M.- 4 P.M. with the last admission at 3 P.M.; Seasonal (call ahead). Closed on Holidays. Group tours and special tours can be arranged by calling our Museum office. The library is open year round 10 A.M. to 4 P.M., on Wednesday, Thursday and Friday. Saturdays by appointment only. $5/day charge to use the library. Members free. Please call ahead and make arrangements with the Librarian. For research, library staff are willing to perform their own search work. Non-Society members are charged $1.00 per hour while members may use the library free-of-charge.

HIGHLANDS, NEW JERSEY

Fort Hancock Museum
P. O. Box 530
Highlands, NJ 07732-0530
(732) 872-5970 Museum direct: (732) 872-5992 Fax: (732) 872-2256
Location: To reach the Highlands take the Garden State Parkway to Keyport. Exit onto SR-36, heading east thirteen miles to Highlands. The Museum is located in Gateway National Recreation Area, one block west of the Sandy Hook Lighthouse on a long spit of sand extending north from the New Jersey shore. The Museum is 100-yards west of the Sandy Hook Lighthouse at Fort Hancock.
Highlights: Museum contains exhibits about Fort Hancock, Sandy Hook Proving Ground, and Sandy Hook Lighthouse, a gift shop, restroom, and park information, **Website:** www.fieldtrip.com/nj/88720115.htm
General Information: The Museum was founded in 1968 when Fort Hancock was still an active military installation. The Museum building was original the Fort Hancock Guardhouse, which was built in 1899. In the future, the Museum will be relocated to the Fort's former barracks. Since 1975 it has been operated by the National Park Service.

The Sandy Hook Lighthouse is the oldest operating lighthouse in America (1764). Even though the Museum contains a limited number of maritime exhibits, the Gateway National Recreation Area is worth visiting because of the additional museums, including the Museum at Navesink Lighthouses.

Robert H. Smith

Admission: No entry fee. Open weekends throughout the year 1 P.M.-5 P.M., and everyday during July and August 1 P.M.-5 P.M. From Memorial Day Weekend through Labor Day Sandy Hook charges a parking fee to park in the park's oceanside parking lots. Parking free in Fort Hancock. Tell fee collectors at park entrance that you are headed for Fort Hancock.

NORTH WILDWOOD, NEW JERSEY

Hereford Inlet Lighthouse
111 North Central Avenues
North Wildwood, NJ 08260
(609) 522-4520
Location: North Wildwood is four-miles east of Exit 6 of the Garden State Parkway.
Highlights: Fourth-order Fresnel lens on display,
Website: http://user.aol.com/houselite/hereford.htm
   General Information: The Hereford Inlet Lighthouse, designed by Paul J. Pelz, architect of the Library of Congress and constructed in 1874 by the U.S. Army Corps of Engineers, is a restored historic Victorian lighthouse which overlooks the wide Hereford Inlet. It leads from the Atlantic Ocean to the famed Intracoastal Waterway linking Maine to Florida.
   The lighthouse was the focus of the development of the Hereford Inlet Life-Saving Station No. 36 serving Great Egg Harbor to the north and south to the mouth of Delaware Bay. 57.5 feet high, the lighthouse was automated and re-activated in the 1980s by the Coast Guard.
   Admission: No entry fee. Open daily, Summer hours are 9 A.M.-5 P.M., Fall and Spring, 10 A.M.-4 P.M. January to March, call for hours.

ATLANTIC CITY, NEW JERSEY

Historic Gardner's Basin
New Hampshire Avenue and the Bay
Atlantic City, NJ 08401
(609) 348-2880 E-mail: jack@oceanlifecenter.com
Location: The basin is situated at the northeast end of Atlantic City on North New Hampshire Avenue.
Highlights: Aquarium/Marine Education Center, Daily sightseeing cruises, Deep Sea Fishing, restaurants and an antique shop,
Website: www. gardner'sbasin.com **or** www.oceanlifecenter.com
   General Information: Historic Gardner's Basin, founded in 1976, is a maritime village within the Atlantic City waterfront homes that pre-date 1900.

The site where Atlantic City was founded was both the center of South Jersey's fishing industry and the hub of rum-running.

The visitor will find maritime artifacts, seafaring memorabilia; working and living exhibits on lobstermen; sculpture, paintings, and working and living exhibits of the clammer (clam digger).

Activities: Eco-tours, salt marsh and beach excursions, ecology cruises and festivals.

Admission: Entry fee but memberships are available. Group rates available. Open daily, year round, 9 A.M.-5 P.M.. Closed Christmas and New Year's Day and Thanksgiving.

GREENWICH, NEW JERSEY

John Dubois Maritime Museum
Ye Greate Street
P. O. Box 16
Greenwich, NJ 08323
(856) 455-4055 E-mail: lummis2@juno.com
Location: Greenwich is five miles off Rte. 49 from Bridgeton in southern New Jersey.
Highlights: Local maritime history,
Website: www.njht.org/profiles/john-dubois-maritime-museum.html

General Information: The John Dubois Maritime Museum is housed in the 1852 Lecture Room, 949 Ye Great Street of the Cumberland County Historical Society. It features displays of tools and equipment related to the days when Cumberland County was noted for the construction of the schooners which transported cargo to ports along the coast of America or were used to harvest oysters from the Delaware Bay.

Owner of the Mauricetown Shipyard for 30 years, John Dubois presented many shipyard items to the Society, including the scaled-down model of the *Samuel H. Sharp* schooner — complete with blueprints for the first ship built in Mauricetown in 1862. There are shipbuilding tools, the rigging mast equipment, fish net buoys, and the sister hooks that also fill the room.

The Warren Lummis Genealogical and Historical Research Library offers researchers books, maps, deeds, cemetery, church and Bible records, genealogy records, and information on South Jersey history.

Admission: No entry fee but donations accepted. Open April-December, Sundays 1:30 P.M.-4:30 P.M.

Robert H. Smith

LINWOOD, NEW JERSEY

Linwood Maritime Museum
Linwood Library
Maple and Davis Avenues
Linwood, NJ 08221
(609) 927-2023

Location: From I-295 (north or south), off on to Atlantic City Expressway forty-five miles to Rte. 50, then four miles south to Linwood where the Museum is located in the lower level of the Library.

Highlights: Boat models (Thomas E. Adams Collection), *Sinda* (bark) history, bay clam/oyster harvesting

General Information: The Museum is dedicated to preserving the artifacts of the shipwrights, watermen, and seamen who were among Linwood's early inhabitants. Exhibits include maritime artifacts such as the last of the wooden garveys: durable boats which served as platforms for baymen to harvest clams and oysters. The Museum provides a very complete descriptive guide to its exhibits and displays with pen-line drawings of the items for future reference.

Admission: No entry fee. Open Thursday evenings 6:30 P.M.- 8 P.M., July.

From floundering Ships, near to shore, crew and others needed a way to get off the ship. A gun fired a line to the ship, attached it and then the Francis life-saving car was pulled to it. Survivors, up to 7, praised its use. (Photo R. H. Smith)

Smith's Guide to Maritime Museums of North America

   This "Grand Old Champion of the Tides" is a great piece of American sculpture, was built in Barnegat Inlet, Barnegat City, in 1834. The tower, fifty feet high, was built of brick.   (Photo R. H. Smith)

Robert H. Smith

When visiting the Independence Seaport Museum in Philadelphia, right next door is Penn's Landing where you can climb aboard Admiral Dewey's Spanish-American War flagship, *Olympia* and Submarine *Becuna*.   (Photo R. H. Smith)

HACKENSACK, NEW JERSEY

New Jersey Naval Museum/Submarine USS *Ling*
78 River Street
Hackensack, NJ 07601
(201) 342-3268 E-mail: njnavalmus@aol.com
Location: The USS *Ling* is docked at the corner of River and Court Streets in Hackensack, five miles west of the George Washington Bridge (I-80) at Borg Park.
Highlights: USS *Ling* (SS-297) (submarine), WWII Japanese *Kaiten* Submarine, WWII Nazi Seahund Submarine, Bietnam Era PBR, gift shop, overnight encampments, **Website:** www.njnm.com
   General Information: The New Jersey Naval Museum/Submarine USS *Ling* Memorial Association was founded in 1973 as a memorial to those who served aboard submarines during World War II. The Memorial also includes displays of Polaris, Terrier, and Talos missiles; and three smallcraft: a Japanese Kaiten, a German Seehund, and a PBR Mark II.
   The *Ling* was built at Cramp Shipbuilding Company in Philadelphia and outfitted in the Boston Navy Yard. She was commissioned June 8, 1945. When

the *Ling* was struck from the Navy Register in December 1971, she was donated to the Submarine Memorial Association. On January 13, 1973, the Submarine Memorial Association brought the *Ling* to Borg Park in Hackensack.

Activities: Overnight encampments Friday and Saturday nights, Guided tours of the submarine seven days a week

Admission: Entry fee. Open Wednesday-Sunday, 10 A.M.-4 P.M.

OCEAN CITY, NEW JERSEY

Ocean City Historical Museum
1735 Simpson Avenue
Ocean City, NJ 08226
(609) 399-1801 E-mail: ocnjhistomuseum@aol.com
Highlights: *Sindia* shipwreck, gift shop, archives,
Website: www.ocnjmuseum.org/

General Information: An exhibit is located in the city museum on the wreck of the four-masted bark *Sindia,* which ran aground in 1901 just off Ocean City's beaches.

Admission: Call for hours open.

PATERSON, NEW JERSEY

Paterson Museum
2 Market Street
Paterson, NJ 07501
(973) 881-3874 Fax: (973) 881-3435 E-mail: patersonmuseum@hotmail.com
Location: Paterson is sixteen miles west of New York City off I-80. I-80 West to exit for Main St. in Paterson. Turn left onto Main St., then left onto Grand St. Go approx. 4 blocks and turn right onto Spruce St. 2 blocks to Market St., and Museum on corner in the Rogers Locomotive Building. **Highlights:** Submarines *Holland,* Boat I, and *Fenian Ram* (submersible),
Website: www.fieldtrip.com/nj/18813874.htm

General Information: The Paterson Museum presents, in real and graphic form, a record of the City's accomplishments. The Museum was founded in 1925 as a branch of the Paterson Public Library, an adjunct to the Charles Danforth Memorial Library. Displayed are unusual items and artifacts that had been collected by Pattersonians.

Soon the many exhibits and specimens were relocated to the carriage house of former Mayor, Nathan Barnert. That building, located adjacent to the Library, remained home to the Museum for 55 years.

In 1982, Mayor Frank X. Graves, Jr., directed that the Museum be removed to the newly restored, Rogers Locomotive-Erecting Shop at number 2 Market street. This structure, built in 1872 and enlarged in 1878, is owned by Paterson and is located only 1,000-feet away from the focal point of early development, the Great Falls of the Passaic River in Totowa.

John Philip Holland, and Irish mathematician who came to this country in 1873, developed basic designs for submarine boats in the 1870s. The *Holland I*, a test vessel, was operated in the Passaic River above Great Falls. The *Holland II*, a true submersible boat, was built in New York City and operated in New York harbor. That ship, thirty-one-feet long and weighing 19 tons, contained all elements that form a modern submersible boat.

The *Holland II*, launched in 1881, has a torpedo tube that could discharge a six-foot long, Whitehead torpedo. The submarine was powered by a Brayton gasoline engine on the surface and operated by a crew of three men. Underwater, the engine was shut down.

John Holland designed and built six, small, submersible boats between 1866 and 1898. The last unit was purchased by the Navy in 1900 and was renamed the USS *Holland*. The *Fenian Ram* (1881), displayed at Museum, is the first "true" submarine built anywhere. Seldom does the "first:" model of any invention survive for any appreciable time. The *Fenian Ram* is an exception to that rule. It has been "moored" in Paterson since 1927. It's little sister, *Holland I* has been in The Paterson Museum since 1926.

Admission: Entry fee. Open Tuesday-Friday 10 A.M.-4 P.M.; Saturday-Sunday 12:30 P.M.- 4:30 P.M.

KEYPORT, NEW JERSEY

Steamboat Dock Museum
2 Broad Street
P.O. Box 312
Keyport, NJ 07735
(732) 739-6390

Location: Keyport sits on the Raritan Bay about ten miles southeast of Sayreville. The Museum is located on American Legion Drive in the center of town, just at the foot of Broad Street.

Highlights: Model of the *Keyport* (steamboat), oystering displays and photos, aeromarine displays and photos

General Information: The Steamboat Dock Museum, founded in 1976 and a part of the Keyport Historical Society, contains much of the history of the Kearney family, who settled in the area in 1714. A major shipping industry began in 1830, and the town grew and prospered. The Chingarora oyster, harvested from the Raritan Bay, became world famous. In the mid-1800s, not long after Fulton's first steamboat, Benjamin Terry, a builder and entrepreneur, began his steamboat industry, launching more steamboats from the Keyport shores than competitors in Jersey City and Camden.

Admission: No entry fee. Open Sundays, 1 P.M.-4 P.M., Mondays, 10 A.M.-12 Noon, June through September.

TOMS RIVER, NEW JERSEY

Toms River Seaport Society
78 E. Water Street
P.O. Box 1111
Toms River, NJ 08754
(732) 349-9209 Fax: (732) 349-2498
Location: Take the Garden State Parkway to exit 82 onto Rte. 38 E. Then go to the second traffic light and turn right onto Hooper Avenue. Proceed one mile to the museum, which is at east corner of Hooper and Water Streets.
Highlights: Boat models, maritime artifacts, boat restorations of local watercraft, library,
Website: www.fieldtrip.com/nj/83499209.htm

General Information: The Seaport Society's maritime museum displays many artifacts, maintains a maritime library, historic boats, and boat models. Exhibits include the twelve-foot Barnegat Bay sneakbox *Sheldrake* that the late F. Slade Dale sailed from New Jersey to Florida in the 1920's, an eleven-foot moth (c.1915), a 1902 Parrine sneakbox, a Beardslee row boat, two Diamond sneakboxes, and a Barnegat Bay garvey.

Admission: No entry fee. Donations accepted, Open Tuesday and Saturday, 10 A.M.-2 P.M., year-round.

HIGHLANDS, NEW JERSEY

Twin Lights State Historic Site
Lighthouse Road
Highlands, NJ 07732
(732) 872-1814
Location: To reach Highlands take the Garden State Parkway to Exit 117, Keyport. Exit onto SR-36, heading east twelve miles to Highlands. *Highlights:* The Twin Lights, gift shop,
Website: www.fieldtrip.com/nj/88721814.htm

General Information: Twin Lights has served as a beacon for ships since 1828, having been rebuilt in 1862 during Lincoln's term as president. Today, a state-maintained occulting white light is seen from the north tower. The original lighthouse, which houses the nautical and lifesaving museum, is a brownstone structure with towers at both ends.

Robert H. Smith

From Sandy Hook to Cape May, five major lighthouses marked New Jersey's 144-mile Atlantic coastline. Sandy Hook, Navesink (Twin Lights), Barnegat, Absecon, and Cape May lighthouses all had powerful lenses, the beacons of which could be seen eighteen to twenty miles from the shore. The most powerful beacon was installed at the Navesink Light Station (Twin Lights) in 1898. Marking the westerly side of the entrance to New York Harbor, the twenty-five-million-candlepower beam was the brightest in the country and could be seen twenty-two miles away. This lens is now exhibited in the Electric Power House on the grounds.

Activities: Audio stations assist in recounting the site's history. The public may climb sixty-four steps to an observation deck at the top of the north tower.

Admission: No entry fee, but donations accepted. Open daily, 10 A.M.-5 P.M., Memorial Day-Labor Day. Closed Monday & Tuesday during winter.

PENNSYLVANIA

PHILADELPHIA, PENNSYLVANIA

American Philosophical Society Library
105 Fifth Street
Philadelphia, PA 19106
(215) 440-3400 Fax: (215) 440-3423
Location: Near downtown Philadelphia
Highlights: Ship models, library, **Website:** www.amphilsoc.org

General Information: The American Philosophical Society Library, founded in 1743, offers one of America's richest collections of materials on the development of modern science since 1700, early American history to 1840, and native North American languages and culture. A number of unique ship models and instruments are on display with the Society's 247-year-old collection.

Admission: No entry fee. Open Monday through Friday, 9 A.M. to 5 P.M.

WYOMISSING, PENNSYLVANIA

C. Howard Hiester Canal Center
Berks County Heritage Center
2201 Tulpehocken Road
Wyomissing, PA 19610
(610) 374-8839 Fax: (610) 373-7049
Location: Off Red Bridge Road one mile south of Rte. 183 near Reading, PA.
Highlights: Nineteenth-century Union Canal history and memorabilia,
Website: www.berksparkandrec.org

Smith's Guide to Maritime Museums of North America

General Information: The Berks County Parks and Recreation Department operates the C. Howard Hiester Canal Center which is located at Stop No. 8 Berks County Heritage and Wertz's Covered Bridge. The Center chronicles the life of the canal people and how the Union (canal operated 1827-1884) and Schuylkill Canals fit into the larger network of canals that served the Berks County area and Philadelphia. Displays include the pilot house from the tugboat *Dolphin* and a hands-on program in the houseboat *Mildred*.
Admission: Entry fee. Open Tuesday-Saturday 10 A.M.-4 P.M., Sunday, noon-5 P.M., May-October.

GREENVILLE, PENNSYLVANIA

The Canal Museum
Lock 22-Alan Avenue
Greenville, PA 16125
(724) 588-7540
Location: Greenville is located off I-79, I-80, and Ohio Route 11. Follow signs to center of town and look for Canal Museum signs.
Highlights: The *Rufus A. Reed* (forty-foot replica canal barge)
General Information: The Canal Museum in Greenville provides the history of the Erie Extension Canal during its heyday in the 1840s, complete with a full-size replica of an original canal boat. Canal-day artifacts fill the Museum, where hours can be spent reliving this period of western Pennsylvania lore. Exhibits include dioramas of a canal section, working model of a canal lock, and a learning experience for all — children and adults.
Admission: Entry fee. June-August, Saturday-Sunday 1 P.M.-5 P.M., other times by appointment

PHILADELPHIA, PENNSYLVANIA

Cigna Museum and Art Collection
Two Liberty Place TL07E
1601 Chestnut Street
Philadelphia, PA 19192
(215) 761-4907 Fax: (215) 761-5596 E-mail: melissa.hough@cigna.com
Location: The Museum is located at 1601 Chestnut Street in downtown Philadelphia.
Highlights: Ship models, marine paintings (American and British)
General Information: Founded in 1925, Cigna Museum exhibits a collection of eighteenth- and nineteenth-century marine and fire-fighting objects and eighteenth- and nineteenth-century American fine art. Included are paintings, models, prints, equipment, and manuscripts.

Robert H. Smith

Activities: Permanent and changing exhibits, loan exhibits, and guided tours by appointment.
Admission: No fee. Open Monday-Friday 9 A.M.-5 P.M., by appointment only, year-round. Closed national holidays.

ERIE, PENNSYLVANIA

Erie Maritime Museum, Homeport U.S. Brig *Niagara*
Pennsylvania Historical and Museum Commission
Flagship *Niagara* League
150 East Front Street
Erie, PA 16507
(814) 452-2744 Fax: (814) 455-6760 E-mail: sail@brigniagara.org
Location: Erie is a port city on Lake Erie, north of the Junction of I-90 on I-79 where it ends on Bayfront Parkway, Turn north on Holland Street to west on East Front Street.
Highlights: The U.S. Brig *Niagara* (reconstructed ship), interactive exhibits, USS *Wolverine* Exhibit, Shipwright Museum store, Lecture Concert Series, gift shop, **Website:** www.brigniagara.org

General Information: Commodore Oliver Hazard Perry commanded the U.S. Brig *Niagara* as his relief flagship in the Battle of Lake Erie, a major U.S. naval victory during the War of 1812. Reconstructed by the Pennsylvania Historical and Museum Commission between 1988 and 1990, *Niagara* incorporates a few timbers of the original 1813 brig in her hull, and the fully restored vessel now carries six cast 1812-type carronades identical to the 18 she carried originally to defeat the British in the famous Battle of Lake Erie in 1813 near Put-in-Bay on South Bass Island.

The Museum, which is the home port of the U.S. Brig *Niagara*, is a part of the waterfront redevelopment, which includes exhibits on the Live Fire Exhibit, USS *Wolverine* exhibit, the first Iron Hull vessel built by the United States Navy and more recent local Maritime Heritage.

Activities: The *Niagara* sails to commemorate and interpret a significant part of national maritime history; provide the community with an educational tool and cultural amenity; preserve the knowledge and skills of traditional seamanship; and serve as the Commonwealth's flagship and a focal point of Erie's Bayfront development. Guided tours.

Admission: Entry fee. Open Monday-Saturday, 9 A.M.-5 P.M.; Sunday, noon-5 P.M.; **NOTE:** *Niagara* maintains a sailing schedule; however, the site is open with activities when the ship is sailing. Call (814) 452-2744 to check if ship is in port.

Smith's Guide to Maritime Museums of North America
PHILADELPHIA, PENNSYLVANIA

Independence Seaport Museum
211 S. Columbus Blvd. and Walnut Street
Philadelphia, PA 19106-3199
(215) 925-5439 Fax: (215) 925-6713 E-mail: seaport@indsm.org
Location: The Museum is located on Philadelphia's historic Penn's Landing at Walnut Street and Columbus Boulevard on the Delaware River. It is easily accessed from I-95 north/south.
Highlights: Home Port Philadelphia, Divers of the Deep, small craft gallery, rotating exhibit space, shipmodels, Workshop on the Water, research library, National Historic Landmarks, USS *Olympia* and USS *Becuna*, the Lenthall collection — 342 volumes on naval architecture, nautical gift shop, Newsletters: *The Masthead* and *Olympia Update*, **Website:** http://seaport.philly.com

General Information: Independence Seaport Museum captures the Delaware Valley region's maritime heritage with family-oriented interactive exhibits, historic ship tours, working boat shop, and special exhibitions that lead visitors on exciting journeys of discovery through the history and traditions of our maritime past.

The Museum's more than 14,000 artifacts combine with hands-on exhibits, large-scale models and audiovisuals to present a dynamic environment that is both entertaining and educational. It examines the events, people and technologies that shaped the history of the Delaware River and Bay. Through its permanent exhibits Home Port Philadelphia, Divers of the Deep, and On the Rivers, On the Shores: Small Craft of the Delaware River Valley, the Museum explores aspects of maritime history from the commercial shipping and shipbuilding to navigation, immigration, defense, outdoor recreation, the environment, and underwater exploration.

Experience a general-quarters drill on the actual bridge of the destroyer, USS *Lawrence*, which last saw action in the Persian Gulf Conflict. Tour the WWII submarine *Becuna* and climb aboard Admiral Dewey's Spanish-American War flagship, *Olympia*. Watch first-hand as artisans build wooden crafts traditional to our local waterways in Workshop on the Water.

A premier regional research library comprised of more than 14,000 volumes, 35,000 historical photographs and 12,000 boat/ship plans is also housed in the Museum offering research materials to the public by appointment or via mail requests for a nominal fee.

An extensive gift shop is also available offering nautical pieces, ship models, jewelry, books, videos, clothing, and children's items.

Admission: Entry fee. Open daily, 10 A.M.-5 P.M., Sunday 1 P.M.-5 P.M. year-round. Closed Thanksgiving, Christmas, and New Year's. Discounted River

Robert H. Smith

Pass tickets include the Museum and its two ships, and round-trip to the New Jersey State Aquarium in Camden.

EASTON, PENNSYLVANIA

National Canal Museum and Hugh Moore Park
30 Centre Square
Easton, PA 18042-7743
(610) 559-6613 Fax: (610) 559-6690 E-mail: ncm@canals.org
Location: Easton is located where the Lehigh River meets the Delaware River, fifteen miles east of Allentown via I-78 or US 22. Once in town, follow the brown "Canal Boat" signs to the park or the red and gray "Easton Attractions" signs to the Museum.
Highlights: Hugh Moore Park, Lehigh Canal, mule-drawn canal boat, Locktender's House Museum, picnic tables, playground, gift store, National Canal Museum, archives/library, **Website:** www.canals.org/
General Information: The National Canal Museum is located in the Two Rivers Landing building in Centre Square, Easton. The Museum's exhibits tell the stories of America's towpath canal era and modern inland waterways. The archives/library maintains manuscript collections, photo archives, library, and artifacts of the canal era and its related industries. Hugh Moore Park consists of six miles of the restored Lehigh Canal and structures, including a Locktender's House, three locks, waste weirs, and feeder gate. Hugh Moore Park also has a mule-drawn canal boat ride, Chain Dam, the Glendon and Abbott Street industrial ruins, bike and hiking trails, picnic areas, pavilions, playground, and boat rental..
Activities: Annual Canal Festival, Annual Canal History and Technology Symposium, Railroad Film Night, lectures, boat rides, and rentals.
Admission: Entry fee. Memberships are available. National Canal Museum: Open Tuesday-Saturday, 9:30 A.M.-5 P.M., Sunday, 12 P.M.- 5 P.M., extended hours during summer. Closed
Mondays except Martin Luther King, Jr., President's, Memorial, Labor, and Columbus days. Closed New Year's Day, Easter, Thanksgiving, and Christmas Eve and Day.
Canal Boat ride: Open May - September including Memorial Day, Labor Day, and July 4. Please call for exact departure times.

NEW HOPE, PENNSYLVANIA

New Hope Canal Boat Company
149 So. Main
P. O. Box 164
New Hope, PA 18938
(215) 862-2842 Fax: 215-862-0965 E-mail: sales@canalboats.com
Location: Take I-95 and exit on Rte. 32 northwest ten miles to New Hope on the south side of the Delaware River.
Highlights: Mule barge/canal, **Website:** www.canalboats.com/
General Information: In Delaware Canal State Park, the company operates an historic eighty-seven-foot barge on the constantly repaired Delaware Canal.

The Delaware River, stretching from the Delaware Bay to Catsberg, New York, is approximately 300 miles long. The Delaware Canal, which runs parallel to the river, starts at Easton and ends at Bristol. Construction started on the canal in 1827 but it was not fully operational until 1840 for commercial use. The old barges may be seen today and in the warm months; regular barge trips are taken by sightseers leaving from the little village of New Hope, Bucks County, Pennsylvania.

Admission: Entry fee. Open Wednesday, Saturday, and Sunday, 1 P.M.-4:30 P.M., April 1-April 30; daily, 11:30 A.M.-6 P.M., May 1-October 15; Wednesday, Saturday, and Sunday, 11:30 A.M.-4:30 P.M., Oct. 16-Nov. 15.

PHILADELPHIA, PENNSYLVANIA

The Philadelphia Ship Preservation Guild
801 South Columbus Boulevard
Philadelphia, PA 19147-4306
(215) 218-0110 Fax: (215) 463-1875
Location: Penns Landing vicinity. Please contact the Ship Guild for access information and directions.
Highlights: The tall ship *Gazela* and the tug boat *Jupiter,*
Website: www.gazela.org
General Information: The Ship Guild has been in existence since 1972. We own and operate the historic 1902 tug *Jupiter* in conjunction with Penn's Landing Corporation.

The tall ship *Gazela* was built in Cacilhas, Portugal as "*Gazella*" in 1883. Records of current configuration date from a major rebuild in 1900-1901 in Setubal, Portugal. She emerged from that refit as the barkentine we know today and joined the Portuguese Grand Banks/Davis Straits cod fishing fleet. She sailed with that fleet well into the 20th century (her last season: 1969). *Gazela* carried 35 cod fishing dories. After filling their dories with cod (then called the "beef of the sea") weighing 40-60 pounds each, the dorymen would return to *Gazela* to process and preserve the fish with salt. The better the catch, the longer the work day but the bigger the catch, the better their income as they worked on a system much akin to piecework. The fishing season lasted 4-6 months.

Gazela was laid up after the 1969 season having become obsolete for fishing. She was purchased in 1971 for the Philadelphia Maritime Museum (now known as the Independence Seaport Museum) by a wealthy Philadelphian. She is now owned by the volunteer organization that maintains her, the Ship Guild.

Gazela serves as a maritime ambassador for Philadelphia, and a living museum for the preservation of traditional sailing skills. Her crew is volunteer and inter-generational. After participating in OpSail 2000, *Gazela* has become the focus for our new student cadet and apprentice programs, both of which are cooperative ventures with local schools. Major *Gazela* project in 2001 — replace her deck.

The historic tug, *Jupiter* was built in Philadelphia at the Neafie & Levy Shipyard in 1902 and built of charcoal iron and was originally steam powered. During World War II she assisted vessels through the Chesapeake & Delaware Canal. She also towed barges and assisted in laying submarine cable across the Delaware River to prevent German U-Boats from coming upriver. She was the first tug to catch a line from the battleship USS *New Jersey* during her launching. In 1949 *Jupiter* was refitted with a diesel engine from an LST. She worked as a commercial tug until 1989 and continues to function as a tug when needed for such vessels as the *Gazela* and the *Olympia*. *Jupiter* also serves as a Philadelphia maritime ambassador and is tended by her own dedicated volunteer crew.

Activities: Both vessels are boardable when in port.
Admission: Contact the Guild for information.

PITTSBURGH, PENNSYLVANIA

USS *Requin* SS-481 (submarine)
The Carnegie Science Center
1 Allegheny Avenue
Pittsburgh, PA 15212-5850
(412) 237-3400 Fax: (412) 237-3375
Location: USS *Requin* is moored on the banks of the Ohio River in front of The Carnegie Science Center.
Highlights: USS *Requin* (SSR 481) (submarine),
Website: www.CarnegieScienceCenter.org

General Information: The USS *Requin* is a World War II submarine which was converted to the first U.S. Navy Radar Picket Submarine (1946), later converted to a Fleet Snorkel Submarine (1959). The *Requin* is presently restored to her 1968 Fleet Snorkel condition. Visitors are provided with very detailed guided tours emphasizing the science and technology contained in a submarine of this type. The guided tours last approximately 60 minutes.

Activities: Overnight camping program.

Admission: Entry fee. Open Sunday-Friday, 10 A.M.-5 P.M., Saturday, 10 A.M.-5 P.M. Summer hours: Open daily June 19-September 4, 10 A.M.- 6 P.M.; Winter hours, December 8-February 28, weekends, 10 A.M.-5 P.M., closed weekdays. May close during inclement weather. Holiday hours: Open December 26-31, 10 A.M. - 5 P.M., Martin Luther King Day: 10 A.M. - 5 P.M., President's Day: 10 A.M. - 5 P.M. Closed Thanksgiving Day, Christmas Day, New Year's Day.

ERIE, PENNSYLVANIA

Watson Curtze Mansion and Planetarium
356 W. Sixth Street
Erie, PA 16507
(814) 871-5790 Fax: (814) 879-9088 E-mail: ehmp@erie.net

Location: Erie is on the lakefront along I-90, which runs east/west from New York to Ohio. At the junction with I-79 head north to Erie. The Museum is just west of Gannon University Campus on Lake Erie.

Highlights: Planetarium, ship models, library (500 volumes),

Website: www.erie.net/~ehmp/main.html

General Information: The Erie Historical Museum and Planetarium was founded in 1899. The Museum offers exhibits on regional and maritime history. An archive of letters, documents, and books on local history is available for research.

Activities: Guided tours; lectures, films, and a Victorian Christmas show. In addition, a research planetarium has shows Saturday and Sunday 2 P.M. and 3 P.M. From August, Planetarium show hours are 11 A.M., 1, 2, and 3 P.M.

Admission: Entry fee. Memberships available. Open June-August, Tuesday-Friday, 10 A.M.-5 P.M., Saturdays and Sundays, 1 P.M.- 5 P.M., September-May, Tuesday-Sunday, 1 P.M.-5 P.M.

DELAWARE

LEWES, DELAWARE

Cannon Ball Marine Museum
c/o Lewes Historical Society
110 Shipcarpenter Street
Lewes, DE 19958
(302) 645-7670 Fax: (302) 645-9418

Location: Lewes (pn. LOO - is) is on Rte. 9, thirty miles southeast of Dover near the Atlantic coastline.

Highlights: The *Overfalls* (lightship), *U.S. Coast Guard Newsletter*

General Information: Cannonball Marine Museum, founded in 1972, is housed in the Cannonball House, noted for having been hit by a cannonball in the War of 1812. The Lewes Historical Society has been restoring six or seven historical homes in Lewes including the Cannonball House, which now houses maritime exhibits of ship models, a "Pilot Room" devoted to artifacts and items about the ship pilots of the area. The Lightship *Overfalls* is a part of the Museum and is located on the canal at Ship Carpenter Street.

Activities: Lectures, films, annual craft fair, annual flea market, and seminars

Admission: Entry fee. Open Tuesdays, Thursdays, and Saturdays, 10 A.M.-3 P.M., June-September.

At the *Kalmar Nyckel* Shipyard in Wilmington, DE, besides the replica 1629 ship, there is also a twenty-foot Swedish naval whale-boat pictured above. (Photo R. H. Smith)

The oldest lighthouse station in North America, Boston Light has stood as a guiding light into Boston Hrbor for almosts three hundred years—since 1716. Blown up by the British in the Revolutionary War, the lighthouse was rebuilt in 1783. 76 steps to the lantern room to view Boston. (Photo R. H. Smith)

FENWICK ISLAND, DELAWARE

DiscoverSea Shipwreck Museum
708 Ocean Highway (2nd Floor)
Fenwick Island, DE 19944
Toll Free: 1-888-743-5524 (302) 539-9366 E-mail: seashell@dca.net
Location: From Georgetown south on Rte. 113 nineteen miles to Rte. 34. Then east eleven miles to Fenwick Island.
Highlights: Thousands of artifacts from shipwrecks such as the Spanish ship *Atocha*, 1715 Fleet, *Titanic*, *R.M.S. Republic*, *Faithful Steward*, *Edmund Fitzgerald*, China Wreck, and many more. **Website:** www.discoversea.com
   General Information: DiscoverSea Shipwreck Museum is a continuing exhibit which expands and diversifies with the acquisitions of new artifacts as they are recovered. The Shipwreck Museum opened in July 1995 and has a goal of recovering and preserving our maritime heritage. For hundreds of years, the great ports of the Delaware and Chesapeake Bays brought to the Delmarva Peninsula one of the highest concentrations of shipping in the early Americas.

Robert H. Smith

Today, through the use of proper archeology and recovery, you can experience Delmarva's forgotten maritime history.

If the Delaware Coast could talk, its story would be of merchant men and galleons, pirates and privateers, men who sailed the ships and wreckers who laid in wait for them. Other interactive displays include aquariums, and theatre make this a unique gateway to our maritime heritage.

Through your DiscoverSea Shipwreck Museum visit, lecture or beach tour, you will travel through a hands-on experience which will enable you to shake hands with history.

Admission: No entry fee. Open daily Memorial Day-Labor Day - 9 A.M.-9 P.M.; daily September-October - 11 A.M.-4 P.M.; Saturday-Sunday November-March - 11 A.M.-4 P.M.; daily April-Memorial Day - 10 A.M.-4 P.M.

REHOBOTH, DELAWARE

Indian River Life-Saving Station
P.O. Box 949
Bethany Beach, DE 19930
(302) 227-0478 Fax: (302) 227-6438 E-mail: DSPF@splus.net
Location: The Station is located on the ocean side of Route 1, 3.5 miles south of Dewey Beach and 1.5 miles north of the Indian River Inlet *Highlights:* Lifsaving history, **Website:** www.irless.org

General Information: The former Indian River Life-Saving Station building, under the direction of the Delaware Seashore Preservation Foundation, has stood on its current location for more than 100 years. The Station is the object of a restoration effort by a group of local volunteers. The learning center will feature information on the lifesaving history of the Delaware coast focusing on the period of 1905. Also included is information on the Revenue Cutter Service, the U.S. Lifesaving Service, the U.S. Coast Guard Service, and sunken ships, famous rescues, and pirates. The hope is to restore the Venetian red-roofed structure to its original appearance when it was constructed in 1876.

Admission: Entry fee. Open daily Memorial Day-Labor Day. Call for off-season hours rest of year.

WILMINGTON, DELAWARE

***Kalmar Nyckel* Shipyard and Museum**
Kalmar Nyckel Foundation
1124 E. Seventh Street
Wilmington, DE 19801
(302) 429-7447 Fax: (302) 429-0350 E-mail: execdir@kalnyc.org

Location: The Museum is located on a small peninsula on the Delaware and Christina Rivers near downtown Wilmington and can be reached from Rte. 13 on Church Street turning east on E. 7th Street.
Highlights: The *Kalmar Nyckel* (replica ship), small craft (Swedish), wooden boat shop, **Website:** www.kalnyc.org
General Information: The *Kalmar Nyckel* Shipyard and Museum brings to life the heritage of "New Sweden," the first permanent European settlement in the Delaware River Valley. A living history shipyard at the settler's site has been re-established.

The *Kalmar Nyckel* ("the Key of Kalmar," name of fort that protects the city of Kalmar) is a 97-foot, 317-ton replica of a 1629 Dutch pinnace. The ship, launched in September 1997, was constructed at the *Kalmar Nyckel* Shipyard and Museum by shipwrights, blacksmiths, ship riggers, carpenters, and many other trades people. A cadre of volunteers are on sight to assist also.

The Museum exhibits, in what was the lofting building for the construction of the replica ship, seventeenth-century shipbuilding tools, ship plans, flags, navigation, and marine artifacts from 1700 to 1900. The Museum's small-craft include: *Little Key*, an eighteen-foot ship's boat; *King's Launch*, a twenty-foot Swedish naval whale-boat.

Activities: The Shipyard has a community Challenge School, an alternative educational program for at-risk youth teaching boat-building skills; Delaware Valley History Program; teaching cruises and Summer In-Service Programs.

Admission: Entry fee. Summer hours: due to sailing schedule, call or check website for hours open. Open Thursday-Sunday, 10 A.M. to 4 P.M., winter hours only.

PORT PENN, DELAWARE

Port Penn Interpretive Center
P.O. Box 155
Port Penn, DE 19731
(302) 836-2533 Fax: (302) 836-2539
Location: The Center is located at the intersection of Delaware Rte. 9 and New Castle County Road 2 (Port Penn Road) in the old schoolhouse.
Highlights: Decoy exhibits, floating fishing cabin, Fort Delaware State Park, Port Penn Wetland Trail,
General Information: The village of Port Penn is one of the many stops along Delaware's Coastal Heritage Greenway. This Greenway, which extends from urban Fox Point State Park to the beaches of Cape Henlopen State Park, encompasses many of Delaware's finest cultural and natural resources.

Throughout its history, Port Penn has looked to the Delaware River and its marshes for sustenance and contact with the outside world. The Interpretive

Robert H. Smith

Center focuses on life during the eighteenth and nineteenth centuries and how the landscape evolved over time in this Delaware Riverbank community.

Since settlement in 1764, the people of Port Penn have relied on the wetlands through such enterprises as hunting, fishing, and trapping. And original dikes built by the Dutch settlers provided fresh-water farming. Nearby is the Chesapeake & Delaware Canal (C & D Canal) from the Delaware River to the head of the Chesapeake Bay, a major shipping route. The wetlands have played a major role in the lives of Port Penners — then and now.

Floating cabins: one- or two-room watermen's houses mounted on shallow-draught hulls that were once a common maritime tradition in the Delaware River area. The one cabin that remains gives a glimpse of a tradition that almost disappeared without being recorded.

The Port Penn Interpretive Center is administered by nearby Fort Delaware State Park. On Pea Patch Island, the state park provides programs about the fort focusing on the period between 1863-1864 (Civil War) and emphasizes learning history through examining abundant records of the guards and prisoners. Besides the fort and its living history program, Pea Patch Island hosts an intricate habitat. A walk along the nature trail takes you through the area which in Civil

War times was the prisoners and guards barracks (a replica is being completed)

GEORGETOWN, DELAWARE

Treasures of the Sea Exhibit
Delaware Technical & Community College
Rte. 18, P. O. Box 610
Georgetown, DE 19947
(302) 856-5700 or 5482 Fax: (302) 858-5462
Location: The Treasures exhibit is located in the Delaware Technical & Community College library building, Rte. 18, Georgetown.
Highlights: Gold, jewels, and silver from a Spanish galleon *Atocha*, gift shop,

General Information: Treasures of the Sea Exhibit contains the lost treasures of the ill-fated *Nuestra Senora de Atocha*, a Spanish galleon that was helplessly driven by hurricane-force winds into a coral reef, off Key West, Florida, ripping a hole in her bow. May 20, 1973, treasure hunters discovered 1,500 silver coins dated no later than 1621. On July 4, 1973, three silver bars and a coral and gold necklace were recovered; numbers on one of the silver bars matched those listed on the *Atocha's* manifest located in the library in Seville, Spain. July 13, 1975, saw the recovery of nine bronze cannons with markings that confirmed Mel Fisher* had discovered the *Atocha*. However, it was not until July 20, 1985, that the "motherlode" of the *Atocha* was found, a cargo estimated to be worth $400 million.

Melvin Joseph, a Georgetown investor, and others assigned their stock or investment interest to the Delaware Technical and Community College Education Foundation, which made it possible for the establishment of the Treasures of the Sea Exhibit.

Admission: Entry fee. Open Monday, Tuesday, 10 A.M.-4 P.M.; Friday, noon-4 P.M.; Saturday, 9 P.M.-1 P.M. Suggest phoning to verify days and times exhibit is open. *-See also Mel Fisher Maritime Heritage Society, Key West, FL. and Mel Fisher Treasurer Museum, Sebastian, FL.

Lowell's Boat Shop (since 1793) at Amesbury, MA, operates as a museum and working boat-building shop to preserve the knowledge and history of the traditional craft of building small wooden boats. (Photo R. H. Smith)

Robert H. Smith

Part 1

CANAL PARKS

LISTED BELOW ARE THE NAMES OF SELECTED CANAL PARKS. FOR MORE INFORMATION ABOUT A SPECIFIC PARK, PLEASE WRITE TO THE FOLLOWING:

The American Canal Society
117 Main Street
Freemansburg, PA 18017

or

Virginia Canals and Navigation Society
6826 Rosemont Drive
McLean, VA 22101

Black River Canal (New York)
Blackstone Canal (Massachusetts)
Cayuga-Seneca Canal (New York)
Champlain Canal (New York)
Chemung Canal (New York)
Chenango Canal (New York)
Delaware and Raritan Canal (New Jersey/Pennsylvania)
Genesee Valley Canal (NY)
Lehigh Navigation (Pennsylvania)
New Haven and Northampton (Connecticut)
Schuylkill Navigation (Philadelphia, Pennsylvania)
Susquehanna and Tidewater (Pennsylvania)

Part 1

ALPHABETICAL LIST OF MUSEUMS

Absecon Lighthouse, Atlantic City, New Jersey 182
Adirondack Museum, Blue Mountain Lake, New York 139
Age of Sail Heritage Center, Port Greville, Nova Scotia-Canada 5
Albert County Museum, Hopewell Cape, NB 1
Alfred S. Brownell Collection of Atlantic Coast Fishing Craft Models
    Atlantic Coast Fishing Craft Models Providence, RI 117
American Merchant Marine Museum/U.S.
    Merchant Marine Academy, Kings Point, NY 140
American Philosophical Society Library, Philadelphia, PA 196
Antique Boat Museum, Clayton, NY 141
Aquarium and Marine Centre, (Centre Marin de Shippagan) Shippagan, NB 1
Archelaus Smith Museum, Certreville, NS 5
Assiginack Historical Museum and SS *Norisle* Heritage Park,
    Manitowanin, ONT 20
Atlantic County Historical Society Museum, Somers Point, NJ 182
Atlantic Statiquarium Marine Museum, Louisbourg 6
Barn Museum, Bellport, NY 142
Barnegat Bay Decoy & Baymen's Museum, Tuckerton, NJ 183
Barnegat Lighthouse, Barnegat light, NJ 184
Basin Head Fisheries Museum Souris PEI 49
Battleship Cove, Fall River, MA 76
Battleship *New Jersey* Historical Museum Society, Camden, NJ 185
Beavertail Lighthouse & Museum, Jamestown, RI 118
Bernier Maritime Museum (Musée Maritime Bernier), L'Islet-sur-mer, Québec,
    QBC 44
Beverly Historical Society and Museum, Beverly, MA 77
Binghamton (Ferry), Edgewater, NJ 185
Block Island Southeast Lighthouse & Museum Block Island, RI 119
Boothbay Region Historical Society, Boothbay Harbor, ME 51

Robert H. Smith

Border Historical Society, Eastport MA 53
Boston Marine Society, Boston, MA 78
Boston Tea Party Ship and Museum, Boston, MA 78
Brick Store Museum, Kennebunk, ME 54
Buffalo and Erie Counties Naval and Servicemen's Park, Buffalo, NY 142
Bytown Museum, Ottawa, ONT..21
C. Howard Hiester Canal Center, Wyomissing, PA...196
Canadian Canoe Museum, Peterborough, ONT 21
Canal Museum, Greenville, PA...197
Canal Society of New Jersey Museum at Waterloo Village, Morristown, NJ ...186
Canal Society of New York State, Syracuse, NY...143
Canastota Canal Town Museum, Canstota, NY 143
Cannon Ball Marine Museum, Lewes DE..203
Cape Ann Historical Museum, Gloucester, MA 79
Cape May County Historical and Genealogical Society Museum, Cape May, MJ
....186
Capt. Charles H. Hurley Library, Buzzard's Bay, MA 80
Captain Robert Bennet Forbes House, Mitlon, MA 80
Cartier-Brébeuf National Historical Park, Québec, QBC......................................45
Chafee Blackstone National Corridor, Woonsocket, RI......................................119
"Chapel Hill" Museum, Shag Harbor, NS..7
Charlestown Navy Yard, Boston, MA 81
Chautauqua Lakes Historic Vessels Co., Mayville, NY......................................144
Chittenango Landing Canal Boat Museum, Chittenango, NY 146
Churchill House and Marine Memorial Room Museum, Hantsport, NS 7
Cigna Museum and Art Collection, Philadelphia, PA...197
City Island Nautical Museum, City Island, NY...146
Clinton County Historical Museum, Cohasset, MA..147
Cohasset Maritime Museum, Plattsburg, NY...81
Cold Spring Harbor Whaling Museum, Cold Spring Harbor, NY 148
Collingwood Museum, Collingwood, ONT 22
Connecticut River Museum, Essex, CT..131
Coteau-du-Lac National Historic Site, Coteau-du-Lac, Québec, QBC.................47
Counting House-Old Berwick Historical Society, South Berwick, ME...............54
Crown Point State Historic Site/, Crown Point, NY 148
Custom House Maritime Museum of Newburyport, Newburyport, MA 82
Custom House Museum, New London, CT...131
D and H Canal Park, Cuddebackville, NY...165
David M. Stewart Museum, Montréal, Québec, QBC...46
Delaware and Hudson Canal Museum, High Falls, NY......................................150
DiscoverSea Shipwreck Museum, Fenwick Island, DE 205
Discovery Harbour, Penetanguishene, ONT 23

Smith's Guide to Maritime Museums of North America

Dory Shop, Shelburne, NS 8
Dunkirk Historical Lighthouse and Veteran's Park, Dunkirk, NY 151
Dwight D. Eisenhower Lock, Massena, NY 152
East End Seaport Maritime Museum, Greenport, NY 152
East Hampton Town Marine Museum, East Hampton, NY 153
Egan Institute of Maritime Studies, Nantucket Island, MA 83
Erie Canal Museum, Syracuse, NY 154
Erie Canal Village, Rome, NY 154
Erie Maritime Museum Homeport U.S. Brig *Niagara*, Erie, PA 198
Essex Shipbuilding Museum, Essex. MA 84
Expedition *Whydah* (Pirate Ship), Provincetown, MA...................................... 85
Falmouth Historical Society's Museums, Falmouth, MA 86
Fathom Five National Marine Park, Tbermony, ONT 24
Fire Island Lighthouse Preservation Society, Captree, NY 155
Fisheries Museum of the Atlantic, Lunenburg, NS 9
Fishermen's Museum, Musgrave Harbor, NFLND 3
Fishermen's Museum Pemaquid Point Lighthouse, Pemaquid Point, ME........... 55
Fort Hancock Museum, Highlands, NJ 187
Fort Hunter – Schoharie State Historic Site, Fort Hunter, NY 156
Forwarders' Museum, Prescott, ONT 24
Franklin D. Roosevelt Library and Museum, Hyde Park, NY 156
Friendship Museum, Friendship, ME.. 56
Gates House, Machiasport Historical Society, Machiasport, ME 56
Glacier Society Museum, Bridgeport, CT 132
Gloucester Adventure (schooner), Gloucester, MA 86
Grand Banks Schooner Museum, Boothbay, ME 56
Grand Manan Museum and Walter B. McLaughlin Marine Gallery, Grand
    Manan, NB.. 2
Great Harbor Maritime Museum, Northeast Harbor, ME 57
Green Park Shipbuilding Museum, Port Hill, PEI 50
Grosse Ile and the Irish Memorial, National Historic Site, Québec, QBC 47
H. Lee White Marine Museum, Oswego, NY 157
HMCS *Fraser* (DDE), Bridgewater, NS 11
HMCS *Haida* Naval Museum, Toronto, ONT 25
HMCS *Sackville* (K-181), Halifax, NS 11
HMCS *Rose* (Replica Ship), Bridgeport, CT 132
Half Moon Visitor Center/New Netherland Museum, Albany, NY 158
Hamilton-Scourage Project, Hamilton, ONT 26
Hart Nautical Collections, Cambridge MA 87
Hereford Inlet Lighthouse, North Wildwood, NJ 188
Herreshoff Marine Museum/Hall of Fame, Bristol, RI 120
Historic Gardner's Basin, Atlantic City, NJ 188

Robert H. Smith

Historical Society Museum, Wellfleet, MA 88
Historical Society of Old Yarmouth, Yarmouth Port, MA 90
Hudson River Maritime Museum, Kingston, NY 158
Hudson River Slooop *Clearwater*, Inc., Poughkeepsi, NY 159
Hull Lifesaving Museum, Hull, MA 90
Huronia Museum, Midland, ONT 26
Independence Seaport Museum, Philadelphia, PA 199
Indian River Life-Saving Station, Bethany Beach, DE 206
The International Yacht Restoration School, Newport, RI 120
Intrepid Sea-Air-Space Museum, New York City, NY 159
Islesford Historical Museum, Bar Harbor, ME 58
Jamestown Museum, Jamestown, RI 121
John Dubois Maritime Museum, Greenwich, NJ 189
John Hancock Warehouse and Warf/Old York Historical Society, York, ME 58
John Paul Jones House, Portsmouth, NH 71
Jones Falls Defensible Lockmaster's House, Elgin, ONT 27
Kalmar Nyckel Shipyard & Museum, Wilminton, DE 206
Kennebunkport Maritime Museum, Kennebunkport, ME 59
Kittery Historical and Naval Museum, Kittery ME 60
LaHave Island Marine Museum, LaHave Island, NS 10
Lake Champlain Maritime Museum, Basin Harbor 74
Lawrence House, Maritime, NS 10
Lightship *New Bedford*, New Bedford, MA 91
Linwood Maritime Museum, Linwood, NJ 190
Lockmaster's House Museum, Basin Harbor, ... 28
Lockport Canal Museum, Lockport, NY 160
Long Island Maritime Musuem, West Sayville, NY 161
Lowell's Boat Shop, Amesbury, MA 92
Lower Lakes Marine Historical Society, Buffalo, NY 162
Maine Maritime Museum, Bath, ME 61
Marblehead Historical Society, Marblehead, MA 92
Marine Museum at Fall River, Fall River, MA 93
Marine Museum of the Great Lakes at Kingston, Kingston, ONT 29
Mariners' Park Museum, Milford, ONT 29
Maritime & Irish Mossing Museum, Scituate, MA 94
Maritime Aquarium, Norwalk, CT 133
Maritime Command Musuem/Fort Schuyler, Bronx, NY 12
Maritime Industry Museum/Fort Schuyler, Bronx, NY 163
Maritime Museum of the Atlantic, Halifax, NS 12
Marshall Point Lighthouse Museum, Port Clyde, ME 61
Martha's Vineyard Historical Society and Museum, Edgartown, MA 95
Mary Celeste Museum, Marion, MA 96

Mather House Museum, Port Jefferson, NY 163
Medford Historical Society Museum, Medford, MA 96
Merrickville Blockhouse Museum, Merrickville, ONT 30
Middlesex Canal Museum, Lowell, MA 97
Montauk Point Lighthouse Museum, Montauk, NY 164
Moore Museum, Mooretown, ONT 31
Moosehead Marine Museum, Greenville, ME 62
Museum of Newport History, Newport, RI 122
Museum of Science, Boston, MA 97
Museum of the City of New York, New York City, NY 164
Museum of Yachting, Newport, RI 123
Museum of Yarmouth History, Yarmouth, ME 63
Museum Ship *Norgoma*, Sault Ste. Marie, ONT 32
Muskoka Lakes Museum, Port Carling, ONT 32
Mystic Seaport Museum, Mystic, CT 134
Nancy Island Historic Site, Wasaga Beach, ONT 33
Nantucket Life-Saving Museum, Nantucket Island, MA 98
National Canal Museum and Hugh Moore Park, Easton, PA 200
Nautical Museum at Horton Point Lighthouse, Southhold, NY 165
Nautilus and Submarine Force Museum, Groton, CT 135
Naval War College Museum, Newport, RI 124
Neversink Valley Area Museum/D and H Canal Park, Cuddebackville, NY 165
New Bedford Free Public Library, New Bedford, MA 99
New Bedford Whaling Museum, New Bedford, MA 99
New Brunswick Museum, St. John, NB 3
New England Pirate Museum, Salem, MA 100
New Hampshire Antique & Classic Boat Museum, Wolfeboro, NH 72
New Hope Canal Boat Company, New Hope, PA 201
New Jersey Naval Museum/Submarine USS *Ling*, Hackensack, NJ 192
The New-York Historical Society, New York City, NY 166
New York State Canal System, Albany, NY 168
Newfoundland Museum, St. John's, NFLD 4
Noble Maritime Collection, Staten Island, NY 169
Northport Historical Museum, Northport, NY 170
Ocean City Historical Museum, Ocean City, NY 193
Ocean Liner Museum, New York City, NY 170
O'Dell House Museum, Annapolis Royal/Clark's Harbour, NS 14
Old Fort William, Thunder Bay, ONT 33
Old Harbor Life-Saving Station, Wellfleet, MA 101
Old Lighthouse Museum, Stonington, CT 136
Old Sardine Village Museum, Lubec, ME 63
Old State House – The Bostonian Society, Boston, MA 102

Osher Map Library, Portland, ME ... 64
Osterville Historical Society, Osterville, Cape Cod, MA ... 102
Oswego Maritime Foundation, Oswego, NY ... 171
Ottawa House By-the-Sea, Parrsboro, NS ... 14
Owen Sound Marine-Rail Heritage Museum, Owen Sound, ONT ... 34
PT Boat Musuem and Library, Fall River, MA ... 103
Paterson Museum, Paterson, NJ ... 193
Peabody Essex Musuem, Salem, MA ... 103
Peary-MacMillian Arctic Museum, Brunswick, ME ... 65
Penobscot Marine Museum, Searsport, ME ... 65
Peterbororough Centennial Museum, Peterborough, ONT ... 36
Peterborough Hydraulic Lift Lock and Visitor Center, Peterborough, ONT ... 37
Philadelphia Ship Preservation Guild, Philadelphia, PA ... 201
Pilgrim Hall Museum, Plymouth, MA ... 104
Plainville Historic Center, Plainville, CT ... 137
Plimoth Plantation, Plymouth, MA ... 106
Pointe-au-Pére Sea Museum, Pointe-au-Père, Québec, QBC ... 48
Port Colborne Historical and Marine Museum, Port Colborne, ONT ... 38
Port Dover Harbour Museum, Port Dover, ONT ... 38
Port of Portsmouth Maritime Museum, Portsmouth, NH ... 72
Port of Québec in the Nineteenthe Century, National Historic Site, Québec, QBC ... 49
Port Penn Interpretive Center, Port Penn, DE ... 207
Portland Harbor Museum, South Portland, ME ... 66
Portland Head Light, Cape Elizabeth, ME ... 67
Portsmouth Athenaeum, Portsmouth, NH ... 73
Providence (Reproduction-18th Century Sloop), Newport, RI ... 126
Queens County Museum, Liverpool, NS ... 15
QuoddyMaritime Museum, Eastport, ME ... 68
Rhode Island Historical Society Library, Providence, RI ... 127
Rideau Canal Museum, Smiths Falls, ONT ... 39
Rose Island Lighthouse & Museum, Newport, RI ... 128
SS *Nobska* (Coastal Steamer), New Bedford, MA ... 107
Sackets Harbor Battlefield State Historic Site, Sackets Harbor, NY ... 172
Sag Harbor Whaling Museum, Sag Harbor, NY ... 173
Sailor's Memorial Musuem and Lighthouse, Bar Harbor, ME ... 68
St. Catharines Historical Museum, St. Catharines, ONT ... 39
St. Lawrence Islands National Park/Brown's Bay Wreck, Mallorytown, ONT ... 40
St. Mary's River Marine Center, Sault Ste. Marie, ONT ... 41
St. Peters Canal, St. Peters, NS ... 16
Salem Maritime National Historical Site, Salem, MA ... 108
Salt Pond Visitor Center, Eastham, MA ... 108

Smith's Guide to Maritime Museums of North America

Sandy Bay Historical Society & Museums, Rockport, MA 109
Saugerties Lighthouse Museum, Saugerties, NY 174
Schooner *Ernestina* Commission, New Bedford, MA 109
Scituate Lighthouse, Scituate, MA 110
Seal Island Light Museum, Barrington, NS 16
Settler's Museum, Mahone Bay, NS 17
1768 Jeremiah Lee Mansion, Marblehaed, Ma 111
Shelburne Museum, Inc., Shelburne, VT 75
Shore Village Museum, Rockland, ME 70
Sims' Store Museum, Camillus, NY 175
Singlehanded Sailors Hall of Fame, Newport, RI 129
Skenesborough Museum, Whitehall, NY 175
Sodus Bay Lighthouse Museum, Sodus Point, NY 176
South Street Seaport Museum, New York City, NY 177
Southampton Historical Museum, Southampton, Ny 178
Steamboat Dock Museum, Keyport, NJ 194
Stone House, Deep River, CT 137
Strawbery Banke Museum, Portsmouth, NH 73
Submarine Library Museum, Middletown, CT 138
Suffolk Historical Museum, Riverhead, NY 179
The Pier: Toronto's Waterfront Museum, Toronto, ONT 42
Toms River Seaport Society, Toms River, NJ 195
Toronto Port Authority, Toronto, ONT 43
Treasurers of the Sea Exhibit, Georgetown, DE 208
Truro Historical Society Museum, North Truro, MA 111
Tugboat *Urger*, Waterford, NY 179
Twin Lights State Historic Site, Highlands, NJ 195
U.S. Coast Guard Museum, New London, CT 138
USS *Constitution*, Boston, MA 112
USS *Constitution* Museum, Boston, MA 113
USS *New Jersey*, Battleship, Camden, NJ 185
USS *Requin* (SS-481) (Submarine), Pittsburgh, PA 202
USS *Slater* (Destroyer Escort), Albany, NY 180
United States Naval Shipbuilding Museum, Quincy, MA 114
University of Rhode Island, Special Collections, Kingston, RI 130
Vanderbilt Mansion, Marine Museum, Centerport, NY 180
Varnum Memrial Armory, East Greenwich, RI 130
Voyaguer Heritage Centre, Samuel de Champlain Provincial Park
   Mattawa, ONT 43
Waterfront Museum and Showboat Barge, Brooklyn, NY 181
Watson Curtze Mansion and Planetarium, Erie, PA 203
Welland Historical Museum, Welland, ONT 44

Robert H. Smith

Whaling Musuem, Nantucket Island, MA 115
Whaling Museum, Cold Spring, NY 148
Willowbrook at Newfield, Newfield, ME 71
Woods Hole Historical Collection, Woods Hole, MA 116
Yarmouth Coutny Museum, Yarmouth, NS 19

Part 1

SUBJECT INDEX CONTENTS

BED AND BREAKFAST and OVERNIGHT ENCAMPMENTS

BOAT/SHIP BUILDING
GIFT/BOOK SHOPS
HALLS OF FAME
LIBRARIES
LIGHTHOUSES / LIGHTSHIPS
LOCKS AND CANALS
NAVY YARDS
NEWSLETTERS & PERIODICALS
SCRIMSHAW
SHIP CHANDLERS
SHIP MODELS
SHIPS AND BOATS
CANOES
CANAL BOATS/BARGES
ICE BREAKERS
IRONCLADS
LIGHTSHIPS
SMALLCRAFT
SUBMARINES
TUGBOATS
WHALING

BED AND BREAKFAST and OVERNIGHT ENCAMPMENTS

Alexander Henry (210-foot icebreaker) Mid-May to Labour Day
Marine Museum of Great Lakes/Kingston (Kingston, ONT) 29
New Jersey Naval Museum/Submarine USS *Ling*
                (Hackensack, NJ) 192
Rose Island Lighthouse (Newport, RI) 128
Saugerties Lighthouse Museum (Year-round) (Saugerties, NY) 174

Robert H. Smith

USS *Little Rock* - Cruiser Capacity: 250 (Buffalo, NY) 142
USS *Massachusetts* -Battleship Capacity: 400 youths, 100 adults.
Min. age: 6 (Fall River, MA) 76
USS *Requin* - Submarine Capacity: 30 youths, 10 adults
Minimum age: 10 (Pittsburgh, PA) 202
USS *Salem* - Cruiser Capacity: 250, Minimum age: 5
 (Quincy, MA) 114
USS *Slater* Museum Ship (DE-766) (For youths) (Albany, NY) 180

BOAT/SHIP BUILDING

Adirondack Museum	(Blue Mountain Lake, NY)	139
Age of Sail Heritage Center	(Port Greville, NS)	5
Archelaus Smith Museum	(Centerville, NS)	5
Atlantic County Historical Soc. Museum	(Somers Point, NJ)	182
Antique Boat Museum	(Clayton, NY)	141
City Island Nautical Museum	(City Island, NY)	146
Dory Shop	(Lunenburg, NS)	9
Dory Shop	(Shelburne, NS)	8
East End Seaport Maritime Museum	(Greenport, LI, NY)	152
East Hampton Town Marine Museum	(East Hampton, NY)	153
Green Park Shipbuilding Museum	(Port Hill, PEI)	50
Hull Lifesaving Museum	(Hull, MA)	90
Independence Seaport Museum	(Philadelphia, PA)	199
International Yacht Restoration School	(Newport, RI)	120
Kalmar Nyckel Shipyard and Museum	(Wilmington, DE)	206
Lake Champlain Maritime Museum	(Basin Harbor, VT)	74
Lawrence House	(Maitland, NS)	10
Lowell's Boat Shop (dories)	(Amesbury, MA)	92
Maine Maritime Museum	(Bath, ME)	61
Maritime & Irish Mossing Museum	(Scituate, MA)	94
Maritime Aquarium at Norwalk	(Norwalk, CT)	133
Muskoka Lakes Museum	(Port Carling, ONT)	32
Mystic Seaport	(Mystic, CT)	134
Ottawa House By-the-Sea	(Parrsboro, NS)	14
Queens County Museum	(Liverpool, NS)	15
The Pier: Toronto's Waterfront Museum	(Toronto, ONT)	42
United States Naval Shipbuilding Museum	(Quincy, MA)	114

GIFT/BOOK SHOPS

Adirondack Museum	(Blue Mountain Lake, NY)	139
Age of Sail Heritage Center	(Port Greville, NS)	5
Antique Boat Museum	(Clayton, NY)	141

Aquarium and Marine Center	(Shippagan, NB)	1
Barn Museum	(Bellport, NY)	142
Barnegat Bay Decoy and Baymen's Museum	(Tuckerton, NJ)	183
Basin Head Fisheries Museum	(Souris, PEI)	49
Battleship Cove	(Fall River, MA)	76
Bernier Maritime Museum	(L'Islet-sur-Mer, QBC)	44
Boston Tea Party Ship and Museum	(Boston, MA)	78
Brick Store Museum	(Kennebunk, ME)	54
Brig *Niagara* (reconstructed ship)	(Erie, PA)	198
Bytown Museum	(Ottawa, ONT)	21
Canadian Canoe Museum	(Peterborough, ONT)	21
Canal Society of New Jersey Museum	(Morristown, NJ)	186
Cape Ann Museum	(Gloucester, MA)	79
Cape May Historical Society	(Cape May, NJ)	186
Chittenango Landing Canal Boat Museum	(Chittenango, NY)	146
Clinton County Historical Museum	(Plattsburg, NY)	147
Cold Spring Harbor Whaling Museum	(Cold Spring Harbor, L.I., NY)	148
Collingwood Museum	(Collingwood, ONT)	22
Connecticut River Museum	(Essex, CT)	131
Coteau-du-Lac National Historic Site	(Québec, QBC)	47
Custom House Maritime Museum	(Newburyport, MA)	82
David M. Stewart Museum	(Montréal, QBC)	46
Discovery Harbour	(Penetanguishene, ONT)	23
East End Seaport Maritime Museum	(Greenport, NY)	152
Erie Canal Museum	(Syracuse, NY)	154
Erie Canal Village	(Rome, NY)	154
Erie Maritime Museum/Homeport U.S. Brig *Niagara*	(Erie, PA)	198
Essex Shipbuilding Museum	(Essex, MA)	84
Expedition *Whydah* (Pirate Ship)	(Provincetown, MA)	85
Fisheries Museum of the Atlantic	(Lunenburg, NS)	9
Fort Hancock Museum	(Highlands, NJ)	187
Forwarder's Museum	(Prescott, ONT)	24
Franklin D. Roosevelt Library and Museum	(Hyde Park, NY)	156
Gloucester Adventure	(Gloucester, MA)	86
Grand Manan Museum	(Grand Manan, NB)	2
Green Park Shipbuilding Museum	(Port Hill, PEI)	50
HMCS *Haida* (WW II Cutter)	(Toronto, ONT)	25
HMCS *Sackville* (K-181)	(Halifax, NS)	11
Hamilton-Scourge Project	(Hamilton, ONT)	26
Herreshoff Marine Museum	(Bristol, RI)	120
Hudson River Maritime Museum	(Kingston, NY)	158

Hull Lifesaving Museum	(Hull, MA)	90
Independence Seaport Museum	(Philadelphia, PA)	199
Intrepid Sea-Air-Space Museum	(New York, NY)	159
John Hancock Warehouse and Wharf	(York, ME)	58
Jones Falls Defensible Lockmaster's House	(Elgin, ONT)	27
Kalmar Nyckel Shipyard & Museum	(Wilmington, DE)	206
Kennebunkport Maritime Museum	(Kennebunkport, ME)	59
Kittery Historical/Naval Museum	(Kittery, ME)	60
Lake Champlain Maritime Museum	(Basin Harbor, VT)	74
Lockmaster's House Museum	(Chaffeys Lock, ONT)	28
Maine Maritime Museum	(Bath, ME)	61
Marblehead Historical Society	(Marblehead, MA)	92
Marine Museum at Fall River	(Fall River, MA)	93
Marine Museum of the Great Lakes	(Kingston, ONT)	29
Maritime & Irish Mossing Museum	(Scituate, MA)	94
Maritime Aquarium	(Norwalk, CT)	133
Maritime Industry Museum/Fort Schuyler	(Bronx, NY)	163
Maritime Museum of the Atlantic	(Halifax, NS)	12
Marshall Point Lighthouse	(Port Clyde, ME)	61
Museum of Science	Boston, MA)	97
Museum of Yachting	(Newport, RI)	123
Museum of Yarmouth History	(Yarmouth, ME)	63
Museum Ship *Norgoma*	(Sault Ste. Marie, ONT)	32
Mystic Seaport Museum	(Mystic, CT)	134
Nantucket Lifesaving Museum	(Nantucket Island, MA)	98
National Canal Museum and Hugh Moore Park	(Easton, PA)	200
Nautilus and Submarine Force Museum	(Groton, CT)	135
Naval War College	(Newport, RI)	124
Neversink Valley Area Museum	(Cuddebackville, NY)	165
New Bedford Whaling Museum	(New Bedford, MA)	99
New Brunswick Museum	(Saint John, NB)	3
New Jersey Naval/USS *Ling* (Submarine)	(Hackensack, NJ)	192
New-York Historical Society	(New York, NY)	166
Northport Historical Museum	(Northport, L.I., NY)	170
Ocean City Historical Museum	(Ocean City, NJ)	193
Old State House	(Boston, MA)	102
PT Boat Museum and Library	(Fall River, MA)	103
Peabody Essex Museum	(Salem, MA)	103
Penobscot Marine Museum	(Searsport, ME)	65
Pilgrim Hall Museum	(Plymouth, MA)	104
Plainville Historical Center	(Plainville, CT)	137
Plimoth Plantation	(Plymouth, MA)	106

Smith's Guide to Maritime Museums of North America

Port Colborne Historical & Marine Museum	(Port Colborne, ONT)	38
Quoddy Maritime Museum	(Eastport, ME)	68
Sag Harbor Whaling Museum	(Sag Harbor, NY)	173
Sailor's Memorial Museum, Grindle Point Light	(Islesboro, ME)	68
St. Catharines Historical Museum	(St. Catharines, ONT)	39
Salem Maritime National Historical Site	(Salem, MA)	108
Saugerties Lighthouse Museum	(Saugerties, NY)	174
Shelburne Museum	(Shelburne, VT)	75
Shore Village Museum	(Rockland, ME)	70
Skenesborough Museum	(Whitehall, NY)	175
Sodus Bay Lighthouse	(Sodus Point, NY)	176
South Street Seaport Museum	(New York, NY)	177
Suffolk Historical Museum	(Riverhead, NY)	179
Treasures of the Sea Exhibit	(Georgetown, DE)	208
Truro Historical Society Museum	(N. Truro, MA)	111
Twin Lights State Historic Site	(Highlands, NJ)	195
U.S. Coast Guard Museum	(New London, CT)	138
USS *Constitution* Museum	(Boston, MA)	112
USS *Slater* Museum Ship (DE-766)	Albany, NY)	180
Vanderbilt Mansion	(Centerport, NY)	180
Waterfront Museum and Showboat Barge	(Brooklyn, NY)	181
Watson Curtze Mansion and Planetarium	(Erie, PA)	203
Willowbrook at Newfield	(Newfield, ME)	71
Woods Hole Historical Collection	(Woods Hole, MA)	116
Yarmouth County Museum	(Yarmouth, NS)	19

HALLS OF FAME

American Merchant Marine Museum	(Kings Point, NY)	140
America's Cup Museum	(Bristol, RI)	120
Single-Handed Sailors Hall of Fame (Mus/Yachting	(Newport, RI)	123

LIBRARIES

Alfred S. Brownell Collection	(Providence, RI)	117
American Philosophical Museum	(Philadelphia, PA)	196
Antique Boat Museum	(Clayton, NY)	141
Atlantic County Historical Society Museum	(Somers Point, NJ)	182
Battleship Cove	(Fall River, MA)	76
Bernier Maritime Museum	(L'Islet-sur-Mer, QBC)	44
Beverly Historical Society and Museum	(Beverly, MA)	77
Brick Store Museum	(Kennebunk, ME)	54
Canal Society of New York State, Inc.	(Syracuse, NY)	143
Cape Ann Historical Museum	(Gloucester, MA)	79

Cape May County Historical Museum	(Cape May, NJ)	186
Capt. Charles H. Hurley Library	(Buzzards Bay, MA)	80
Chittenango Landing Canal Boat Museum	(Chittenango, NY)	146
City Island Nautical Museum	(Bronx, NY)	146
Connecticut River Museum	(Essex, CT)	131
Counting House	(South Berwick, ME)	54
Custom House Maritime Museum	(Newburyport, MA)	82
Egan Institute of Maritime Studies	(Nantucket Island, MA)	83
Erie Maritime Museum	(Erie, PA)	198
Fisheries Museum of the Atlantic	(Lunenburg, NS)	9
Franklin D. Roosevelt Library and Museum	(Hyde Park, NY)	156
Gates House/Machiasport Historical Society	(Machiasport, ME)	56
Grand Manan Museum	(Grand Manan, NB)	2
H. Lee White Marine Museum	(Oswego, NY)	157
HMCS *Haida* (WW II cutter)	(Toronto, ONT)	25
Hudson River Maritime Museum	(Kingston, NY)	158
Huronia Museum	(Midland, ONT)	26
Independence Seaport Museum	(Philadelphia, PA)	199
John Dubois Maritime Museum	(Greenwich, NJ)	189
John Hancock Warehouse and Wharf	(York, ME)	58
Kalmar Nyckel Shipyard and Museum	(Wilmington, DE)	206
Kendall Institute	(New Bedford, MA)	99
Kynett Library and Research Center(Life Saving)	(Nantucket, MA)	98
Kittery Historical and Naval Museum	(Kittery, ME)	60
Lake Champlain Maritime Museum	(Basin Harbor, VT)	74
Linwood Maritime Museum	(Linwood, NJ)	190
Long Island Maritime Museum	(West Sayville, L.I., NY)	161
Lower Lakes Marine Historical Society	(Buffalo, NY)	162
Maine Maritime Museum	(Bath, ME)	61
Marine Museum at Fall River	(Fall River, MA)	93
Marine Museum of the Great Lakes at Kingston	(Kingston, ONT)	29
Maritime Command Museum	(Halifax, NS)	12
Maritime Industry Museum at Fort Schuyler	(Bronx, NY)	163
Maritime Museum of the Atlantic	(Halifax, NS)	12
Martha's Vineyard Historical Society and Museum	(Edgartown, MA)	95
Museum of Newport History	(Newport, RI)	122
Museum of the City of New York	(New York, NY)	164
Museum of Yachting	(Newport, RI)	123
Museum of Yarmouth History	(Yarmouth, ME)	63
Mystic Seaport Museum	(Mystic, CT)	134
Nantucket Life-Saving Museum	(Nantucket, MA)	98
National Canal Museum and Hugh Moore Park	(Easton, PA)	200

Naval War College Museum	(Newport, RI)	124
New Bedford Free Public Library	(New Bedford, MA)	99
New Bedford Whaling Museum	(New Bedford, MA)	99
New-York Historical Society	(New York, NY)	166
Noble Maritime Collection	(Staten Island, NY)	169
Old State House-Bostonian Society	(Boston, MA)	102
Osher Map Library	(Portland, ME)	64
Osterville Historical Society	(Osterville, Cape Cod, MA)	102
Oswego Maritime Foundation	(Oswego, NY)	171
Owen Sound Marine-Rail Museum	(Owen Sound, ONT)	34
PT Boat Museum and Library	(Fall River, MA)	103
Peabody Essex Museum(Phillips Library)	(Salem, MA)	103
Peary-MacMillan Arctic Museum	(Brunswick, ME)	65
Penobscot Marine Museum	(Searsport, ME)	65
Peterborough Centennial Museum	(Peterborough, ONT)	36
Plainville Historic Center	(Plainville, CT)	137
Plimoth Plantation	(Plymouth, MA)	106
Portsmouth Athenaeum	(Portsmouth, NH)	73
Rhode Island Historical Society Library	(Providence, RI)	127
Sackets Harbor	(Sackets Harbor, NY)	172
Sag Harbor Whaling Museum	(Sag Harbor, NY)	173
St. Catharines Historical Museum	(St. Catharines, ONT)	39
St. Mary's River Marine Center	(Sault Ste. Marie, ONT)	41
Scituate Lighthouse	(Scituate, MA)	110
Shelburne Museum	(Shelburne, VT)	75
South Street Seaport Museum	(New York, NY)	177
Southampton Historical Museum	(Southampton, NY)	178
Submarine Library Museum	(Middletown, CT)	138
Suffolk Historical Museum	(Riverhead, NY)	179
The Pier: Toronto's Waterfront Museum	(Toronto, ONT)	42
Toms River Seaport Society	(Toms River, NJ)	195
Toronto Port Authority	(Toronto, ONT)	43
Treasures of the Sea Exhibit	(Georgetown, DE)	208
U.S. Coast Guard Museum	(New London, CT)	138
USS *Constitution* Museum	(Charlestown, MA)	112
University of Rhode Island	(Kingston, RI)	130
Waterfront Museum and Showboat Barge	(Brooklyn, NY)	181
Watson Curtze Mansion and Planetarium	(Erie, PA)	203
Whaling Museum	(Nantucket Island, MA)	115
Woods Hole Historical Museum	(Woods Hole, MA)	116
Yarmouth County Museum	(Yarmouth, NS)	19

LIGHTHOUSES / LIGHTSHIPS

Absecon Lighthouse	(Atlantic City, NJ)	182
Ambrose (lightship)	(New York, NY)	177
Aquarium & Marine Center	(Shippagan, NB)	1
Barnegat Lighthouse	(Barnegat Light, NJ)	184
Beavertail Lighthouse Museum	(Jamestown, RI)	118
Block Island Southeast Lighthouse and Museum	(Block Island, RI)	119
Cannon Ball Museum	(Lewes, DE)	203
Cape Cod Lighthouse	(N. Truro, MA)	111
Cape May County Historical and Genealogical Society Museum		
	(Cape May, NJ)	186
Champlain Lighthouse	(Crown Point, NY)	148
Colchester Reef Lighthouse	(Shelburne, VT)	75
Derby Wharf Lighthouse	(Salem, MA)	108
Dunkirk Historical Lighthouse	(Dunkirk, NY)	151
False Duck Island Lighthouse (Mariners Park Mus.)	(Milford, ONT)	29
Fire Island Lighthouse Preservation Society	(Captree Island, NY)	155
Fishermen's Museum	(Musgrave Harbor, NFLND)	3
Fishermen's Museum and Pemaquid Point Lighthouse		
	(Pemaquid, ME)	55
Fort Hancock Museum	(Highlands, NJ)	187
Grindel Point Lighthouse (Sailor's Memorial Museum)		
	(Islesboro, ME)	68
Hereford Inlet Lighthouse	(North Wildwood, NJ)	188
Hudson River Maritime Museum	(Kingston, NY)	158
Lightship *New Bedford*	(New Bedford, MA)	91
Lightship *Overfalls*	(Lewes, DE)	203
Marshall Point Lighthouse	(Port Clyde, ME)	61
Montauk Point Lighthouse Museum	(Montauk, NY)	164
Nancy Island Historic Site	(Wasaga Beach, ONT)	33
Nautical Museum at Horton Point Lighthouse	(Southold, L.I., NY)	165
Old Lighthouse Museum	(Stonington, CT)	136
Pemaquid Point Lighthouse	(Pemaquid Point, ME)	55
Point Gratiot Lighthouse	(Dunkirk, NY)	151
Pointe-au-Père Sea Lighthouse	(Point-au-Père, QBC)	48
Portland Head Light	(Cape Elizabeth, ME)	67
Rondout Lighthouse	(Kingston, NY)	158
Rose Island Lighthouse and Museum	(Newport, RI)	128
Sailor's Memorial Museum, Grindle Point Light	(Islesboro, ME)	68
Salem Maritime National Historic Site	(Salem, MA)	108
Sandy Hook Lighthouse	(Highlands, NJ)	187
Scituate Lighthouse	(Scituate, MA)	110

Seal Island Light Museum	(Barrington, NS)	16
Shelburne Museum	(Shelburne, VT)	75
Sodus Bay Lighthouse	(Sodus Point, NY)	176
Spring Point Lighthouse	(South Portland, ME)	66
Twin Lights State Historic Site	(Highlands, NJ)	195
Valcour Island Lighthouse	(Plattsburg, NY)	147

LOCKS AND CANALS

Blackstone Canal	(Woonsocket, RI)	119
Bytown Museum	(Ottawa, ONT)	21
C. Howard Hiester Canal Center	(Wyomissing, PA)	196
Canal Museum	(Greenville, PA)	197
Canal Society of New Jersey Museum at Waterloo Village	(Morristown, NJ)	186
Canal Society of New York State	(Syracuse, NY)	143
Canastota Canal Town Museum	(Canastota, NY)	143
Chafee Blackstone National Corridor	(Woonsocket, RI)	119
Chaffeys Lock	(Chaffeys Lock, ONT)	28
Champlain Canal - Skenesborough	(Whitehall, NY)	175
Chittenango Landing Canal Boat Museum	(Chittenango, NY)	146
Coteau-du-Lac Canal	(Coteau-du-Lac, QBC)	47
Delaware and Hudson Canal Museum	(High Falls, NY)	150
Dwight D. Eisenhower Lock	(Massena, NY)	152
Erie Canal	Canastota, NY)	143
Erie Canal	(Chittenango, NY)	146
Erie Canal	(Fort Hunter, NY)	156
Erie Canal	(Lockport, NY)	160
Erie Canal Museum	(Syracuse, NY)	154
Erie Canal Village	(Rome, NY)	154
Farmington Canal	(Plainville, CT)	137
Fort Hunter-Schoharie Crossing; State Historic Site	(Fort Hunter, NY)	156
H. Lee White Marine Museum	(Oswego, NY)	157
Jones Falls Defensible - Lockmaster's House	(Elgin, ONT)	27
Lake Champlain Canal	(Whitehall, NY)	74
Lockmaster's House Museum	(Chaffeys Lock, ONT)	28
Lockport Canal Museum	(Lockport, NY)	160
Merrickville Blockhouse Museum	(Merrickville, ONT)	30
Middlesex Canal Museum	(Lowell, MA)	97
Muskoka Lakes Museum	(Port Carling, ONT)	32
National Canal Museum and Hugh Moore Park	(Easton, PA)	200
Neversink Valley Area Museum/D and H Canal Park		

Robert H. Smith

	-(Cuddebackville, NY)	165
New Hope Canal Boat Company	(New Hope, PA)	201
New York State Canal System	(Albany, NY)	168
Oswego Canal	(Oswego, NY)	171
Peterborough Centennial Museum	(Peterborough, ONT)	36
Peterborough Hydraulic Lift Lock/Visitor Center		
	(Peterborough, ONT)	37
Plainville Historic Center	(Plainville, CT)	137
Port Colborne Historical and Marine Museum	(Port Colborne, ONT)	38
Rideau Canal Museum	(Smiths Falls, ONT)	39
St. Catharines Historical Museum	(St. Catharines, ONT)	39
St. Mary's River Marine Center	(Sault Ste. Marie, ONT)	41
St. Peters Canal	(St. Peters, NS)	16
Schoharie Crossing State Historic Site	(Fort Hunter, NY)	156
Sims' Store Museum	(Camillus, NY)	175
Skenesborough Museum	(Whitehall, NY)	175
Welland Canal	(Port Colborne, ONT)	44
Welland Historical Museum	(Welland, ONT)	44

NAVY YARDS

Charlestown Navy Yard	(Boston, MA)	81
Sackets Harbor Battlefield State Historic Site	(Sackets Harbor, NY)	172

NEWSLETTERS & PERIODICALS

A Whaling Account (Whaling Museum Society)
    (Cold Spring Harbor, L.I., NY)   148
American Neptune (Peabody Essex)   (Salem, MA)   103
Canal Currents (newsletter) (Erie Canal Museum)   (Syracuse, NY)   154
Constitution Chronicle (newsletter) (USS *Constitution* Museum)
    (Boston, MA)   112
Dorymates (bi-annual newsletter) (Fisheries Museum of Atlantic)
    (Lunenburg, NS)   9
Fall River Line Journal (quarterly) (Marine Museum at Fall River)
    (Fall River, MA)   93
Forbes House Jottings (Capt. Robert Bennet Forbes House)
    (Milton, MA)   80
Friends of HMCS Haida   (Toronto, ONT)   25
LCMMnews (Lake Champlain Maritime Museum)
    (Basin Harbor, VT)   74
Maritimes (newsletter)   (Oswego, NY)   171
Niagara League News (Erie Maritime Museum)   (Erie, PA)   154
OMF Ontario, Maritimes   (Oswego, NY)   171

Smith's Guide to Maritime Museums of North America

Olympia Update (Independence Seaport Museum) (Philadelphia, PA)		199
Portland Harbor Museum	(South Portland, ME)	66
Rose Island Lighthouse News (Rose Island Lighthouse Museum) (Newport, RI)		128
Shelburne Museum, Inc.	(Shelburne, VT)	75
Shore Village Museum (newsletter) (Shore Village Museum) -(Rockland, ME)		70
Slater Signals (USS *Slater*)	(Albany, NY)	180
Spinnaker (Museum of Yachting)	(Newport, RI)	123
Steamboat Log (newsletter) (Connecticut River Museum) (Essex, CT)		131
Tea Times (newsletter) (Boston Tea Ship and Museum) (Boston, MA)		78
The Bay Chronicle (Penobscot Marine Museum)	(Searsport, ME)	65
The Bay Stater (USS *Massachusetts*)	(Fall River, MA)	76
The Broadside (Boston National Historical Park)	(Boston, MA)	112
The Bulletin from Johnny Cake Hill (New Bedford Whaling Museum) (New Bedford, MA)		99
The Dolphin (Long Island Maritime Museum)	(West Sayville, NY)	161
The Icebreaking News (The *Glacier* Society)	(Bridgeport, CT)	132
The Lock Tender (newsletter) (Natl. Canal Museum)	(Easton, PA)	200
The Log (Mystic Seaport)	(Mystic, CT)	134
The Manifest (newsletter) (American Merchant Marine Museum) (Kings Point, NY)		140
The Masthead (Independence Seaport Museum) (Philadelphia, PA)		199
The PT Boater (PT Boats, Inc.)	(Fall River, MA)	103
The Ship's Bell (Discovery Harbor)	(Penetaguishene, ONT)	23
The Windrose (Mystic Seaport)	(Mystic, CT)	134
Towpath Topics (Middlesex Canal Museum	(Lowell, MA)	97
US Coast Guard Newsletter	(New London, CT)	138
Woods Hole Historical Museum	(Woods Hole, MA)	116

SCRIMSHAW

Alfred S. Brownell Collection	(Providence, RI)	117
Barn Museum	(Bellport, NY)	142
Cold Spring Harbor Whaling Museum (Cold Spring Harbor, L.I., NY)		148
Custom House Maritime Museum	(Newburyport, MA)	82
Kennebunkport Maritime Museum	(Kennebunkport, ME)	59
Mystic Seaport Museum	(Mystic, CT)	134
New Bedford Whaling Museum	(New Bedford, MA)	99

New Brunswick Museum	(Saint John, NB)	3
Old State House	(Boston, MA)	102
Peabody Essex Museum	(Salem, MA)	103
Sag Harbor Whaling Museum	(Sag Harbor, NY)	173
Shelburne Museum	(Shelburne, VT)	75
Shore Village Museum	(Rockland, ME)	70
Whaling Museum	(Nantucket Island, MA)	115

SHIP CHANDLERS

Cohasset Historical Museum	(Cohasset, MA)	81
Discovery Harbour	(Penetanguishene, ONT)	23
Robertson & Son Ship Chandlery (Maritime Museum of the Atlantic)	(Halifax, NS)	12

SHIP MODELS

Albert County Museum	(Hopewell Cape, NB)	1
Alfred S. Brownell Collection of Atlantic Coast Fishing Craft Models	(Providence, RI)	117
American Merchant Marine Museum	(Kings Point, NY)	140
American Philosophical Society Library	(Philadelphia, PA)	196
Atlantic County Historical Society Museum	(Somers Point, NJ)	182
Atlantic Statiquarium Marine Museum	(Louisbourg, NS)	6
Barn Museum	(Bellport, NY)	142
Battleship Cove	(Fall River, MA)	76
Bernier Maritime Museum	(L'Islet-sur-Mer, QBC)	44
Boston Marine Society	(Boston, MA)	78
Brickstore Museum	(Kennebunk, ME)	54
Buffalo and Erie County Naval and Military Park	(Buffalo, NY)	142
Capt. Charles H. Hurley Library	(Buzzards Bay, MA)	80
Captain Robert Bennet Forbes House	(Milton, MA)	80
Churchill House & Marine Memorial Room Museum	(Hantsport, NS)	7
Cigna Museum and Art Collection	(Philadelphia, PA)	197
Cohasset Maritime Museum	(Cohasset, MA)	81
Collingwood Museum	(Collingwood, ONT)	22
Connecticut River Museum	(Essex, CT)	131
Counting House	(South Berwick, ME)	54
David M. Stewart Museum	(Montreal, QBC)	46
East Hampton Town Naval Museum	(East Hampton, NY)	153
Essex Shipbuilding Museum	(Essex, MA)	84
Fishermen's Museum	(Musgrave Harbour, NFLD)	3
Fishermen's Museum	(Pemaquid Point, ME)	55

Smith's Guide to Maritime Museums of North America

Franklin D. Roosevelt Library and Museum	(Hyde Park, NY)	156
Gates House/Machiasport Historical Society	(Machiasport, ME)	56
Grand Manan Museum	(Grand Harbor, NB)	2
Gundalow ship models (Countinghouse)	(South Berwick, ME)	54
H. Lee White Marine Museum	(Oswego, NY)	157
Hart Nautical Collections	(Cambridge, MA)	87
Herreshoff Marine Museum	(Bristol, RI)	120
Historical Society Museum	(Wellfleet, MA)	88
Independence Seaport Museum	(Philadelphia, PA)	199
Intrepid Sea-Air-Space Museum	(New York, NY)	159
Kennebunkport Maritime Museum	(Kennebunkport, ME)	59
Kittery Historical and Naval Museum	(Kittery, ME)	60
Linwood Maritime Museum	(Linwood, NJ)	190
Long Island Maritime Museum	(West Sayville, NY)	161
Marine Museum at Fall River	(Fall River, MA)	93
Maritime Industry Museum at Fort Schuyler	(Bronx, NY)	163
Maritime Museum of the Atlantic	(Halifax, NS)	12
Medford Historical Society Museum	(Medford, MA)	96
Moore Museum	(Mooretown, ONT)	31
Museum of Newport History	(Newport, RI)	122
Museum of Science	(Boston, MA)	97
Museum of the City of New York	(New York, NY)	164
Museum of Yachting	(Newport, RI)	123
Muskoka Lakes Museum	(Port Carling, ONT)	32
Mystic Seaport Museum	(Mystic, CT)	134
Nancy Island Historic Site	(Wasaga Beach, ONT)	33
Nautilus and Submarine Museum	(Groton, CT)	135
Naval War College Museum	(Newport, RI)	124
New Bedford Whaling Museum	(New Bedford, MA)	99
New Brunswick Museum	(Saint John, NB)	3
Old Lighthouse Museum	(Stonington, CT)	136
Old Sardine Village Museum	(Lubec, ME)	63
Old State House	(Boston, MA)	102
Owen Sound Marine-Rail Museum	(Owen Sound, ONT)	34
Peabody Essex Museum	(Salem, MA)	103
Penobscot Marine Museum	(Searsport, ME)	65
Portsmouth Athenaeum	(Portsmouth, NH)	73
Sag Harbor Whaling Museum	(Sag Harbor, NY)	173
Sandy Bay Historical Society and Museums	(Rockport, MA)	109
Settler's Museum	(Mahone Bay, NS)	17
Shore Village Museum	(Rockland, ME)	70
Skenesborough Museum	(Whitehall, NY)	175

Steamboat Dock Museum (Keyport, NJ) 194
Strawbery Banke (Portsmouth, NH) 73
Submarine Library Museum (Middletown, CT) 138
Suffolk Historical Museum (Riverhead, NY) 179
Toms River Seaport Society (Toms River, NJ) 195
Truro Historical Society Museum (N. Truro, MA) 111
USS *Constitution* Museum (Boston, MA) 112
United States Shipbuilding Museum (Quincy, MA) 114
Vanderbilt Mansion (Centerport, NY) 180
Watson Curtze Mansion and Planetarium (Erie, PA) 203
Willowbrook at Newfield (Newfield, ME) 71

SHIPS AND BOATS
Acadia, CSS (Canadian Hydrographic Survey Vessel)
   (Maritime Museum of the Atlantic) (Halifax, NS) 12
Adventure (sailing fishing schooner) (Gloucester, MA) 86
Alexander Henry (icebreaker) (Kingston, ONT) 29
Batteau (flat-bottom freight boat) (Wasaga Beach, ONT) 33
Beaver II, Tea Party Ship (Boston, MA) 78
Bee (schooner) (Penetanguishene, ONT) 23
Bemus Point-Stowe ferry (cabledrawn)
   (Chautauqua Lakes Historic Vessels Co.) (Mayville, NY) 144
Binghamton (ferry) (Edgewater, NJ) 185
Bluenose, Schooner (Fisheries Museum of Atlantic)
   (Lunenburg, NS) 9
Bras d'Or (hydrofoil) (Bernier Maritime Museum)
   (L'Islet-sur-Mer, QBC) 44
Buoy Tender (USCG) (CG 52303) (Basin Harbor, VT) 74
CSS *Acadia* (hydrographic survey vessel) (Halifax, NS) 12

CANAL BOATS/BARGES
Canal boat (Erie Canal Museum) (Syracuse, NY) 154
Canal barge (New Hope, PA) 201
Chief Engineer of Rome (horse-drawn canal packet-boat)
   (Erie Canal Village) (Rome, NY) 154
Capt. Edward H. Adams (open-decked barge) (Portsmouth, NH) 73
Steam canal barge (Oswego, NY) 171

CANOES
Canadian Canoe Museum (Peterborough, ONT) 21
H. Lee White Marine Museum (Oswego, NY) 157
Ice Canoe (1920s) (Grosse Ile/Irish Memorial National Historic Site)

Shelburne Museum	(Québec, QBC)	47
	(Shelburne, VT)	75

Cape Sable (Trawler/dragger)	(Lunenburg, NS)	9
Charles W. Morgan (whaleship)	(Mystic, CT)	134
Chautauqua Belle (sternwheeler) (Chautauqua Lakes Hist. Vessels)		
	(Mayville, NY)	144
Clearwater Hudson River Sloop	(Poughkeepsie, NY)	159
Coast Guard Buoy Tender (Lake Champlain Maritime Museum)		
	(Basin Harbor, VT)	74
Daisy (whaleboat)	(Cold Spring Harbor, L.I., NY)	148
Derrick Boat No. 8 (H. Lee White Marine Museum)	(Oswego, NY)	171
Dixie II (Gold Cup racer) (Antique Boat Museum)	(Clayton, NY)	141
Eagle (training barque) (U.S. Coast Guard Museum)		
	(New London, CT)	138
Lapointe (icebreaker) (Bernier Maritime Museum)		
	(L'Islet-sur-Mer, QBC)	44
Evelina M. Goulart (schooner) (Essex Shipbuilding Museum)		
	(Essex, MA)	84
Gasela (tall ship) (Independence Seaport Museum)		
	(Philadelphia, PA)	199
Growler (guided missile submarine) (*Intrepid* Sea-Air-Space Museum)		
	(New York, NY)	159
Gunboat (War of 1812)	(Mallorytown, ONT)	40
HMCS *Fraser* (DDE-233)	(Halifax, NS)	11
HMCS *Haida*	(Toronto, ONT)	25
HMCS *Sackville* (K-181)	(Halifax, NS)	11
HMS *Rose* (replica ship)	(Bridgeport, CT)	132
Halve Maen (*Half Moon*) (replica ship)	(Albany, NY)	158
Hiddensee (Russian Naval vessel)	(Fall River, MA)	76

ICE BREAKERS

Alexander Henry (ice breaker)	(Kingston, ONT)	29
Ernest Lapointe (icebreaker)	(L'Islet-sur-Mer, QBC)	44
Glacier Society Museum, The	(Bridgeport, CT)	132
Japanese submarine	(Fall River, MA)	76
Joseph Conrad (fishing schooner)	(Mystic, CT)	134
Kalmar Nyckel (replica ship) (*Kalmar Nyckel* Shipyard/Museum)		
	(Wilmington, DE)	206

Robert H. Smith

Katahdin (steamboat) (Moosehead Marine Museum)
(Greenville, ME) 62
La Grande Hermine (Cartier flagship)
(Cartier-Brébeuf Natl. Hist. Park) (Québec, QBC) 45
Lifeboat (from S.S. *Hochelaga*) (Port Colborne, ONT) 38

LIGHTSHIPS
Ambross (lightship) (New York, NY) 177
Barnegat (Independence Seaport Landing) (Philadelphia, PA) 199
New Bedford, Lightship (New Bedford, MA) 91
Overfalls (Cannon Ball Marine Museum) (Lewes, DE) 203

Mary Celeste (ship) (Marion, MA) 96
Mathilda (an 1898 steam tug) (Hudson River Maritime Museum)
(Kingston, NY) 158
Mayflower II (replica ship) (Plimoth Plantation) (Plymouth, MA) 106
Miss Canada III (Gold Cup racer) (Antique Boat Museum)
(Clayton, NY) 141
Miss Kathy (motor launch) (Wilmington, DE) 206
Modesty (oyster sloop) (West Sayville, NY) 161
Ned Hanlan (tugboat) (Toronto, ONT) 42
New Hampshire Antique & Classic Boat Museum (Wolfeboro, NH) 72
Niagara (1812 reconstructed brig) (Erie, PA) 198
Norgoma (museum ship) (Sault Ste. Marie, ONT) 32
Norisle, SS (Assiginack Historical Museum) (Manitowaning, ONT) 20
OMF Schooner) (Oswego, NY) 171
PT boats (Battleship Cove at Fall River) (Fall River, MA) 76
Peking (bark) (New York, NY) 177
Perseverance (bateau) (Penetanguishene, ONT) 23
Perseverance (schooner replica) (Thunder Bay, ONT) 33
Philadelphia II (Revolutionary War gunboat) (Lake Champlain
Maritime Museum) (Basin Harbor, VT) 74
Pioneer (Schooner) (New York, NY) 177
Priscilla (oyster vessel) (West Sayville, NY) 161
Providence (replica sloop) (Newport, RI) 126
Rufus S. Reed (replica canal barge) (Greenville, PA) 197
Russian Naval vessel *Hiddensee* (Fall River, MA) 76
SS *Nobska* (coastal steamer) (New Bedford, MA) 107
SS *Norisle* Heritage Park (Manitowaning, ONT) 20
SS *Ticonderoga* (lake paddle-wheeler) (Shelburne, VT) 75
Sackville, HMCS (Halifax, NS) 11
Salem, USS (heavy cruiser) (Quincy, MA) 114

Schooner *Bluenose* (Lunenburg, NS) 9
Schooner *Ernestina* Commission (New Bedford, MA) 109
Sea Lion (16th-century merchant ship)
  (Chautauqua Lakes Historic Vessels) (Mayville, NY) 144
Sherman Zwicker (Grand Banks Schooner)
  (Maine Maritime Museum) (Bath, ME) 61

SMALLCRAFT COLLECTIONS
Barnegat Bay Decoy and Baymen's Museum (Tuckerton, NJ) 183
Basin Head Fisheries Museum (Souris, P.E.I.) 49
Maine Maritime Museum (Bath, ME) 61
Toms River Seaport Society (Toms River, NJ) 195
Willowbrook at Newfield (Newfield, ME) 71
Woods Hole Historical Collection (Woods Hole, MA) 116
Snow Squall (clipper) (South Portland, ME) 66

SUBMARINES
American Turtle (first submarine) (Essex, CT) 131
Holland I, Holland II, Fenian Ram (Paterson, NJ) 193
USS *Albacore* (Portsmouth, NH) 72
USS *Becuna* (Philadelphia, PA) 199
USS *Croaker* (Buffalo, NY) 142
USS *Growler* (New York, NY) 159
USS *Holland* (replica) (Greenport, NY) 152
USS *Ling* (Hackensack, NJ) 192
USS *Lion Fish* (Fall River, MA) 76
USS *Nautilus* (nuclear sub) (Groton, CT) 135
USS *Requin* (Pittsburgh, PA) 202
Tecumseh (bateau) (Discovery Harbour) (Penetanguishene, ONT) 23
Theresa E. Connor (salt bank schooner)
  (Fisheries Museum of Atlantic) (Lunenburg, NS) 9

TUGBOATS
Charlotte (1880s tugboat)
  (Long Island Maritime Museum) (West Sayville, NY) 161
Ned Hanlan (The Pier: Toronto's Waterfront Museum)
  (Toronto, ONT) 42
Tugboat *Urger* (Waterford, NY) 179
Tugboat (LT-5) (World War II) (H. Lee White Marine Museum)
  (Oswego, NY) 171

U.S. Brig *Niagara* (Erie, PA) 198

Robert H. Smith

USS *Cassin Young* (WW II destroyer)	(Boston, MA)	112
USS *Constitution* ("Old Ironsides")	(Boston, MA)	112
USS *Edson* (destroyer) *(Intrepid* Air, Sea, and Space Museum)	(New York, NY)	159
USS *Intrepid* (aircraft carrier)	(New York, NY)	159
USS *Joseph P. Kennedy, Jr.*	(Fall River, MA)	76
USS *Little Rock* (cruiser)	(Buffalo, NY)	142
USS *Massachusetts* (BB 59) (Battleship Cove)	(Fall River, MA)	76
USS *New Jersey* (BB-62)	(Camden, NJ)	185
USS *Olympia* (flagship) (Penn's Landing)	(Philadelphia, PA)	199
USS *Salem* (CA 139) (US Naval Shipbuilding Museum)	(Quincy, MA)	114
USS *Slater* (destroyer escort)(DE-766)	(Albany, NY)	180
USS *The Sullivans* (destroyer)	(Buffalo, NY)	142
Wavertree (full-rigged ship)	(New York, NY)	177
Whaleboat	(Edgartown, MA)	95
Whaleboat	(East Hampton, NY)	153
Whaleboat (Sag Harbor Whaling Museum)	(Sag Harbor, NY)	173
Whydah, Expedition	(Provincetown, MA)	85

WHALING

Young American (tall ship) (Historic Gardner's Basin)	(Atlantic City, NJ)	188
Alfred S. Brownell Collection	(Providence, RI)	117
Barn Museum	(Bellport, NY)	142
Canadian Canoe Museum	(Peterborough, ONT)	21
Cold Spring Harbor Museum Society	(Cold Spring Harbor, L.I., NY)	148
East Hampton Town Marine Museum	(East Hampton, NY)	153
Egan Institute of Maritime Studies	(Nantucket, MA)	83
Falmouth Historical Society's Museums	(Falmouth, MA)	86
Historical Society Museum	(Wellfleet, MA)	88
Martha's Vineyard Historical Society and Museum	(Edgartown, MA)	95
Mystic Seaport Museum	(Mystic, CT)	134
New Bedford Free Public Library	(New Bedford, MA)	99
New Bedford Whaling Museum	'(New Bedford, MA)	99
Old Lighthouse Museum	(Stonington, CT)	136
Peabody Essex Museum	(Salem, MA)	103
Rhode Island Historical Society Library	(Providence, RI)	127
Sag Harbor Whaling Museum	(Sag Harbor, NY)	173
Southampton Historical Museum	(Southampton, NY)	178
Suffolk Historical Museum	(Riverhead, NY)	179
Whaling Museum	(Nantucket Island, MA)	115

A NOTE TO MUSEUM DIRECTORS

An effort was made to include all the maritime museums in North America, but in all likelihood some were missed. If you'd like a listing for your museum in the next edition, please complete the form below.

The following maritime museum was not included in this guide.

_____
(Name of museum, lighthouse, canal museum)

_____
(Street and/or Post Office Box number)

_____
(City/State or Province/Zip or Canadian Mail Code)

_____
(Phone number[s], FAX numbers, e-mail address)

The museum is important because:

_____

_____

Please send to:
R. H. Smith
P.O. Box 176
Del Mar, CA 92014-0176
(858) 755-7753 FAX: (858) 755-1722
E-mail: rhs2@ix.netcom.com

About the Author

ROBERT H. SMITH is a longtime supporter of marine and maritime organizations and the author of two popular cruising guides to harbors, anchorages, and marinas in Northern and Southern California. Formerly, he was assistant to the Chancellor of the University of California, San Diego (the home of Scripps Institution of Oceanography, and vice-president of development at Scripps Clinic and Research Foundation in La Jolla, California. For many years he has traveled extensively visiting, photographing, and writing about the museums contained in the three-part Smith's Guide to Maritime Museum of North America.

Here, at last, is the one essential guide, now in three parts, (Part 1 Canadian Maritime Provinces/New England/Mid-Atlantic, Part 2 Southern/Gulf Coast, Part 3 Mid-West/Canada/West Coast) sought by all lovers of maritime history, of ships, canals, and the sea. Robert H. Smith thoroughly describes more than 620 maritime, lighthouse, and canal lock museums in the North American Continent, giving such essential information as location; directions for motorists; telephone, fax, and e-mail numbers; visiting hours; collection highlights; history of the institutions; special activities such as lectures and film shows; admission policies; and gift shops. Several elaborately cross-referenced indexes will guide the reader to any area of specialized interest, such as geographical locations, location by state, specialized interest index, such as submarine, ships, scrimshaw, research libraries and photographic collections. Robert H. Smith has written four other maritime and boat guides, all well received by the public and specialists alike. He travels extensively visiting the museums he describes, from his home base in Del Mar, California.